INVESTIGATING LANGUAGE ATTITUDES

Investigating Language Attitudes

SOCIAL MEANINGS OF DIALECT,
ETHNICITY AND PERFORMANCE

Peter Garrett, Nikolas Coupland
and Angie Williams

UNIVERSITY OF WALES PRESS
CARDIFF
2003

© Peter Garrett, Nikolas Coupland and Angie Williams, 2003

All rights reserved. No part of this book may be reproduced, stored in a retrieval system, or transmitted, in any form or by any means, electronic, mechanical, photocopying, recording or otherwise, without clearance from the University of Wales Press, 10 Columbus Walk, Brigantine Place, Cardiff, CF10 4UP.
www.wales.ac.uk/press

British Library Cataloguing-in-Publication Data
A catalogue record for this book is available from the British Library.

ISBN 0-7083-1803-7

The rights of Peter Garrett, Nikolas Coupland and Angie Williams to be identified as authors of this work have been asserted by them in accordance with sections 77 and 78 of the Copyright, Designs and Patents Act 1988.

Typeset by Bryan Turnbull
Printed in Great Britain by Dinefwr Press, Llandybïe

Contents

List of tables and figures		vii
Acknowledgements		ix
1	Introduction: the scope of language attitudes	1
2	Direct approaches	24
3	Indirect approaches	51
4	An integrated programme of language attitudes research in Wales	82
5	Mapping and labelling	111
6	Attitude scales and 'social advantage' items	128
7	The narratives study: performances, responses and evaluations	148
8	Keyword responses	179
9	Recognition of dialects	198
10	Conclusions	211
References		229
Index		247

List of Figures and Tables

Figures

2.1	Subjective dialect division	47
2.2	Perceptual culture regions	49
3.1	Language and identity in Wales, based on the 'three-Wales' model	76
4.1	County boundaries of Wales at the time of data collection	91
4.2	Locations of the 'place-tags' in the questionnaire, and of English urban centres close to the border with Wales	94
4.3	Main towns and cities of Wales	95
4.4	Current county boundaries of Wales	96
6.1	Regional voting patterns in the 1997 referendum for a Welsh assembly	141
7.1	MDS and clusters for teachers: 'How interesting does this story sound?'	157
7.2	MDS and clusters for teenagers: 'How interesting does this story sound?'	158
7.3	MDS and clusters for teachers: 'Do you think this speaker is a good laugh?'	161
7.4	MDS and clusters for teenagers: 'Do you think this speaker is a good laugh?'	162
7.5	MDS and clusters for teachers: 'Do you think this speaker does well at school?'	165
7.6	MDS and clusters for teenagers: 'Do you think this speaker does well at school?'	165

7.7 MDS and clusters for teenagers: 'How Welsh do you think this speaker sounds?' 166

7.8 MDS and clusters for teachers: 'How Welsh do you think this teacher sounds?' 167

9.1 Variable independent continua of the modes of non-linguists' language awareness 205

Tables

5.1 Label-sets for Welsh English regions invoked by teachers 114–15

5.2 Frequencies of categorized comments 121

6.1 Means and standard deviations of teachers' judgements of the accent/dialect communities 130

6.2 Means and standard deviations for Welsh versus non-Welsh speakers 132

6.3 Means and standard deviations by area of employment of teachers (north versus south) 134

7.1 Welsh teenagers' evaluations of regional speakers 150

7.2 Teachers' evaluations of regional speakers 152

7.3 Transcripts of responses from focus-group discussions with students 169–72

8.1 Keyword 'boring' comments about speakers 184

8.2 Number of keyword references to Welshness and Englishness used by teenage judges 186–7

8.3 Number of references to 'farmer', 'country-type', 'sheepshagger' etc. in the six judging communities 191

9.1 Responses to question concerning where the speaker was from 199

9.2 Percentage of young adults who achieved correct recognition of where speaker was from 200

9.3 Mean scores for 'How Welsh do you think this speaker sounds?' 203

9.4 Rank orders on the Welshness scale and the Welshness mean scores 204

Acknowledgements

Much of our research that we discuss in this book was funded by an award from the University of Wales Intercollegiate Fund, and we thank them for their financial support. We thank the many schools in Wales and England, and their students, teachers and headteachers, who kindly assisted us in various ways in our data collection. Special mention should be made of those courageous teenagers who narrated their stories to their classmates while we recorded them, and to the many teachers who took the time to complete questionnaires for us. We are also grateful to Jackie Guendouzi, Cathryn Williams, Virpi-Ylänne-McEwen and other colleagues who helped us to collect, code and analyse data at various times.

We are indebted to Alun Williams in the Map Library of the Welsh Assembly Government for providing us with maps of Wales relevant to this book. For permission to use the picture on the cover of this book – *Before the Dance, Great Lawn II* – we thank the Marlborough Gallery New York (www.marlboroughgallery.com), and we would particularly like to express our appreciation to the artist himself, Bill Jacklin (www.bjacklin.com).

Several chapters of this book develop material that we have previously published as journal articles or as contributions to edited collections. In particular, chapters 5 and 6 develop Coupland, Williams and Garrett (1994; 1999), Garrett, Coupland and Williams (1995), and Williams, Garrett and Coupland (1996). Chapters 7, 8 and 9 build on Garrett, Coupland and Williams (1999; forthcoming), and Williams, Garrett and Coupland (1999). Chapters 4 and 10 develop aspects of all of these.

Many colleagues have contributed, through comments and discussion, to the final shape of this book and to the ideas we set out in it. Some have been anonymous reviewers, and some have been participants at conferences. Some have been closer colleagues and friends. We have benefited greatly from their engagement. The responsibility for any weaknesses and errors lies with us.

Peter Garrett, Nikolas Coupland, and Angie Williams
Centre for Language and Communication Research
Cardiff University
Wales

1

Introduction: the scope of language attitudes

We begin this book with a critical review of the main methods employed in language attitudes research, in order to discuss their various strengths and weaknesses. Some of the methodological issues raised in this review we then explore and develop in a series of investigations that we have conducted into language attitudes in Wales over recent years, focusing mainly on how the main regions of Wales and their associated patterns of English speech are characterized and evaluated. Within this structure, the book has three parallel aims. The first is to provide an overview of approaches to investigating language attitudes. The second is to introduce a range of linked empirical studies, focusing on the Welsh context, demonstrating two broad methodological approaches. The third is to develop a dialogue between these first two aims, to explore how sociolinguistic interpretations are both guided and constrained by the different empirical approaches. Through this, we will address the issue of, and indeed demonstrate, how different research methods produce different insights into language attitudes and sociolinguistic structure, contributing to a multi-faceted account of the 'subjective life' of language varieties.

In this first chapter, we begin by considering the nature of language attitudes, since it is their complex and rather elusive nature that brings to the fore the methodological issues considered in this book. We then move on to consider why, for sociolinguistics, it is necessary to study language attitudes, and so why it is necessary to grapple with these methodological problems. We then introduce the main approaches to studying language attitudes, as they have developed mainly since the 1960s. Finally, we set out the main research questions to be addressed in this book, and provide a plan of the book as a whole.

The nature of language attitudes

Let us begin by considering the concept of 'attitude' generally, without being concerned too much at this stage about whether it relates to language or to other objects, processes, or behaviours. Despite attitude being one of the most distinctive and indispensable concepts in social psychology (Perloff, 1993: 26), and, indeed, a pivotal concept in sociolinguistics ever since Labov's (1966) pioneering work on the social stratification of speech communities, defining the concept is by no means straightforward. Researchers have offered a number of definitions. The difficulty undoubtedly stems from the latent nature of attitudes. Allport's work in the 1930s commented on this hampering characteristic of attitudes research in the following way: 'Attitudes are never directly observed, but, unless they are admitted, through inference, as real and substantial ingredients in human nature, it becomes impossible to account satisfactorily either for the consistency of any individual's behaviour, or for the stability of any society' (1935: 839).

Some authors settle for brief and somewhat general definitions. For example, Henerson, Morris and Fitz-Gibbon (1987: 13) write: 'In this book, the word "attitude" will be used quite broadly to describe all the objects we want to measure that have to do with affect, feelings, values and beliefs.' Others offer more elaborate definitions. Oppenheim (1982) includes in his definition some of the many outcomes, including behaviours, from which people try to infer other people's attitudes. For him, an attitude is:

> a construct, an abstraction which cannot be directly apprehended. It is an inner component of mental life which expresses itself, directly or indirectly, through such more obvious processes as stereotypes, beliefs, verbal statements or reactions, ideas and opinions, selective recall, anger or satisfaction or some other emotion and in various other aspects of behaviour.
> (Oppenheim, 1982: 39)

For our present purposes, we will follow the practice of Cargile, Giles, Ryan and Bradac (1994: 221), albeit with more elaboration, and take a general and simple 'core' definition that has an adequate basis of agreement for proceeding, and then establish some of the qualities of attitudes on which there is considerable consensus. Sarnoff's (1970: 279) statement can be used as a starting point, that an attitude is 'a

INTRODUCTION: THE SCOPE OF LANGUAGE ATTITUDES

disposition to react favourably or unfavourably to a class of objects'. We take it as axiomatic, then, that an attitude is an evaluative orientation to a social object of some sort, but that, being a 'disposition', an attitude is at least potentially an evaluative stance that is sufficiently stable to allow it to be identified and in some sense measured.

Beyond this, it is widely claimed that attitudes have a tripartite structure, in that they are said to have cognitive, affective, and behavioural components (for example, Edwards, 1982). They are cognitive in that they contain or comprise beliefs about the world (for example, that learning the Welsh language will help me to get a better job in Wales). They are affective in that they involve feelings about an attitude object (for example, enthusiasm for poetry written in the Welsh language). And they are systematically linked to behaviour, because they predispose us to act in a certain way (for example, to learn Welsh).

In language attitudes, cognitive processes are likely to be shaped by the individual and collective functions arising from stereotyping in intergroup relations. Linguistic forms, varieties and styles can set off beliefs about a speaker, their group membership, and can lead to assumptions about attributes of those members. This sort of categorization is said to serve a number of functions (Tajfel, 1981). At the individual level, the complex social world is made more orderly, and so more manageable and more predictable. Whether they are favourable or prejudiced, attitudes to language varieties and their users at least provide a coherent map of the social world. One way in which this is achieved is through stressing similarities within a category and differences between and amongst categories, simplifying the complex array of individual experiences in social life. At the intergroup level, stereotypes can serve two major social collective functions: a social-explanatory function and a social-differentiation function. The former is the creation and maintenance of group ideologies that explain and defend relations between groups, in particular evaluations and treatment of members of outgroups. The latter concerns the creation, preservation and enhancement of favourable differentiations between the ingroup and relevant outgroups. The contents of stereotypes vary from one intergroup context to another, and are defined by which group function or functions they fulfil in any specific social context. Hence it is possible for people to construct almost any evaluation of a speaker to fit their collective cognitive needs. That is, we have a situation where social stereotypes tend to perpetuate themselves, acting as a repository of 'common-sense' beliefs or filters through which social life is transacted and interpreted. In summary, 'stereotypes constitute a crucial aspect of intergroup communication' (Hewstone and Giles, 1997: 278).

The affective component of attitudes can sometimes appear to determine an attitude, to the exclusion of the cognitive component (Mackie and Hamilton, 1993). For example, a person may hear a language or linguistic variety which they are unable to identify, but may nevertheless consider it 'pleasant', or 'ugly', and this may affect their response during the encounter (van Bezooijen, 1994). In contrast, however, Cargile et al. (1994) consider it rare for the cognitive component to evoke judgements that are devoid of affective content, and indeed most would claim that attitudes always have a strong affective component (Perloff, 1993: 28). The third component – behaviour – is where much controversy lies in the study of attitudes, and this issue is dealt with separately in the next section.

Although most theorists appear to agree that there are affective, cognitive and behavioural aspects to attitudes, a number of models thread these together in different ways. The simple 'tripartite model', which is so often referred to in language attitudes work, was outlined by Rosenberg and Hovland (1960), and supported by subsequent studies by Ostrom (1969), Kothandapani (1971) and Breckler (1984). This model claimed that affect, cognition, and behaviour emerge as separate and distinctive components of attitude, and it has been criticized for prejudging a relationship between attitude and behaviour (Zanna and Rempel, 1988). For many professional persuaders, most notably advertisers and politicians, this is the relationship by which much of the justification for the study of attitudes stands or falls (Perloff, 1993; 79); will surveys of attitudes allow them to predict actual behaviour?

Where do attitudes come from?

> When we talk about attitudes, we are talking about what a person has *learned* in the process of becoming a member of a family, a member of a group, and of society that makes him [*sic*] react to his social world in a *consistent* and *characteristic* way, instead of a transitory and haphazard way. (M. Sherif, 1967: 2)

This view locates attitudes as a fundamental part of what is learned through human socialization. It also emphasizes the durable qualities

INTRODUCTION: THE SCOPE OF LANGUAGE ATTITUDES

of attitudes as socially-structured and socially-structuring phenomena. However, there is by no means unanimous agreement on these points. The persuasion literature (for example, Sears and Kosterman, 1994: 264) points to differing levels of commitment in attitudes. Some attitudes are superficial and less stable, and others are more enduring. Evaluative responses may be so superficial and unstable that they might be labelled 'non-attitudes' (Ostrom et al., 1994), where people might just make up an evaluation on the spot, perhaps as a first-reaction phenomenon to a new topic, or to one that is too complex to evaluate fully. On the other hand, attitudes that are enduring are sometimes seen as being acquired early in the lifespan and unlikely to change much in later life (Sears, 1983). As we shall argue later, there is evidence that, like language itself, some language attitudes are acquired at an early age, and so, following the point above, are likely to be relatively enduring.

Nevertheless, the claim that attitudes can even potentially be stable and enduring is itself by no means uncontroversial. Potter and Wetherell (1987), for example, arguing for a discourse analytic perspective, paint a picture of individuals' evaluative stances unfolding in social interaction, and changing from moment to moment, demonstrating considerable variability and indeed volatility. They claim that traditional attitude measurement misses this dynamic and constructive process. We address the link between attitude and discourse in the series of investigations we report in the second part of this book. We certainly agree with Potter and Wetherell that discourse – in the sense of spontaneous face-to-face social interaction through language – is a rich and dynamic locus for doing social categorization and social evaluation. More than that, what we are calling 'language attitudes' can themselves be stereotyped responses to community-bound ways of speaking, to discourse styles as well as to dialect varieties in the conventional sense. On the other hand, we see no value in restricting the study of social evaluation to the qualitative analysis of talk in interaction, as Potter and Wetherell imply we should. These arguments are caught up in much wider debates about quantitative/qualitative and empiricist/ interpretive designs for research, and we return to some aspects of them in later chapters. But our starting point for the volume is an open stance on method and interpretation, and one that includes attempts to generalize about *community-level* phenomena, including subjective phenomena. The methodological concerns of this book are anchored more in the group-focused empirical work in sociolinguistics and the social psychology of language. The research discussed in the latter half of the book is concerned with attitudes of *groups* about other *groups*. In particular, we aim to construct a geolinguistic atlas of attitudes in regional Welsh communities, rather than to conduct an in-depth investigation of individuals' attitudes and how these may be variably constructed in social interaction. The theoretical issues of attitude stability/ephemerality, and of context-dependent versus context-independent attitudes, are nevertheless important. Even when social evaluations can be shown to be variable across or within social situations, this does not preclude the existence of stable subjective trends existing at higher levels. In much attitudes research, a degree of variability or 'systematic variation' (Potter and Wetherell, 1987: 45) is not seen as seriously prejudicial to the notion of durability, any more than systematic language variation in the speech of an individual severely problematizes the notion of someone 'having a dialect', sharing features with others at the level of the community. Social judgement theory (for example, C. Sherif and M. Sherif, 1967), which is often employed as an explanatory framework for attitude change, suggests that people operate with an 'anchor' position, but will tend to move comfortably within a finite latitude of evaluations that they find acceptable. This issue is revisited when considering attitudes and behaviour below.

Another generally accepted characteristic of attitudes is how they function as both input to and output from social action. This is of particular importance in educational research, and in areas such as language planning, but it can also be invoked to explain the role of attitude in both the reception and production of language. For example, Baker (1992: 12), focusing on Welsh-language education, sees attitude towards Welsh as an important input factor. A strongly favourable attitude towards Welsh may provide the impetus to high achievement in a Welsh-language programme. Conversely, success in a Welsh-language course for beginners may foster a more favourable attitude towards the language. Educationists and language planners often work with such issues in the hope that attitudes will ultimately serve a double function, as both a presage (input) and a product (output) ingredient. Beyond the educational context, in terms of the everyday language use of individuals, since language attitudes and the sociocultural norms that they constitute are an integral part of communicative competence (Hymes, 1971), they would be expected not only to affect our responses to language users around us, but also to

INTRODUCTION: THE SCOPE OF LANGUAGE ATTITUDES

allow us to anticipate others' reactions to our own language use. So we may modify our speech in an attempt to gain from others particular reactions that we seek (for example, to be seen as trustworthy, educated, from a particular region, competent, an ideal person to employ, or to gain approval from the teacher, etc.). Here too then, attitudes may be seen in terms of input and output, completing a cycle of influence between language variation and social cognition. Indeed, it has been argued from this dynamic relationship between 'language' and 'language attitudes' that the two need not be separated conceptually (Giles and Coupland, 1991: 59). However, when attitudes are considered in terms of input and output in this way, they again are being considered in relation to (as input to, or output from) behaviour.

Attitudes are also seen as complex phenomena in the sense that they can have many facets and manifestations. For example, if we wanted to investigate 'students' attitudes towards their Spanish-language lessons at school', we would need to identify the relevant facets of such attitudes: what do we mean – and what do the students mean – by 'Spanish-language lessons'? Facets are likely to include a host of components of communicative events, such as teachers, classmates, teaching methods, course materials, perhaps even the room in which the lessons are held, quite apart from the Spanish language itself. Manifestations concern how we think these attitudes will reveal themselves: that is, what will we look for empirically in our studies and try to assess? We might interview the students individually or in pairs or groups. We might get them to write essays for us about their Spanish-language lessons. We might ask them to circle numbers on attitude-rating scales. We might try to infer their attitudes from their productivity in these lessons. We might try to assess their level of attention in the lessons (for example, by counting how many times students put up their hands to ask relevant questions), and infer attitudes from this behaviour. We might want to assess a number of different manifestations to see if they tell us the same story, or to see if they seem to tell us different things. Comparing different manifestations is a central concern of this book.

The problematic relationship between attitudes and behaviour

A common-sense view about the relationship between attitudes and behaviour can lead people to assume that if they are able to change someone's attitude towards something, they will also change that person's behaviour. It can also lead people to assume that they can confidently infer someone's attitudes from the way that that person behaves. In addition, the assumption is sometimes made that if we can get someone to behave in a certain way, their attitudes will 'look after themselves'.

Much advertising and marketing, in fact, bases itself on such assumptions. To take the first of the above, an advertiser might, for example, try to get men to associate a certain make of car with speed and masculinity, on the assumption that such changes in attitudes towards the car will lead to more men buying that make. To take the last point in the previous paragraph, marketing managers are keen to get us to try out free samples, on the assumption that, having tried out the product, we will then develop favourable attitudes towards the product. Indeed, Festinger's (1957) theory of 'cognitive dissonance' proposes that we prefer to keep our beliefs, attitudes and behaviour aligned.

However, there is considerable evidence from attitudes research that attitudes and behaviours may at times be far removed from such alignment (for example, Wicker, 1969; Hanson, 1980). Various explanations are provided for this. Many of these reflect the method or context of attitude measurement (the main focus of this book). For example, Ajzen and Fishbein's (1980) 'theory of reasoned action' stresses the social context within which any individual operates, and how this may affect the relative importance of private attitudes. Hence we might be deterred from behaving in accordance with our attitudes by the anticipated hostile reactions of significant others. Furthermore, even if we have every intention of acting in line with our attitudes, we might be prevented from doing so by any number of circumstances (too busy, competing priorities, bad weather, absent-mindedness, etc.). Other examples are concerned with notions of 'deindividuation', the tendency of respondents at times to report socially desirable attitudes rather than their own private attitudes, to show acquiescence in attitudinal responses by giving the response they assume the researcher wants, or on some occasions simply to be swept along in their behaviour by the scripted nature of some situations, without any thought about what their attitudes are (for example, Baker, 1988; Perloff, 1993; Ostrom et al., 1994). Some of these ideas will be considered more fully in the next chapter.

Before ending this general review section, there are two important points to draw out, both relating once again to the issue of stability and durability of attitudes. Firstly, the lack of accord that one sometimes finds between attitude and behaviour may be attributable to a failure to gather reliable and valid data on attitudes. In other words, although there may be a gap at times between what we take to be someone's attitude on the one hand, and what we know to be their behaviour on the other, it may be the case that there is no discord whatsoever between their behaviour and their 'real' or dominant attitude, but that we have simply failed to identify what their 'real' or dominant attitude is. We emphasized earlier that there are genuine difficulties in confidently identifying such latent variables. Secondly, although some commentators claim that 'there wouldn't be much point in studying attitudes if they were not, by and large, predictive of behaviour' (Gass and Seiter, 1999: 41), in the field of language attitudes the lack of accord is often very much of interest. For example, links between people's attitudes towards language varieties and their behaviours are likely to differ according to the complexity of domains. Learning a language or forming a friendship, for example, involves a long-term commitment, compared to, say, deciding to buy a car. Attitudes may be in competition: a candidate at an interview for a job may strategically adjust their speech style in a way that diverges from (or conceals) the dialect to which they otherwise have a strong loyalty, if they feel this enhances their chances of getting the job, thus helping them to fulfil their career ambitions, and/or to please significant others, such as a partner or parent.

Attitudes and related terms

No doubt relating to some of the difficulties of definition outlined above, along with the fact that 'attitude' is a term in common usage, there are a number of other concepts that are in some contexts used almost interchangeably with 'attitude'. It will be useful to identify and, as far as possible, distinguish these here. To some extent, to define a concept is to state not only what it is, but also how it differs in meaning from other concepts with which it is closely linked. The following discussion focuses on the concepts: habits, values, beliefs, opinions and ideologies.

Like attitudes, *habits* are learned and, like some attitudes, they are also enduring. But the most significant difference is that attitudes are not generally considered to be intrinsically behavioural (though there may, as discussed above, be links with behaviour). Habits, on the other hand, are usually viewed as behavioural routines. Perloff (1993: 29) claims that individuals are likely to be less aware of their habits than they are of their attitudes, and so are more likely to able to talk about their attitudes than about their habits. However, there are certainly different levels of reflexive awareness with attitudes, too. The main methodological challenge of language attitudes research is to assess whether specific manifestations or indices of evaluative stances to language varieties or users are reliable indicators of underlying social tendencies. Reflexivity is what allows us to access attitudes empirically, but it is also a potential source of systematic error in measuring attitudes.

Values are usually seen as superordinate ideals that we strive towards. Rokeach (1973) distinguishes *terminal values* (such as freedom, equality) from *instrumental values* (such as the importance of being honest, responsible). A terminal value such as 'equality' may underlie a number of highly differentiated attitudes (attitudes towards equal-opportunities legislation, income tax, an inter-ethnic war overseas, a political party, a bilingual policy, etc.). Oskamp (1977) refers to values as 'the most important and central elements in a person's system of attitudes and beliefs', and judges them to be more global and general than attitudes are.

Beliefs are said to be fundamentally cognitive in nature. However, it is usually argued that, even if beliefs do not have any affective content, they may trigger and indeed be triggered by strong affective reactions.

Opinion is the most difficult to differentiate from attitude. As Baker (1992: 14) has pointed out, the two terms tend to be synonymous in everyday usage, and Perloff (1993: 29) notes that many researchers, too, use the terms interchangeably. Some make a distinction, claiming that opinions are cognitive, lacking any affective component. Baker (1992: 14) and Perloff (1993: 30) both make this assertion. Baker also claims that 'opinions are verbalisable, while attitudes may be latent, conveyed by non-verbal and verbal processes' (1992: 14). Hence we can regard opinion as a more discursive (or 'discursable') entity – a view that can be developed about something, while attitudes may be potentially less easy to formulate, needing to be accessed indirectly as well as directly. Although Baker does not include any illustration of this distinction, it does appear at least to leave open the possibility of a distinction in terms of a person's expressed opinion not necessarily reflecting their attitude. Such issues will be returned to when considering the problematic relationship between attitude and behaviour (for example, verbalization), and some of the methodological questions that underlie this book.

The concept of *ideology* has come to the fore in social science and in sociolinguistics through renewed interest in the political climates in which social life is conducted. Distanced from its original Marxist sense of 'false consciousness', ideology generally refers to a patterned but naturalized set of assumptions and values associated with a particular social or cultural group. We might identify, for example, a right-wing political ideology which represents the privileges associated with powerful and affluent social groups as 'freedom of action' and represents left-wing political policies as evidence of 'the nanny state'. Ideology has been taken up as a key concept in, for example, critical discourse analysis (see Fairclough, 1995), where the often hidden values that structure modes of linguistic representation are opened up to critical scrutiny (see Jaworski and Coupland, 1999).

In sociolinguistics *language ideology* is emerging as an important concept for understanding the politics of language in multilingual situations, such as in relation to immigration and social inclusion/exclusion generally (for example, Blommaert and Verschueren, 1998), and indeed as a politically more sensitive backdrop to any investigation of language variation and change (see Gal and Irvine, 1995; Irvine 2001; Irvine and Gal 2000; Woolard, 1998). Language ideology is coming to be seen as a key part of the 'ethnoscapes' (Appadurai, 1996) in which language codes and varieties function. The field of language ideology is not tied to a particular methodological tradition of research, although what we are labelling language attitudes research in this book constitutes a coherent and, we would argue, central set of methodological options for ideology analysis. One of our ambitions for the book is in fact to show how particular methods in the study of language attitudes, in combination with each other, can build richly differentiated accounts of the ideological forces at work in a community – in our case, contemporary Wales – and how they coalesce around distinctive regional dialects and ways of speaking.

Why study language attitudes?

The field of *language* attitudes encompasses a broad range of focuses, and in specific terms, reasons for studying language attitudes depend on the particular focus. Baker (1992: 29) points to the following focuses of language attitudes research over the years:

1. Attitude to language variation, dialect and speech style
2. Attitude to learning a new language
3. Attitude to a specific minority language (such as Welsh)
4. Attitude to language groups, communities, minorities
5. Attitude to language lessons
6. Attitude of parents to language learning
7. Attitude to the uses of a specific language
8. Attitude to language preference

The main focus in this book is on the first of these. However, even if the empirical studies considered in the latter section of this book concern attitudes to varieties of English in Wales and to their respective dialect communities, the bilingual nature of the Welsh context inevitably draws in references to and implications for the Welsh language and Welsh-language speakers (and so to 3, 4 and 8 above). As regards 4, it is generally difficult to distinguish attitudes to language varieties from attitudes to the groups and community-members who use them. This is so for particular, important theoretical reasons. Language varieties and forms have indexical properties which allow them to 'stand for' communities, metonymically. Language is often, therefore, more than just 'a characteristic of' or 'a quality of' a community. It is able to enshrine what is distinctive in that community, or, we might even say, constitutes that community.

From a sociolinguistic perspective, one important goal of sociolinguistic research is to construct a 'record of overt attitudes towards language, linguistic features and linguistic stereotypes' (Labov, 1984: 33). Language attitudes research, for Labov, provides a backdrop for explaining linguistic variation and change. It could be argued, though, that attitudes to language varieties underpin all manner of sociolinguistic and social psychological phenomena: for example, the group stereotypes by which we judge other individuals, how we position ourselves within social groups, how we relate to individuals and groups other than our own. There may be behavioural consequences, in the short – and long – term, and serious experiential outcomes. For example, do language attitudes lead to certain groups (such as speakers of regional dialects, speakers of minority languages) doing better or worse in the labour market, in health care, in the courts, in the educational system? And how, in turn, might awareness of such consequences impact on attitudes or behaviours? Will people speak a minority language less, eventually leading to language death, and perhaps even cultural assimilation? Or will psychological reactance set in (J. Brehm and S. Brehm, 1981) and concerted efforts be made to protect and promote the language, to change attitudes and behaviours, and to rescue and re-establish linguistic and cultural continuity? As we will see, issues of this sort are very much to the fore in contemporary Wales, a traditionally fragmented community which is presented with new opportunities to achieve more integration and coherence.

The study of language attitudes seeks to do more than to discover simply what people's attitudes are, and what effects they might be having in terms of behavioural outcomes. A further concern is to understand what it is that determines and defines these attitudes. Particular linguistic forms have understandably received a great deal of attention, particularly from sociolinguists. Labov's early work focused on the evaluative meanings of specific phonological sociolinguistic variables, most famously, the postvocalic (r) on the eastern seaboard of the USA. Social psychologists have often tended to work at a less specific level regarding linguistic features, working at times with the notion of a 'whole language' (for example, French, in Lambert, Hodgson, Gardner and Fillenbaum, 1960; Classical Arabic, in El Dash and Tucker, 1975), or with a 'whole' or 'generalized' variety such as a 'south-Welsh accent of English' (for example, Giles, 1970). Other researchers, particularly sociolinguists, have sometimes felt that terms such as 'Welsh English' are too unspecific. For example, there are certainly many regional dialect communities of English speakers within Wales, and so it may not be clear enough to which of these the attitudinal data refers. For that reason, they have often offered a description of some of the most salient phonological features of the language variety being evaluated in the study (for example, Knops, 1988; Garrett, 1992; Levin, Giles and Garrett, 1994). Other studies have focused on the use of features of grammar rather than phonology: for example, tag questions (Petty, Cacioppo and Heesacker, 1981), the ordering of clauses (Levin and Garrett, 1990). The studies discussed in the second half of this book focus on a range of dialects of English in Wales, reflecting the broad pattern of dialect differentiation that emerges from the descriptive work set out in Coupland (1990). We overview phonological and other differences between major varieties on p. 70, following.

Attitude studies can also tell us about within-community and cross-community variation and cultural differences. Many studies have found language attitudes differing according to the social characteristics of the people making the judgements (the 'judges'). If attitudes are learned and based on people's earlier experiences, information and inferences, these sources are of course related to social-group membership. Ethnic and regional groups have received much attention from researchers, and attitudinal differences between such groups have often been found to be the most salient compared to other dimensions of group belonging, such as gender (for example, Gorter and Ytsma, 1988), perhaps because individual members of such groups are under more pressure to conform to their speech communities (Saville-Troike, 1982). Earlier language attitudes work in Wales, focusing mainly on attitudes to the Welsh language, to Standard British English (or at least its phonological level of Received Pronunciation), and to Welsh English dialects, showed an ambiguous (or even seemingly contradictory) mixture of findings, culminating in Price, Fluck and Giles (1983) arguing for a survey of attitudes over a larger geographical area (such as all of Wales), capturing a spread of regional communities. The studies detailed in the second half of this book are in part a response to their call to investigate the regional variation of attitudes over a number of communities throughout Wales.

Language attitudes research sometimes also seeks to understand how evaluative judgements are affected by properties of the context in which language use occurs (Hymes, 1972). For example, Received Pronunciation (RP) speakers are associated with prestige, intelligence, a good job, etc., in many situations. However, in certain legal contexts, they may be associated with embezzlement and fraud (Seggie, 1983). Our own research focuses mainly on the educational context, with data gathered from teachers and students all over Wales. In chapter 3, further components in the context of our research are considered, such as discourse goals, the content of talk, and interlocutor features, such as age.

Main approaches to the study of language attitudes

Approaches to researching language attitudes are usually grouped under three broad headings (for example, see Ryan, Giles and Hewstone, 1988): the analysis of the *societal treatment* of language varieties

INTRODUCTION: THE SCOPE OF LANGUAGE ATTITUDES

(relabelled 'content analysis' by Knops and van Hout, 1988: 6); *direct measures*; and *indirect measures* (sometimes referred to as the 'speaker-evaluation paradigm', or 'the matched-guise technique' by Lambert et al., 1960). Each of these approaches inevitably has its own strengths and weaknesses. For the purposes of this introductory chapter, these approaches will be briefly outlined and distinguished. While we do not pursue the societal-treatment approach any further after this introduction (for reasons which are explained below), the direct and indirect approaches will be examined more closely in chapter 2.

The *societal treatment approach* is in fact often overlooked in contemporary discussions of language attitudes research, but it is undoubtedly an important source for gaining insights into the relative status and stereotypical associations of language varieties. The approach generally involves a content analysis of the 'treatment' given to languages and language varieties, and to their speakers within society. Studies falling under this heading typically involve observational, participant observation and ethnographic studies, or the analysis of a host of sources in the public domain. Examples include government and educational language-policy documents and their view on the use of various languages in schools (Cots and Nussbaum, 1999); job advertisements and the occupational demands for Anglophone and Francophone bilinguals in Montreal (Lieberson, 1981); the use of dialect by various characters in novels (Rickford and Traugott, 1985); media output, such as the ethnocultural stereotypes projected through the use of foreign languages in advertisements in Japan (Haarmann, 1984, 1986) and in Switzerland (Cheshire and Moser, 1994); variations in English usage in newspaper-style books (Metcalf, 1985), cartoons, proverbs and etiquette books, and what they have to say to and about women (Kramer, 1974; Kramarae, 1982). Although many of the studies under this rubric are largely qualitative in approach, some of them also use formal sampling procedures and at least provide some descriptive statistics (for example, Lieberson, 1981; Cheshire and Moser, 1994).

In spite of there being relatively little mention in the language attitudes literature of studies employing this approach, this may well not be a function of any dearth of such work. It seems more likely that there is a great deal of attitudinal data in a good number of ethnographic studies, for example, which simply do not get properly reviewed in 'mainstream' accounts. The predominant view of societal treatment research amongst many language attitudes researchers, especially those working in the social psychological tradition, is that much of it is too informal, and that it can therefore serve mainly as a preliminary for more rigorous sociolinguistic and social psychological studies (Ryan et al., 1988: 1069), perhaps as a source of convergent validity to data collected through direct or indirect methods (Knops and van Hout, 1988: 7). Knops and van Hout argue that this approach may be appropriate in situations where restrictions of time and space do not allow direct access to respondents, or where respondents can be accessed only under highly unnatural conditions. It should be pointed out, of course, that the flood of work in discourse analysis and text analysis makes the very different assumption that this work stands independent of these other approaches.

The *direct approach* is generally far more obtrusive than societal-treatment methods. It is characterized by elicitation: the asking of direct questions about language evaluation, preference etc., usually through questionnaires and/or interviews. Knops and van Hout (1988: 7) see the main difference between this and the societal-treatment approach being that it is not the researcher who infers attitudes from the observed behaviours, but the respondents themselves who are asked to do so. Later in this book, we describe and discuss recent attitudinal research employing perceptual dialectological and folklinguistic techniques (Preston, 1989, 1999), and we also include these under the direct approach rubric.

One can of course nevertheless argue that answering interview questions, ticking boxes or circling numbers on questionnaires are all themselves merely behaviours from which the researcher has to infer attitudes. However, they are at one remove from the behavioural reactions in the data analysed in societal-treatment research. As with the societal-treatment approach, the direct approach embraces a considerable array of methods and techniques. The strengths and weaknesses of these, as well as their use in researching language attitudes in Wales, will be considered in chapter 2.

The *indirect approach* to researching attitudes involves engaging in more subtle, and sometimes even deceptive, techniques than directly asking questions. In attitudes research generally, three broad strategies are used under this heading (Dawes and Smith, 1985). These are: observing subjects without their awareness that they are being observed; observing aspects of people's behaviour over which one can presume that they have no control (see, for example, Cacioppo, Petty, Losch and Crites, 1994, on physiological reactions); successfully fooling subjects, for example, into believing that the questioner is examining

INTRODUCTION: THE SCOPE OF LANGUAGE ATTITUDES

something that has nothing to do with their attitudes. Subject to these deceptions being considered acceptable, this is considered a particularly useful approach where it is too intrusive, for some reason detrimental, or not possible to administer direct questions through an interview or questionnaire (Perloff, 1993: 44). Ethical issues concerning such deception are generally dealt with through debriefing (defined by Smith and Mackie, 2000: 52, as 'informing research participants – as soon as possible after the completion of their participation in research – about the purposes, procedures, and scientific value of the study, and discussing any questions participants may have').

In language attitudes research, however, the indirect approach is generally seen as synonymous with the *matched-guise technique* (MGT) developed in the late 1950s by Lambert and his colleagues in Canada (for example, Lambert et al., 1960), and approaches deriving from it. Arguably, this technique does not quite fit Dawes and Smith's categories associated with the indirect approach in attitudes research generally, as outlined above. There are two ways in particular in which it differs. Firstly, in many matched-guise studies respondents do indeed answer questions, usually filling in attitude-rating scales on questionnaires. Hence it is essentially an elicitation task. Secondly, respondents actually are typically aware that their attitudes are being studied. However, matched-guise studies are usually designed in such a way that the respondents are deceived into thinking that the researchers are investigating attitudes other than those that they are actually researching, which is why this is regarded as an indirect method.

Typically (as an illustration of the above points), respondents in matched-guise studies hear an audiotape recording of a single speaker reading out the same text a number of times, differing on each occasion in one respect only. For example, if the focus of the study is on regional or social accent variation, then the text will be read in a number of relevant accents, but with other features remaining constant as far as possible (such as speech rate, pauses and hesitations, etc.). Respondents are told that they will be listening to a number of different speakers. They are not told that the speaker is in fact the same person speaking in different 'guises', and it is assumed that this deception lasts for the duration of the evaluation task. They are asked to listen to each speaker, pausing after each one in order to fill in attitude-rating scales. Attitude-rating questionnaires are therefore used in such studies, and listeners are aware that this is an attitude-rating task, though they believe they are rating the various people, rather than the accents.

A great deal of language attitudes research has been conducted since the 1960s using the MGT. It is fair to say that in the social psychological wing of language attitudes research, and also to a large extent in the sociolinguistic field, it has tended to be the dominant approach. However, despite its strengths, it has by no means escaped criticism, especially of its decontextualized presentation of language varieties and its arguable over-reliance on attitude-rating scales. In the next chapter we examine this approach further, and we review some of the relevant research in Wales. The review of the MGT in chapter 2 will lay some of the groundwork to explain why, in the studies set out in the latter half of the book, alternative methods are explored, despite their arguably lacking the rigour of the MGT.

Researching attitude variation in Wales

Wales has long been a focus for research into language attitudes. On the one hand, a considerable body of research has investigated the attitudinal foundations and outcomes of the use of the Welsh language and of the promotion of bilingualism in educational contexts (for example, Jones, 1949, 1950; Sharp, Thomas, Price, Francis and Davies, 1973; Lewis, 1975; Price-Jones, 1982; Baker, 1992; Garrett, Griffiths, James and Scholfield, 1992, 1994). The implications for the survival and revival of Welsh have, of course, been of particular importance in this agenda (see, for example, Baker, 1988, 1992). A further body of research has worked more in the domain of monolingual sociolinguistic variation and social psychology, investigating the social meanings attached to Welsh, Welsh English, and (primarily) RP (reviewed, for example, in Giles, 1990).

The value of both these lines of research has extended far beyond the Welsh context. For the former strand, Wales has been a 'rich research ground', serving as a 'rich microcosm of minority language problems, practices and potentialities' (Baker, 1992: 6). In relation to monolingual variation, attitude research in Wales has contributed greatly to the proliferation of studies in many parts of the world over the last thirty years, to help advance our understanding of the cultural processes at work in language, and how language both reflects and manufactures social meanings, personal and social identities in context. Such understanding has obvious bearings on language change, maintenance, death or revival, cultural continuity and, as we will see later, also on perceptions of cultural authenticity.

Matched-guise studies published in the 1970s and early 1980s threw up a confusion of findings as regards the relative evaluative profiles of speakers of Welsh, Welsh English and RP. These will be reviewed more closely in chapter 3. Suffice it to say here that, given that the relative statuses of these speakers differed so much between the various studies (for example, compare Giles, 1970; Bourhis, Giles and Tajfel, 1973; Bourhis and Giles, 1976), Price et al. (1983), whose own results differed once again, ultimately called for larger-scale studies that would cover different regions within the same country or state in an effort to build a geolinguistic atlas of the social meanings of linguistic varieties. In their view, this would enable us to appreciate potentially significant regional and contextual differences in groups' responses to varieties of language use.

There may, however, be a number of reasons why results from these earlier studies produced such a mixture of findings, and not all of them necessarily relate to the possible regional diversity that led Price et al. (1983) to suggest a geolinguistic atlas of attitudes. Different findings may also have reflected the varying ages and social groups of the respondents. One further feature of the studies in the second part of the book, therefore, is that they are confined to the educational domain, collecting attitudinal data from teachers and from teenage school-students. One reason for selecting the education domain was that it has long been shown to be a context in which language attitudes can have a considerable impact on life-opportunities (for example, Seligman, Tucker and Lambert, 1972; Choy and Dodd, 1976; Edwards and Giles, 1984). Another was to gain insights from an attitudinal comparison between the teachers' attitudes, which one might expect to form the basis of their classroom interventions in the language use of the students, and those of the teenagers, who have the competing concern of identity negotiation during this period. This aspect of adolescent communication and identity building will be considered in more depth in chapter 3, when the empirical work is introduced. Within the context of Wales and concerns of the survival of the Welsh language, this period of identity formation in the early teens has long been seen as a critical period in terms of changing attitudes towards the Welsh and English languages (Baker, 1988, 1992).

The more general rationale for studying language attitudes in Wales is to contribute to our understanding of the country's fascinating and delicate sociolinguistic ecology. The sociolinguistics of Wales is usually defined in relation to the decline, and more recently the stabilization and revitalization, of the Welsh language (see, for example, Williams, 1995, 2000). The findings of the 2001 census are documenting the next chapter in the language's story, and these demographic shifts, of course, provide a crucial backdrop to any treatment of language and society in Wales. At the same time, ethnolinguistic identity in Wales is as much bound up with use of the English language as with use of Welsh.

The historical imprint of the anglicization of Wales – in the linguistic sense of the relentless attrition of Welsh through the nineteenth and twentieth centuries, and in the wider cultural sense – is a feature that colours *both* of Wales's main languages. Welsh has come to be principally associated with different 'heartland' territories in Wales, mainly in the north-west, especially the county of Gwynedd, and parts of the south and the south-west of the country (Aitchison and Carter, 1994). This sociolinguistic territorialization of Wales is reflected in a complex system of sociocultural perceptions of different parts of the country, not least involving assessments of where 'the real Wales' and 'properly Welsh' parts of Wales are to be found. As we shall see, this areal pattern gives Wales much of its rich cultural distinctiveness, even though it also leads to problems of national incohesiveness and disputes over regional and national policy, with language often implicated in them. The English accents and dialects of Wales have come to symbolize the most fundamental cultural divides, not least those between communities of the north, mid-Wales and the south, between rural and urban zones, and between traditionally Welsh-speaking and non-Welsh-speaking areas. Wales sustains a rich array of sociolinguistic stereotypes, which vary across significant geographical and cultural fault-lines. These lie at the heart of the studies we report later.

For contemporary Wales, describing and modelling the perceptual tendencies that support such cultural differences are in our view important tasks, especially at this point in time. Several decades of fitful initiatives by politicians and political parties in Wales, but more efficaciously by non-governmental pressure groups and cultural agencies, have produced highly significant shifts in governmental policy and institutions. The National Assembly for Wales, devolved from the Westminster Parliament and assuming many of the functions of the traditional Welsh Office government department, has for four years (at the time of writing) brought the potential for more autonomous control of some socio-economic functions, but also cultural developments in Wales. The trajectory of the Welsh language appears to be much more favourable now than in recent decades, with rapidly increasing institutional support for the language following the implementation of the 1993 Language Act. It is often said that Wales is beginning to be 'more confident', more secure in its national identity and perhaps more adventurous in its sociocultural ambitions. References to 'cool Cymru' may prove to be short-lived, but they suggest the possibility of new, less traditional and more positive meanings for Welshness. A fundamental question, then, is whether Wales can reconcile its internal cultural differences, or at least find ways to accommodate the diversity of 'Welshnesses' that are currently in evidence. A first step in this direction is to document the Welshnesses that exist on the ground in people's stereotyped conceptions, and how they are articulated.

Research questions of this book

This book, then, is concerned with the following questions, which we can group under two broad subheadings.

A. Methodological and conceptual issues in language attitudes research
1. What are the theoretical underpinnings, strengths and constraints of some of the main approaches to the study of language attitudes?
2. To what extent can different methods be expected to provide different insights into language attitudes?
3. Can methods employing other less highly controlled modes of speech presentation than the matched-guise technique still lead to valid and significant findings?
4. What advantages might accrue from the gathering of open-ended response data rather than relying upon attitude-rating scales?

B. Sociocultural issues for groups and communities
5. What is the nature of the attitudinal profiles of the English dialect communities across Wales, and how can they be accessed?
6. Is there systematic variation in language attitudes among respondents according to variables such as their regional location, Welsh/English bilingualism, whether they are teachers or teenagers; and how can this variation be accessed?
7. Do data on teenagers' language attitudes provide us with any

insights into their identity formation, and what methods can best tap into their sociolinguistic worlds?
8. What are the general implications of patterns of young people's language attitudes in Wales for 'Welshness' and the changing socio-political face of Wales?

Outline of this book

Reflecting this movement in the book from issues of method to issues of cultural difference, the next two chapters contain a critical review of the main methods employed in language attitudes research, and a review of studies that have employed such methods, in particular where they relate to Wales. In chapter 2, we look at direct approaches. This review not only includes the traditional direct elicitation of attitudes through conventional questionnaires and interviews, but also extends to recent innovative approaches promoted and further developed by Preston (1989, 1999) in the area of folklinguistics and perceptual dialectology. In chapter 3, we then go on to review the MGT, which has been perhaps the dominant and the most controversial method employed during the last thirty years.

In later chapters, we move on to report our own empirical research, with a description and explanation of the variety of methods employed to gather various kinds of language attitudinal data from teachers and teenagers in secondary schools across Wales. We also provide some additional contextualization of the empirical work, to elaborate further on why teachers and teenagers are the selected respondents in this work, and to explain the significance of some lines of elicitation. The empirical work falls broadly into two separate, complementary sets of studies, each using different sets of methods. In the first set, a series of questionnaires was distributed to teachers in secondary schools selected from all over Wales. We refer to this study as 'the questionnaire study'. Dialects were presented only conceptually in this phase, and a range of data was gathered from attitude-rating scales, open-ended questions, perceptual maps and labelling tasks. In the other set of studies, dialect samples, based on narratives told by teenagers, were played to teachers and to teenagers of the same age in similar schools all over Wales, and attitude data were collected from attitude-rating scales, open-ended items, and focus-group interviews. We refer to this study as 'the narratives study'. The results from those two studies are discussed in chapters 5 to 9. Chapter 10 concludes the book with a summary discussion of findings, returning to the main questions set out in the previous section, and then assesses the contribution of this work to this long-established research area.

2

Direct approaches

We begin this chapter by elaborating on what is meant by a 'direct approach' to researching language attitudes. We consider various data-collecting procedures typically employed in this approach, and some of the main issues in their design and use. We then review a number of direct-approach studies that have been conducted in Wales using these procedures. We also include in this chapter the recently emerging 'perceptual dialectology' and folklinguistic methods, since these can also be generally classified under the 'direct approach' heading. The perceptual dialectology procedures are somewhat different from the ones we consider in the earlier part of this chapter, and so we introduce them after our review of research in Wales using the earlier procedures. We then conclude with a review of perceptual dialectological research relevant to Wales.

Direct approaches to language attitudes research

In the previous chapter, the societal-treatment approach to researching language attitudes was referred to briefly. We mentioned that two of the properties of this approach were its unobtrusiveness, and the fact that it is the researcher who infers attitudes from observed behaviours, document analysis, etc. The direct approach to investigating language attitudes, by contrast, is characterized by a high degree of obtrusiveness, and by the fact that it is the informants themselves who are asked to report their attitudes. One central methodological issue involved here concerns 'whether subjects' verbal statements of their attitudes and their behavioural reactions in concrete situations can indeed both be interpreted as manifestations of the same underlying dispositions' (Knops and van Hout, 1988: 7).

Assuming this can be resolved, language attitudes can be measured directly with interviews and/or questionnaires concerning specific aspects of language. An early and well-known example of such research is to be found in Labov's (1966) work in which he asked New York City respondents to choose which of two alternative pronunciations they used and which they felt they should use. The direct approach has been used across a whole range of contexts: to predict second-language learning (Gardner and Lambert, 1972; Gardner, 1982), and relative language use (Gardner and Lambert, 1972; Hidalgo, 1984), to examine policy issues such as bilingual education (Mosley, 1969; Carranza, 1976). It has also been employed to study people's attitudes to the preservation or promotion of whole languages (rather than particular varieties or features), such as Gaelic (MacKinnon, 1981) and Irish (CILAR, 1975; O'Riagain, 1993), or attitudes to two languages in bilingual contexts, such as Welsh and English (Jones, 1949, 1950; Sharp et al., 1973; Lewis, 1975; Baker, 1992; Garrett, Griffiths et al., 1992, 1994), and Spanish and English in the USA (Ryan and Carranza, 1980), and to study the impact of language legislation in such contexts (Bourhis, 1983). According to Cargile et al. (1994: 213), direct approaches have facilitated research into more languages, language varieties and linguistic features than have been covered by societal-treatment analyses.

Data-collection procedures

Central to the direct approach is the question of whether to collect data through 'word-of-mouth' techniques, or through 'written response' techniques, to use the broad dichotomous terms employed by Henerson et al. (1987). It is important to deal in this chapter with the main relative merits of these with particular regard to research that investigates attitudes at the group level. Some of the issues that will be raised also relate to the indirect approach, which we consider in the next chapter. Similarly, although some attention is given to statistical analysis of quantitative data here, we return to statistical methods in chapter 3 in relation to the interval data gathered from semantic-differential scales. Beyond this, in the research we report later, we deal with statistical matters as they arise.

In the category of 'word of mouth' procedures, Henerson et al. (1987: 24) list 'interviews, surveys and polls'. They define a poll as simply a headcount, where respondents are simply presented with a limited number of options, such as 'do you think MORE or LESS French should be taught in secondary schools?' This type of 'word-of-mouth' technique is seldom used in language attitudes research, so we do not consider it further. Henerson et al. distinguish 'interviews' from 'surveys' by stating that the latter is a 'highly structured interview' that need not be face-to-face (for example, it may take place over the telephone). For our purposes, however, as word-of-mouth procedures, these will both be considered as interviews. Interviews and focus-group interviews can usefully be distinguished, however, and we deal with this distinction later.

Henerson et al.'s 'written-response' procedures include 'questionnaires and attitude-rating scales' (p. 27). We make no distinction here, though, since attitude-rating scales are an integral part of questionnaires in much language attitudes research. Henerson et al. separate into a different category of procedures less formal written accounts, such as logs, journals, diaries, etc. (p. 29). However, such less-structured sources can also be useful for attitudinal data in direct-approach studies, and so we also include them in this chapter. For instance, questions requiring short essay-type accounts or other kinds of qualitative data sometimes occur on questionnaires.

The procedures considered below, then, are dealt with under the broad headings of questionnaires and interviews, with some separate consideration of focus-group interviews. These data collection techniques will be discussed and compared against a number of different qualities and merits. There is of course a substantial literature on the design and execution of questionnaires and interviews generally (for example, Burroughs, 1971; Cohen and Manion, 1994), and on focus-group interviews specifically (see Vaughn, Schumm and Sinagub, 1996; Morgan, 1997), with some concerned with their use in attitude research in particular (for example, Triandis, 1971; Oppenheim, 1992). Here, we consider just a selection of the main issues that are involved in the decisions that have to be made in their design and implementation. We begin by considering general difficulties with the direct approach. Some of these issues are rather basic, and betray a lack of linguistic sensitivity in the literature, but they nevertheless relate to some of the research questions set out in chapter 1, in particular those concerning the strengths and constraints of approaches, the expectations we might have of the insights provided by different methods, and the pros and cons of gathering data from open-ended or closed-ended items.

Common issues affecting direct-approach studies

Whether questionnaires or interviews are used, there are a number of general difficulties of which researchers need generally to be mindful when designing direct-approach studies. These pitfalls include: hypothetical questions, strongly slanted questions, multiple questions, social-desirability bias, acquiescence bias, characteristics of the researcher, the language employed in the process of data collection and group polarization. The first three of these are directly related to the formulation of questions, and hence become extremely important in the preparation of questionnaires and of interview schedules. The remainder are connected more with common tendencies in respondents, for which researchers need to be on their guard in the process of data collection, and which they can sometimes anticipate in the design of their studies. Since some of these difficulties also feature in the indirect approach to language attitudes research, some of the studies we cite below as illustrations are ones that have used the indirect approach.

Hypothetical questions

Hypothetical questions ask how people *would* react to a particular event or action. They are often poor predictors of people's future reactions or behaviour in a situation where such an event or action is actually encountered (see, for example, Breckler's 1984 study on attitudes towards snakes, in which one group was asked how they would react if they encountered one, and a comparable group's reactions were recorded when they did actually encounter one). Hence, if one is investigating attitudes with a view to gaining insights into likely behaviour arising from them, the use of hypothetical questions is less likely to allow such insights.

Strongly slanted questions

These are questions that employ relatively 'loaded' items that tend to push people into answering one way. Oppenheim (1992: 130, 137) lists a number of terms that are often viewed as best to avoid: for example, 'Nazi', 'Reds', 'bosses', 'strike-breakers', 'healthy', 'natural'. Questions may also be slanted less by individual loaded items, but more by their overall leading content: for example, 'Do you disagree that Welsh children should be perfectly entitled to learn Welsh?'

Multiple questions
Multiple questions are either questions where a positive answer can refer to more than one component of the question, or double negative questions, to which a negative answer would be ambiguous. Baker (1988) points to one such instance in MacKinnon's (1981) survey of opinion on Scottish Gaelic. One of the survey items was: 'Should children in any part of Scotland be able to learn Gaelic at school if they or their parents want it?' The question conflates children and parents in the conditional clause, making the interpretation of answers difficult. There are arguably two questions in one here, and the responses to it differed considerably from those to other questions in his survey. On most of the major points covered by the survey, approximately 40 per cent to 50 per cent of the total sample were positive towards Gaelic and the remainder were neutral or negative. But about 70 per cent of the responses to the above question were positive, suggesting the double-barrelled nature of the question may have combined responses relating to both children and parents.

Social-desirability bias
This is the tendency for people to give 'socially appropriate responses' to questions. Cook and Sellitz (1964: 39), working in the United States, reported that people are often motivated to give replies that make them appear 'well-adjusted, unprejudiced, rational, open-minded and democratic'. Questions aimed at tapping attitudes towards racial, ethnic and religious minorities are often hampered by a social-desirability bias. Respondents harbouring negative views towards a particular group may not wish to admit to the researcher, or even to themselves, that they hold such feelings, and so 'they may avoid giving answers that would make them look like bigots' (Perloff, 1993: 44). One of the reasons for guaranteeing anonymity or confidentiality to respondents, of course, is to reduce the risk that they will merely provide socially desirable responses, but one cannot be certain that even this in itself will be entirely effective. Social-desirability bias is deemed to be of greater significance in interviews than in questionnaires (Oppenheim, 1992: 126), and logically, one might expect the greatest risk of social-desirability bias in interviews with whole groups of

respondents (for example, focus group interviews) where there is no individual anonymity.

Acquiescence bias

Acquiescence bias (Ostrom et al., 1994) is a further difficulty. Some respondents may tend to agree with an item, regardless of its content. They may see this as a way of gaining the researcher's approval. This, too, then means that the responses do not reflect the respondent's actual personal evaluation of the attitude statement, and therefore raises issues of validity. Acquiescence bias can occur in response to questionnaire or interview items, although some claim that it is especially pronounced in oral face-to-face interviews (Gass and Seiter, 1999: 45). It would seem plausible that acquiescence bias would be reduced where group discussion is encouraged, and group polarization (see below) is more likely to occur, but we know of no research into this issue.

Social desirability and acquiescence are features that arguably impact on some attitudes more than others, and on some people more than others. For example, it may well be that they have a greater effect where the issues are of some personal sensitivity, or where the issues are less likely to have been well thought through. And in terms of the respondents themselves, there is evidence to suggest that people who are more 'ego-involved' are less likely to articulate or even tolerate a view that is not in accord with their own (see, for example, Bettinghaus and Cody, 1994: 168ff.). Nevertheless, these are features of language attitudes research that can prevent researchers tapping into the 'private attitudes' of respondents, and it was these sorts of difficulties, and the importance of accessing such private attitudes, that led Lambert and his colleagues (for example, Lambert, 1967) to develop an indirect approach to language attitudes research (the MGT), which is examined in the next chapter. The issue of social desirability is also considered again in chapter 6 when weighing up possible interpretations of some of the results of the research discussed there.

Characteristics of the researcher

Qualities of the researchers themselves may also affect the validity of attitude data, reflecting what might be termed an 'Interviewer's Paradox' (compare with Labov's 'Observer's Paradox'). Responses to questions posed by the researcher may be affected by the ethnicity and gender of both sides, for example. Webster (1996) investigated these issues in relation to Anglo and Hispanic males and females in the US. She found that better response rates were achieved when interviewers and respondents shared the same ethnicity (especially in the case of Anglos, and especially when questions related to cultural issues). There was a tendency for self-reported biographical data to be distorted where ethnicities were not matched, and also where sexes were not matched. Hispanic men were found to exaggerate upwards their socio-economic status when interviewed by either Hispanic women or by Anglo men. Investigating attitudes in an employment context, Dunnette and Heneman (1956) found that respondents were more open about their attitudes towards superiors when interviewed by a university researcher than when interviewed by a personnel manager. Wolfson (1976) also stresses the impact of power and solidarity attributes, such as sex, age and perceived social status, on the quality of data gleaned from interviews in particular. Similarly, recent language attitudes research in Wales conducted by a Japanese researcher has thrown up results that differ from comparable data collected by Welsh or English researchers (Bellin, Matsuyama, and Schott, 1999). Not entirely unrelated to this is the finding that the language employed in data collection may also have an impact on the results, particularly where language is a salient dimension of intergroup comparison (for example, Price et al., 1983).

Effects of prior discussion
Questionnaire results have been found to be affected by whether discussion of the questions is permitted before respondents complete questionnaires. In particular, there has been some investigation of the group polarization phenomenon (see, for example, Myers and Arenson, 1972; Myers and Lamm, 1976), which maintains that groups can make people more extreme in their decisions. Giles, Harrison, Creber, Smith and Freeman (1983), found significant differences in their study of language attitudes of Bristol schoolchildren when children were given time to discuss questionnaire items before completing them. It should be noted here that people tend not to have qualitatively different attitudes in such conditions. Rather, for example, on an attitude scale, a slightly negative rating – say, a 3 on a seven-point scale – is more likely to shift in the group condition to a 1, or a positive rating of 5 to a 7, suggesting that respondents have more confidence in their judgements after group discussion, or that they wish to differentiate themselves from the average that they see within the group. (If this is a regular

pattern, it would suggest that group discussion would not counter acquiescence effects in the way speculated above.) For a fuller discussion of the theoretical debate around the group polarization effect, see, for example, Boster, 1990 and Pavitt, 1994.

A similar but more specific phenomenon has been investigated by Alderfer (1968), but this time the questionnaire completion was preceded, not by group discussion, but by an interview with the researcher. He found that attitudes expressed about peers were significantly more negative in that condition. Alderfer concluded that the additional familiarity with the researcher in this condition enabled them to provide more valid data regarding these more intimate attitudes. Prior interviews did not produce different data in the case of other attitudes involving less intimacy (for example, financial rewards).

'Word-of-mouth' and 'written-response' procedures

In this section, we look at various properties of data-gathering procedures that need to be considered in designing language attitudes surveys. Many of these issues are of a very practical nature, but they are basal considerations in selecting methods.

When 'written response' cannot be used

There are, of course, research contexts where questionnaires simply cannot be employed, and where interviewing is the only option available. Questionnaires have to assume adequate respondent literacy in the language in which the questionnaire is written. This cannot always be safely assumed. Young children, for example, may have to be interviewed. Furthermore, some languages have no written script. Even where speakers of such languages have competence in a more widely used scripted language, their reading and writing competence in that language may not be developed enough for a researcher to be sure that they would be able to understand the questionnaire and express their responses reliably.

This is not to say, of course, that interviewing in such cases is necessarily straightforward either. Interviewing young children can be encumbered with its own difficulties (for example, Aldridge and Wood, 1998). And Schmied (1991: 163), while pointing to the difficulties that often arise in using questionnaires in language attitudes research in Africa, also points to the fact that in many instances populations are unused to being interviewed by outsiders. Wolfson (1976), too, mentions and exemplifies effects of power differentials on what happens in interviews, even where respondents have literacy in the language used.

Dynamics: individual and group
Most commonly, data in language attitudes research are collected from individuals rather than from groups of people together, whether the data are collected through written responses on questionnaires, or through spoken responses to interview questions. The individual responses are then analysed, through statistical analysis, for example, or through various forms of content analysis to identify patterns at the group level. Wolfson (1976) notes that native English speakers generally define interviews in English as having a question–response format, most often between two people. In this aspect of dynamics, questionnaires and interviews tend to share the same property.

However, focus-group interviews are also used in such research. This has been a popular research technique in marketing and business for more than thirty years, but its use has nowadays extended into other fields, such as psychology, communication and politics (Cannon, 1994). Market researchers viewed the use of focus-group interviews as an insightful complement to surveys, since they could provide a better understanding of why people felt the way they did, not simply the number of individuals who felt a particular way (Bellenger, Bernhardt and Goldstucker, 1976; Calder, 1977).

There are a number of definitions of focus groups. Vaughn et al. (1996: 5) set out the following core elements in definitions:

1. The group is an informal assembly of target persons whose points of view are requested to address a selected topic.
2. The group is small, six to twelve members, and is usually homogeneous.
3. A trained moderator with prepared questions and probes sets the stage and induces participants' responses.
4. The goal is to elicit perceptions, feelings, attitudes and ideas of participants about a selected topic.
5. A focus group does not generate quantitative information that can be projected to a larger population.

Focus-group interviews are used in a variety of research designs. Morgan (1997) sets out how they can be linked to studies involving individual interviews, for example by generating a range of informants' thoughts and experiences prior to the individual interviews, or employing individual interviews to generate ideas to provide a basis for subsequent focus-group interviews. Focus groups can also be linked to experimental research to help in the search for explanations of unexpected findings, for example. With surveys, they may typically be used as a preliminary, to help ensure that the survey items capture all the domains needed, to provide item wordings, and even to contribute to hypotheses. Or they may also be used as a follow-up to data collection to pursue exploratory aspects of analysis or speculative interpretations.

Krueger (1981: 1) describes focus-group interviews as organized group discussions focused around a single theme, and it is this element of group discussion that, according to Vaughn et al. (1996: 4), tends to distinguish focus groups from other interview procedures.

In the context of focus groups, it is worth noting concerns that have been expressed about the large amounts of data that such interviews usually generate. Various ways have been proposed to content-analyse the transcripts from focus group interviews. Vaughn et al. (1996: 105ff.) outline a five-step procedure. Step 1 is the identification (perhaps during or immediately following the interview) of the strongest themes emerging from the data. Step 2 involves breaking down the data into 'units': the smallest amount of information (a phrase, sentence, or paragraph) that is informative in itself. In step 3, these units are organized into categories, perhaps by two coders working independently who then, in step 4, compare their categories and negotiate a final set. In step 5, the researcher considers whether the strong themes from step 1 are supported by these categories. Relevant theories or models are employed for interpreting the categories and findings, if indeed they have not been used much earlier on for developing data analysis (Yin, 1989).

Such group dynamics are more a feature of 'word-of-mouth' data collection than 'written-response' procedures in language attitudes research. However, group discussion itself has sometimes been encouraged immediately prior to the filling in of attitudes questionnaires (for example, Giles et al., 1983), as was mentioned earlier in this chapter.

Numbers of respondents
One of the advantages of using questionnaires is that data can be collected from a large number of people simultaneously. For example, if

100 people can be accessed in a single location to fill in questionnaires requiring fifteen minutes to complete, only one researcher needs to be present to collect a substantial amount of data in a short period of time. Depending on the nature of the study, of course, a researcher may find that such a session enables them to collect all the data they need in order to address their research question adequately. To interview such a large sample of people would almost inevitably take either a great deal of time, or involve a large number of trained interviewers, or even both, and therefore require considerably more resources.

Distance
Where it is not possible or not desirable to access respondents in a single location, it is possible to post questionnaires. This is usually a less satisfactory way of issuing questionnaires than the above, because return rates on posted questionnaires are generally notoriously low. However, in some instances, it is the only option open, and can nevertheless provide sufficient data without involving an interviewer in the financial and temporal costs of travel. In the research that we discuss later in this book, the postal solution to distance was used and return rates were indeed low initially.

Uniformity
Using questionnaires is a relatively uniform procedure, compared with an interview, and the claim is sometimes made that this gives questionnaires a reliability advantage over interviews (for example, Burroughs, 1971: 103). Whereas an interviewer may (even unintentionally) put questions in different ways to different people and/or on different occasions, a questionnaire is free from these and other interviewer effects. Of course, this does not mean that one can be certain that all the respondents will interpret the questions in the same way, or that they will respond unambiguously. On the other hand, proper piloting of a questionnaire is aimed at minimizing such problems.

Anonymity
Questionnaires can offer more anonymity for respondents than interviews. Possibly, as was mentioned earlier, this reduces the likelihood of responses being affected by social desirability.

Interactive nature and response rates
Perhaps one of the greatest advantages of interviews over written-

response methods is that, through being on the spot, interviewers are able to combat reluctance in respondents, and so achieve better response rates compared to, say, posted questionnaires. It is also often invaluable to be able to exploit the interactive nature of the interview context. Most obviously, it is easy to identify and pursue any differences in interpretation of questions, to encourage respondents to clarify any unclear responses, to pursue responses in more depth, and spontaneously to take up any unanticipated but interesting points that are raised in the course of the interview (especially in focus-group interviews). Interviews in general also allow greater scope for people to respond in their own terms rather than being confined to predetermined categories, which is often a feature of questionnaires.

Perhaps because of the better opportunities for expressing oneself in one's own terms, the argument is sometimes made that interviewing better allows an assessment of the strength of an attitude. Henerson et al. (1987: 25), for example, say that, whereas on a questionnaire a respondent may tick a 'no' box on a yes/no item, when asked the same question in an interview, they might respond with a 'no way', or a 'you must be joking'. However, this argument is not totally convincing, since the problem in their example lies more with the choice of a yes/no item (which could also be used in an interview) than with limitations inherent in questionnaires. As will be seen below, and indeed, paradoxically, as Henerson et al. themselves point out later in their book (p. 84ff.), there are ways in which attitude strength has been investigated through written responses. And in the research discussed in chapter 6, it will be seen that written responses on questionnaires can also enable respondents to express themselves in their own terms and display the strength of their attitudes.

Structured/unstructured designs
The degree of structure in data collection is an issue that in general concerns interviews more than questionnaires, although less structured forms of written response (such as essays or diaries on the research topic) are sometimes sought. Unstructured interviews, though perhaps resembling a casual conversation, are based on a general notion of topics that need to be covered, a hidden agenda, but the interviewer also feels free to 'go with the tide', where interesting directions crop up of their own accord. Hence, this differs significantly from, say, an open-ended written response, in that the researchers or interviewers themselves are free to explore in an unstructured fashion. Oppenheim

(1992: 52) sees open-ended interviewing as a preliminary and exploratory stage in research, but others would doubtless see this as a valuable study in itself, rather as there are 'strong' and 'weak' views of ethnography (van Lier, 1988). The same kind of discussion is heard in relation to focus-group interviews (for example, Morgan, 1997).

Interviews can, however, be very highly structured, to the point where they become an orally transacted questionnaire with a set sequence of fixed-worded questions. MacKinnon's (1981) survey interviews appear to have followed this format, allowing the advantage of having several trained interviewers relatively independently conducting the survey of opinions on Scottish Gaelic over the whole of Scotland while still maintaining a high degree of reliability.

Open/closed-endedness

To some extent (though not necessarily) related to the degree of structure is the open- or closed-endedness of responses designed into the interview or questionnaire. A closed-ended response gives respondents a restricted choice of alternative replies, whereas open-ended responses allow the possibility, as with unstructured designs above, of unanticipated and valuable factors coming to the fore, and gives the researcher more opportunity to probe. An open response on a questionnaire might be invited in the form of a few words, a few sentences, or an essay. Where research issues are more open to socially desirable responses, Oppenheim (1992: 127) claims that open-ended questions in an interview are especially sensitive to this kind of bias.

One is of course not restricted to using *either* closed-ended *or* open-ended items. There can be advantages to using both in the same study, with an open-ended item immediately following a particular closed-ended item, in an effort to gain deeper insights into the closed-ended response. As we will show in the studies that we consider later, such a combination can be very illuminating. On a more modest scale, there are parallels with the advantages that focus-group interviews bring to surveys.

It is fair to say that open-ended items are often easier to ask, require more effort to answer, and involve even more work and time to analyse (consider the processing and analysis of focus-group data earlier). Hence the choice between open-ended items and closed-ended items may be influenced by how many respondents will be involved in the study, and the temporal, human, and/or financial resources available for processing and interpreting the data. Closed-ended items may take longer to prepare, but require little time to ask and to answer. They are generally easier to process and analyse. Oppenheim (1992: 115) also suggests that they make group comparisons easier. Disadvantages often cited are that they are more likely to irritate or frustrate respondents if they feel that they are not being given the chance to answer as fully or as accurately as they would wish and, of course, that they do not allow some of the advantages of spontaneity.

To return to the debate about the nature of attitudes, set out in the first chapter, most important in this consideration of closed- and open-ended responses is what they have to say about how attitudes are held and accessed. Arguably, the two alternatives imply two different models of attitudes. Closed-ended items in this direct approach (whether the data are spoken or written) suggest that attitudes can be elicited as simple propositions (perhaps, where rating scales are used, with an indication of the strength with which they are held, although this is not uncontroversial, as we argue below). Open-ended items, whether in a one-to-one interview or focus-group interview, or in written form, such as a short essay as part of a questionnaire, rest on a more discursive model of attitudes, in which attitudes are considered to be best accessed in a more contextualized form, allowing the explicit weighing up of contrasting viewpoints, and the expression of modality. For example: 'A lot of people complain about Welsh being compulsory at school because they could be learning more of something else, and I can see the point they're making, but I think learning Welsh is as, if not more, important, because it's part of our national identity, and everyone ought to be learning it.' Or: 'I know that I really shouldn't say this, but I used to think the Birmingham accent sounded appalling. But now I've lived here a few years, I think it sounds OK.' Or: 'If you're asking me how much status this accent has, I'd say it probably has a great deal of status among some of the key people in the company where I work. But, sadly, it can't have much amongst the people I go to football matches with.' Or: 'I haven't really ever given this any thought, but I suppose I would be against having newsreaders with regional accents.' This more discursive model is likely to be most evident in the interactive and less structured environment of focus-group discussions. Indeed, the group polarization phenomenon, referred to earlier, might be seen as one aspect of the construction and negotiation of attitudes through discourse. However, as social psychologists have shown with group polarization, and as marketing, communication and political consultants have shown with focus groups, this discursive model may not in itself be a viable alternative to the group-based simplified aggregates and trends that surveys seek to find. On the other hand, it can, as in the examples above, provide some clues as to the likelihood of bias due to social desirability or 'non-attitudes'. Indeed, the two models of attitudes can work in parallel to provide a deeper and more revealing understanding of such group-based trends. This is the main rationale for combining open- and closed-ended procedures in the research that we discuss in the later chapters.

Response format: types of closed-ended responses
The simplest of closed-ended items are forced-choice two-way questions, requiring a response of either 'yes' or 'no', 'true' or 'false', 'for' or 'against', etc. This is, at times, all a survey needs to find out. Tabulation of responses is an easy task. And it is possible to treat this as nominal data on which a simple statistical test, such as chi square, can be conducted, if this is desirable. The disadvantage of such dichotomous items is that they might be used where the two-way format is not revealing enough. For example, to the question: 'Since the establishment of the Welsh Assembly, do you think that people in Wales are speaking more Welsh than before?', the answer 'no' leaves open two possible interpretations: that people are speaking Welsh the same as before, or that they are speaking less Welsh. And it may well be that the researcher also needs to resolve that ambiguity.

Multiple-choice responses are a further type of closed-ended item. These are useful when there are several firmly predetermined possible responses, and the researcher wants to make sure that the respondent is aware of all the possibilities that the researcher has thought of. Although these feature in attitudes research (see, for example, Henerson et al., 1987: 67), they tend not to be used in language attitudes research. Rank ordering, allowing preferences and priorities to be seen from a number of items, is also seen to a lesser degree in this field of research. Probably one important reason for the relative absence of such response formats is that they place considerable restrictions on the type of statistical analysis that can be conducted on the data to explore associations and differences.

Attitude-rating scales are probably the most widely used type of closed-ended item in language attitudes research. While the above 'yes/no' items and ranking scales provide nominal and ordinal data respectively, rating scales have the advantage of giving interval data, which allow more advanced and revealing statistical analysis (which we will return to in the next chapter). The language attitudes research literature generally refers to three types of attitude-rating scales: *Thurstone*, *Likert*, and *semantic differential*. Semantic-differential scales have become closely associated with the indirect approach discussed in the next chapter, so will be looked at more closely there. Thurstone scales are relatively little used now, so will be dealt with briefly before moving on to Likert scales in this chapter.

Attitude-rating scales

Thurstone scales

The usual method for constructing a Thurstone scale is to construct a pool of relevant attitude statements from the literature and from a pilot study. After that, a group of judges is asked to consider each item individually and place it in one of (usually) eleven piles. What they deem to be the most favourable statements go into pile number one, slightly less favourable ones in pile two, least favourable of all into pile eleven, and so on. The intervals between the piles have to be regarded as subjectively equal.

The next stage is to throw out any statements that different judges have placed in very different piles, on the grounds of unreliability. Of the remainder, through the calculation of medians, a set of statements is arrived at that give an even spread, covering the continuum from highly unfavourable to highly favourable, and providing the number of points the researcher prefers to have on the scale. At this stage, each attitude statement has a scale value. The researcher arranges these final statements in random order on the questionnaire and asks the respondents to indicate which statements they agree with. It is then possible to compute a score for each respondent by finding the mean of the scale values of the statements selected by the respondent (for more detail, see Henerson et al., 1987: 84ff.; Oppenheim, 1992: 190ff.).

Thurstone scales are considered to have an adequate degree of reliability, but, as is clear from the above, they need a great deal of careful preparation in the assembly and pilot-judging of statements to arrive at the scales. It is usually recommended that the group of judges in this preliminary stage are comparable to those who will participate in the main study. These judges are also instructed not to allow their own attitudes to influence the way in which they categorize the statements into eleven piles. It has been found that scale values obtained from quite differing groups of judges correlate well, and that even though it is fairly inevitable that judges will be influenced by their own attitudes in the way they categorize the statements, the effects are generally negligible (Oppenheim, 1992: 195). There can be problems, however, if the scales are used cross-culturally, or if scales used some years ago are used again. In the latter instance, for example, some words may have undergone subtle changes in meaning (Oppenheim, 1992: 195).

Likert scales
Likert scales are seen as giving more reliability (Oppenheim, 1992: 200) and being far less laborious to prepare than Thurstone scales. Preparation involves gathering together (for example, from a group of people comparable to the respondents anticipated for the main study) a number of statements about the attitude one wishes to measure, and then asking a sample of people to rate whether they agree with them or not. There is a balance of positive and negative statements, and responses are scored on a scale of, for example, 1 to 5, with, say, 5 for the most favourable and 1 for the least favourable response. This means that responses are scored differently depending on whether the statement reflects a negative or a positive attitude. Hence favourable statements might be scored 5 for 'strongly agree' and unfavourable statements are scored 1 for 'strongly agree', etc.

So, measuring attitudes towards Welsh, Baker (1992: 141) included the following Likert-scale statements:

> 'Children should not be made to learn Welsh.'
> 'I would like Welsh to take over from the English language in Wales.'
> 'Welsh has no place in the modern world.'
> 'Welsh should be taught to all pupils in Wales.'
> 'You are considered a lower class person if you speak Welsh.'

Summation of scores on related statements provides a single score for each respondent. Factor analysis is often used on such scale ratings. This is a mathematical procedure employed to see to what extent some scales may be measuring something that they have in common, and to discover whether the number of scales can therefore be reduced to fewer variables. For example, conducting a factor analysis on a number of attitude statements formulated around attitudes to Welsh may identify subcomponents (or 'dimensions'), with some statements factoring, for example, into attitudes towards learning Welsh, and others into attitudes towards Welsh speakers, or towards the Welsh language.

In practice, researchers often prefer to have at least four statements tapping into each attitudinal subcomponent, with two of them worded negatively and two positively. Pilot data are often collected, again from a group of judges comparable to those in the main study, and a factor analysis is then conducted on the pilot ratings to check correlations between the four items on each attitudinal subcomponent, and between the items and the total for each attitudinal component. This shows whether each of the sets of four statements really does coalesce into differentiated subcomponents in the way anticipated, and indicates whether some statements need to be replaced by others that are more appropriate before the questionnaire is used in the main study.

Although Likert (1932) himself proposed a five-point scale, other researchers have preferred to use seven-point scales for the increased variance that such longer scales allow. This can be particularly useful when making comparisons in independent samples or repeated measures designs, since, rather like a ruler with finer gradations on it, a seven-point scale is more sensitive to differences in measurement. There has been considerable discussion, in fact, about the number of points to include on these scales (as is also the case with semantic differential scales, introduced in the next chapter). Having an odd number of points on the scale means there is a mid-point, which arguably allows respondents to indicate their 'neutrality' towards the attitude object. However, as Oppenheim (1992: 200) points out, scores in the middle of the scale are often ambiguous. They might reflect a much-considered weighing of attitudes, for example, or an uncertain response to an issue in which respondents feel little involvement. For this reason, some researchers prefer to use an even number of points. The fact that this then forces the respondents to commit themselves one way or the other, towards agreement or disagreement with the attitude statement, is also controversial, of course, for example because it does not allow them to express a considered commitment to a mid-point. It seems fair to say that in most language-attitudes research, five- and seven-point scales are used, with researchers preferring to live with the ambiguity of the mid-point.

The claim is sometimes made that Likert scales are particularly useful for measuring the *intensity* of attitudes (for example, Henerson et al., 1987: 86): that is, expressing an attitude at either end of the scale reflects a higher degree of attitude intensity than if one selects the mid-point of the scale. This same claim is made for semantic-differential scales (Osgood, Suci and Tannenbaum, 1957). But can one be committed to the mid-point of these scales with the same intensity as to either end of the scale? (See page 66.)

Direct-approach research into language attitudes in Wales

The direct-approach research conducted in Wales has focused to a large extent on schools. Over fifty years or so, such attitudinal research has had quite direct implications for and effects on bilingual educational policies to bolster the position of the Welsh language. The earliest work, conducted in the years following the Second World War, was carried out by Jones (1949, 1950) with children from a 'secondary-modern' school (a lower-ability secondary school) in the Welsh Valleys and from another such school in Cardiff. Jones employed a Thurstone scale to study attitudes towards Welsh in relation to student age. The main finding was that there was a constantly declining attitude towards Welsh as students moved from the first year (aged eleven to twelve) to the fourth year (aged fourteen to fifteen). Furthermore, he concluded that 'attainment in Welsh is increasingly influenced by the pupil's attitude in the later stages of the course' (Jones, 1950: 132). As is evident in table 2.1, there was a particularly noticeable drop in the Cardiff sample from the third to the fourth year.

Table 2.1: Age and average attitude to Welsh in W. R. Jones's research.

Age	*Average Scores* Cwm Rhondda *(Jones, 1949)*	Cardiff *(Jones, 1950)*
1st year (11/12 years)	6.74	6.74
2nd year (12/13 years)	6.23	6.64
3rd year (13/14 years)	5.97	6.41
4th year (14/15 years)	–	5.52

Note: The higher the score, the more positive the attitude. A score of 6 represents a neutral attitude.

Sharp et al. (1973) subsequently conducted a much larger-scale study than that of Jones. They used a stratified sample of 12,000 children aged ten/eleven, twelve/thirteen, and fourteen/fifteen, and this time the 'post-junior' students were drawn from grammar schools (selective state secondary schools) and technical schools, as well as secondary-modern schools. For their attitudinal data collection, Sharp et al. used Thurstone scales, Likert scales and semantic-differential scales. Although, as will be seen in the next chapter, semantic-differential scales have become closely associated with indirect approaches to language attitudes research, they may also be used in a more direct way. In the Sharp study, for example, the instructions given to the students made it very clear what the researchers' objectives were: 'The following exercise is designed to find out what kind of idea you have of *the Welsh language*' (Sharp et al., 1973: 167).

Table 2.2: Age and average attitude to Welsh in Sharp et al.'s (1973) research.

Welsh-speaking population density of neighbourhood	*Average scores*		
	10/11 years	*11/12 years*	*14/15 years*
68–81% Welsh	3.97	4.10	4.98
48–55% Welsh	4.22	4.70	5.14
3–26% Welsh	5.39	5.67	5.80
Children attending designated bilingual schools	3.21	3.55	3.72

Note: Score 0–5 = positive attitude; score 5–6 = neutral attitude; score 6–11 = negative attitude.

Table 2.3: Age and average attitude to English in Sharp et al.'s (1973) research.

Welsh-speaking population density of neighbourhood	*Average scores*		
	10/11 years	*11/12 years*	*14/15 years*
68–81% Welsh	5.87	5.25	4.81
48–55% Welsh	5.66	5.16	4.92
3–26% Welsh	5.06	4.82	4.58
Children attending designated bilingual schools	6.75	6.43	5.76

Note: Score 0–5 = positive attitude; score 5–6 = neutral attitude; score 6–11 = negative attitude.

The findings of this study told a similar, albeit more detailed, story to that of Jones's research. While, at the age of ten/eleven the great majority of children were mildly positive towards Welsh, there was an overall trend to a relatively neutral attitude by the fourth year (see table 2.2). This was paralleled by an increasingly favourable attitude towards English (see table 2.3), creating a 'see-saw' effect. Attitudes towards Welsh in bilingual schools followed a different pattern, however. Despite a decline in positivity, they nevertheless remained on the positive side. It was not clear whether these findings supported bilingual education policies. This is because the creation of bilingual schools resulted from parental pressure, so the positive attitudes in these students might have been fostered as much by their parents, family and community as by the policies themselves. This is suggested by the fact that these latter students also *started* with a comparatively more favourable attitude.

In terms of the ideas we wish to explore in this book, there are two particularly relevant aspects of these findings. Firstly, during these early to mid-adolescent years, research has shown that there can be a significant attitudinal shift with regard to both Welsh and English. In subsequent research, also employing a battery of direct-approach rating scales, Baker (1992) found that the 'pivotal' age when structural change occurs in these language attitudes is thirteen to fourteen, when there is a significant shift. In the studies discussed later in this book, data are collected from groups of school students in their fourth year of secondary education. More research background on this age group is provided in chapter 4.

The second aspect of these findings that we wish to highlight is that language attitudes in Wales (at least with regard to these two 'whole languages', if not also to regional dialects) are different in different regions of Wales: 'there are regional factors affecting attitudes towards Welsh English, as there are towards Welsh itself' (Peate, Coupland and Garrett, 1998: 99). It was shown in the studies reported above that attitudes varied according to the proportion of Welsh speakers in the various areas of Wales. This attitudinal variation will be further considered in the light of the indirect-approach studies reported in the next chapter.

Perceptual dialectology

Recent developments in perceptual dialectology have provided a further set of procedures for gathering data on language attitudes, and these procedures can also be incorporated under the direct-approach rubric. Preston's starting point is essentially Hoenigswald's (1966: 20) assertion that 'we should be interested not only in what goes on (in language), but also in how people react to what goes on (they are persuaded, put off, etc.), and in what people say goes on (talk concerning language)'. This assertion restates the Labovian view on the importance of evaluative data. It also shows how language attitudes constitute an important facet of metalanguage research (Jaworski, Coupland and Galasinski, forthcoming).

An array of folklinguistic procedures has been developed by Preston (1989, 1999). Although language attitudes research contributes to our understanding of a speech community's set of beliefs about language and use, Preston (1989: 3) claims that much of the research is too limited in scope, making it at times difficult to interpret. People's representations of language variation, their articulation of their beliefs about language, language use and language users, give a far more contextualized account of language attitudes than emerges from the relatively structured interviews and questionnaires which are generally characteristic of direct-approach studies, or from the equally highly focused instruments employed in indirect-approach research. These arguably focus on comparatively limited facets of language attitudes. In Preston's view, to study adequately the attitudinal component of the communication competence of ordinary speakers, at least some attention needs to be given to beliefs concerning the geographical distribution of speech, beliefs about standard and affectively preferred language varieties, the degree of difference perceived in relation to surrounding varieties, imitations of other varieties, and anecdotal accounts of how such beliefs and strategies develop and persist (Preston, 1989: 4). This additional component, he argues, will broaden the scope of language attitudes research.

Some of the principal data-gathering procedures developed by Preston (see, for example, Preston, 1999: xxxiv) are set out below. Illustrative studies employing these techniques can be found in Preston (1989, 1993, 1996, 1999); Niedzielski and Preston (2000); Long and Preston (2002).

Draw a map
This procedure is taken from cultural geography (for example, Gould and White, 1986) and applied to dialect perceptions. Respondents draw dialect boundaries on a blank (or almost blank) map around areas

where they believe regional speech zones exist. From these maps drawn by individual informants, composite maps can then be created. Illustrations of this technique can be found in Preston (1989, 1999).

Correct and pleasant
Respondents rank regions for correct and/or pleasant speech, reflecting the prestige and solidarity dimensions well documented in language attitudes research (for example, see Ryan, Giles, and Sebastian, 1982; Zahn and Hopper, 1985). An example of this technique is Preston's (1989: 51–83) studies in which he asked respondents in Indiana to rank the 50 states of the USA, plus Washington DC and New York City, from most to least correct, and from most to least pleasant, in terms of the English spoken there.

Qualitative data
Respondents are asked about the research tasks they have carried out, and are involved in open-ended conversations about their beliefs and practices concerning language varieties, speakers of such varieties, etc.

We use extensions of these kinds of procedures in our own studies, reported later.

Perceptual dialectology research relating to Wales

Other than in our own research, perceptual dialectological work in Wales is almost totally absent. This is surprising, given Wales's long-standing high profile in language attitudes research internationally. There are, however, two studies that we wish to mention here. The first one is a *draw a map* study by Inoue (1999), in which students at Essex university in England were asked to 'draw lines on a British map in order to divide the areas according to the accents or dialects they perceived' (Inoue, 1999: 164). Figure 2.1 shows the composite map for the whole group of respondents (Inoue, 1999: 167). Wales was seen as a single dialect-zone by the group of respondents, and most commonly given the label 'Welsh'. Inoue interpreted these labellings as meaning that the student judges perceived the dialect of Wales (as well as those of Scotland and Ireland) to be different from the dialects of England. He felt that this was possibly a reflection of their knowing that a language other than English is spoken there, but that more probably they were signalling that the difference lay in the English spoken there (Inoue, 1999: 166).

DIRECT APPROACHES

That Wales was seen as a single dialect-zone (as were Scotland and Ireland) is not something that Inoue comments on. It probably results from the tendency for respondents to perceive more distinctions closer to their familiar local areas than in areas further away, and doubtless fewer of the respondents were from these three 'Celtic' areas (though

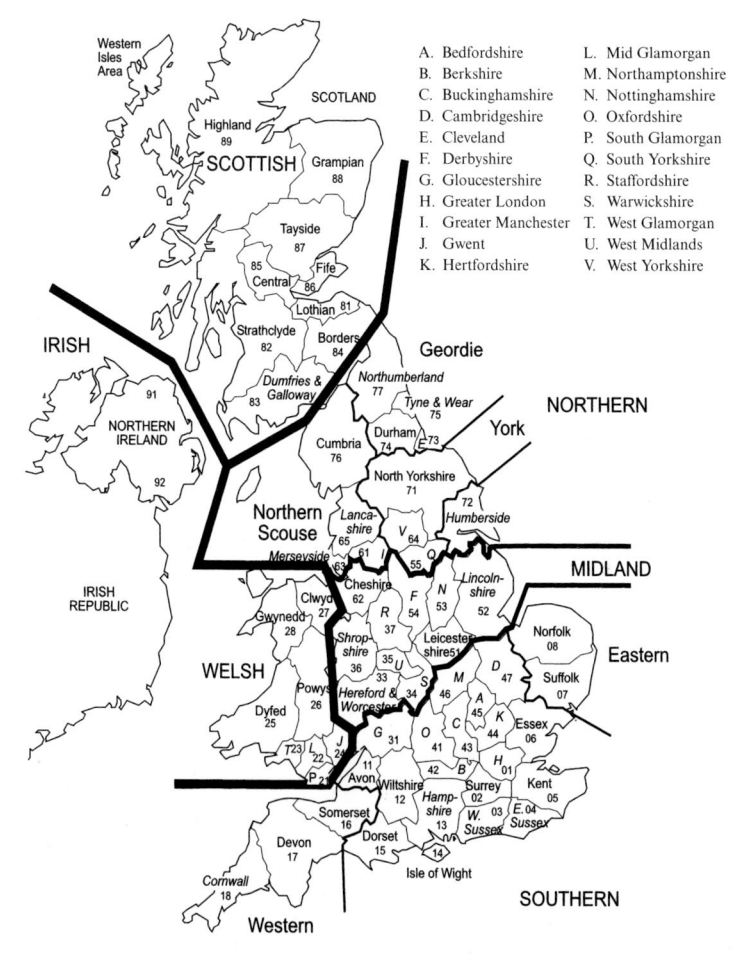

A. Bedfordshire
B. Berkshire
C. Buckinghamshire
D. Cambridgeshire
E. Cleveland
F. Derbyshire
G. Gloucestershire
H. Greater London
I. Greater Manchester
J. Gwent
K. Hertfordshire
L. Mid Glamorgan
M. Northamptonshire
N. Nottinghamshire
O. Oxfordshire
P. South Glamorgan
Q. South Yorkshire
R. Staffordshire
S. Warwickshire
T. West Glamorgan
U. West Midlands
V. West Yorkshire

Source: 'Subjective dialect division in Great Britain', in D. Preston (ed.), *Handbook of Perceptual Dialectology*, Vol. 1, pp. 161–76. By kind permission of John Benjamins Publishing Company, Amsterdam/Philadelphia. www.benjamins.com

Figure 2.1: Subjective dialect division of Great Britain in Inoue's (1999) research

Inoue does not provide precise details about the respondents). There are doubtless additional factors. For example, 'Geordie', too, in the north-east of England, is geographically distant, but more familiar as a distinct urban variety through, perhaps, the broadcasting media, than are many of the specific dialects of Welsh English. This view of Wales by those outside Wales needs more study. If there is a view of the people of Wales all speaking one English dialect, then it would appear to be a product and a source of the intergroup perspective, as we discussed it in chapter 1, that the outgroup are 'all the same'. It is more likely, however, that the methodological constraints of Inoue's study predisposed a view of Wales as a 'single dialect-region', consistent with the broad Great Britain focus and the informants' lack of differentiated experience.

Williams (1985) conducted a study mapping culture regions in Wales, and his study is pertinent to us here because it focuses on language. Specifically, Williams asked schoolchildren all over Wales to identify on a map which towns they judged to be in predominantly Welsh-speaking areas. In his study he was not concerned to show perceived boundaries between zones, but instead produced a set of 'isolines' to reflect percentile rates of inclusion as Welsh speaking. The composite map resulting from his data is shown in figure 2.2. It shows a perceived Welsh-speaking heartland in the north-west of Wales (where the shading indicates the 70 per cent and 80 per cent isolines), with a slightly lesser heartland in the south-west around Carmarthen (the 60 per cent isoline). The significance of this study has to be seen against the fact that people react to a perceived environment (Gould, 1977: 111), and such perceptual studies in contexts such as Wales can help us achieve a better understanding of language maintenance, decay, and revival. In particular, language groups may become demarcated, and territories can take on a number of functions. The following functions are based on Boal (1976), cited in Williams (1985).

- *a defensive* function, establishing 'fortresses', discouraging the entry of outsiders;
- *an avoidance* function, providing havens and sanctuaries for group members;
- *a preservation* function, to defend distinctiveness;
- *a resource base* function, providing a means for trying in time to alter the existing relationship with the dominant group.

As Williams (1985: 276) observes, 'regional distinctiveness and territorial identification can become salient instruments in the defence

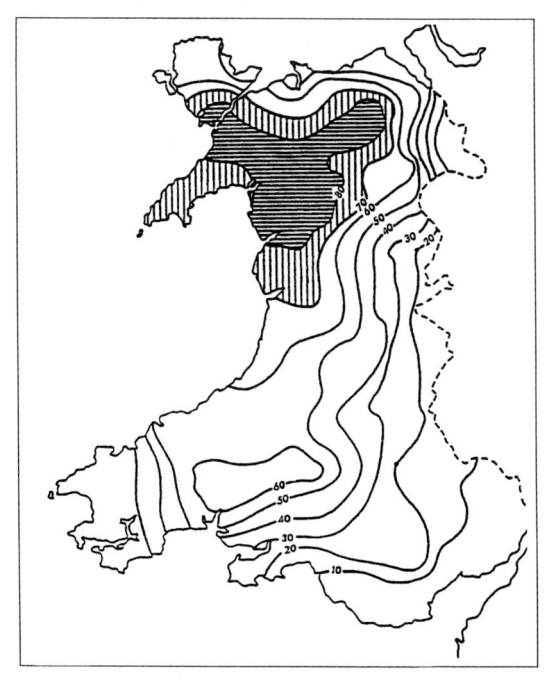

Figure 2.2: Perceptual culture regions in Williams's research (after Williams, 1985)

of minority group cultures'. The underlying consideration is, of course, that it is *perceptions* of community characteristics and of boundaries between communities that will inform critical judgements and policy initiatives, possibly more directly than actual demographic data.

Perceptual dialectological studies therefore appear to have much to offer the study of language attitudes in Wales, as a complement to usage surveys (see Aitchison and Carter, 1994). The level of defensiveness in Welsh-language heartlands may be found to reveal itself in alternative ways – as defensive of the language and the cultural identity, for example, or perhaps primarily of the cultural identity, whether expressed through the Welsh or the English language. The research that we look at later in this book investigates attitudes towards English dialects in Wales, and includes an examination of whether Welsh identity (and the plural 'identities' proves to be far more apposite) are carried through some or all of these. In the competitive language context of Wales, to study attitudes towards English dialects necessarily means considering implications for the Welsh language; hence, mental mapping is perhaps a more complex matter than in monolingual contexts. We revisit these perceptual studies later, and consider them against other maps where, arguably, Welsh identities are in one way or another salient, judging from language-based census data, and from the voting patterns on the question of the establishment of a Welsh Assembly.

3

Indirect approaches

In this chapter, we introduce and give a general description of the core principles of the indirect approach to language attitudes research, specifically the matched-guise technique, the MGT. Some aspects of the MGT design have proved controversial, and we appraise this technique, addressing some theoretically significant issues. We then summarize some of the matched-guise research that has been conducted in Wales and which forms the most immediate backdrop to the empirical research discussed later.

General description of the MGT

We mentioned in the first chapter that the label 'indirect approach' to researching attitudes entails more subtle, and in a sense deceptive, techniques compared to those approaches reviewed in chapter 2, which directly ask questions. We also mentioned that, in language attitudes research, the term 'indirect approach' is more or less synonymous with the MGT (for example, Lambert et al., 1960). Lambert developed this technique because he suspected that the public, overt responses elicited through direct approaches did not match people's privately held attitudes; in other words, direct procedures were arguably not a valid way of researching the language attitudes in which he was interested. In chapter 2, we discussed some of the obstacles to validity, such as social desirability in responses. However, validity is a persistent concern in all empirical research, and the MGT brings its own validity problems.

The MGT is deemed to be comparable with the way in which we form impressions of people as we converse with them on the telephone or listen to them speaking on the radio (Lambert et al., 1960: 44). Typically, the MGT consists of playing audio-recordings to listeners ('judges') who rate each speaker they hear on a number of personality traits. The technique attempts to control out all but the manipulated independent variable, so that only this variable remains to explain variable patterns of response among listeners. Hence, where accent (the phonological speech-style) is the manipulated variable, a single speaker is recorded reading the same 'factually neutral' passage in the required range of accents, and keeping other variables (such as speech rate, pitch, etc.) constant. Thus efforts are made to ensure that any 'interfering' effects of spontaneous speech production are eliminated. These speech samples are then arranged in random order on an audiotape to be used in the experiment itself. Usually, two versions of the stimulus tape are made, with the accents in opposite orders, to minimize any ordering and fatigue effects in subsequent evaluations by judges. The speech samples are presented for validation to a group of independent judges (that is, not involved in the subsequent main study), preferably comparable to the group to be used in the main part of the study. The objective with this is to ensure that what the researchers have taken to be, for example, an RP or Cardiff accent is also seen by others as being so.

The final tapes are then played to a group of judges who are asked to evaluate the speakers on a number of (usually) seven-point bipolar adjective scales. Often, the order of the bipolar adjective scales is reversed on half of the questionnaires, again to reduce possible ordering and fatigue effects. Judges are usually encouraged to fill in these bipolar semantic-differential scales quickly, since they are generally regarded as being a means of measuring judges' general impressions rather than thought-out opinions (see, for example, Henerson et al., 1987: 89). Typically, too, the tape is stopped after each rendition of the text, for judges quickly to complete the appropriate page of attitude scales. This device is deemed to help in the process of making the listeners believe that they are not listening to one and the same person, but are listening to *different people* speaking in their 'normal voices'. (Occasionally, as a further safeguard against judges recognizing that the speaker is always the same person, 'dummy' readings by different people are included on the tape, and are then excluded from the analysis – for example, Price et al., 1983: 154.)

MGT studies, it is claimed, lend themselves to the secure application of statistical measures. Typically, the measurement overlap in the bipolar semantic-differential scales ratings is analysed by factor analysis (which we explained in chapter 2) in order to identify (or confirm) the broader evaluative dimensions with which the judges are operating. The most regular dimensions of judgements attaching to language varieties and their speakers, established across many communities, are prestige (adjectives such as 'educated', 'high status'), social attractiveness (for example, 'friendly', 'sincere', 'kind') and dynamism (for example, 'lively', 'energetic', 'eager') – see Zahn and Hopper (1985). After the factor analysis, a clearly identifiable and arguably isolable independent variable such as accent is then tested through analysis of variance for significant effects on these dimensions.

Variant forms of the MGT

Over the years in which the MGT has dominated so much language attitudes work, there have been many variations on the above 'core' elements, stemming from some of the acknowledged shortcomings and criticisms of the approach. Edwards (1982), for example, claimed that the MGT does not measure language attitudes so much as attitudes to representative speakers of languages and language varieties. This is an issue that is revisited later in the book, when we suggest that attitudes relate to both speakers and varieties together, in performances. The criticism has also frequently been made that the use of decontextualized speech-samples in MGT studies undermines validity. The speech stimuli are said to be too 'contrived' in that, for example, they do not take into account the social meaning of people's ability to modify their speech styles in different contexts and at different linguistic levels. For these and related reasons, some researchers have therefore designed their studies somewhat differently from the 'standard' MGT procedure outlined above. For instance:

1. Some studies have employed a number of different speakers to make the stimulus audio-recordings. This is sometimes referred to as the 'verbal-guise' technique (for example, Gallois and Callan, 1981; Callan, Gallois and Forbes, 1983; Bayard, Weatherall, Gallois and Pittam, 2001). In fact, this design has often been employed out of necessity, since it is not always possible to find a single person who can competently produce the varieties required for the study. For example, in a study by Nesdale and Rooney (1996), there was no possibility of

locating children in Australia who could produce strong and mild Anglo-, Italo- and Viet-Australian guises convincingly and with comparable fluency. But different speakers are also used in order to defend research against the charge of artificiality – for example, Masterson, Mullins and Mulvihill (1983), in their study of Irish-accented English. (As will be seen later in this chapter, however, the corresponding notion of 'authenticity' is still problematic.) Some studies have used 'verbal guises' for both these reasons. For example, Garrett (1992), in a study of reactions to the English pronunciation of foreign learners of English, was able to find French speakers of English who could produce English spoken with 'broad', 'mild' and 'hyper-correct' accents, and, for comparison, Spanish speakers who could do likewise with Spanish-accented English. But it would have been both futile and doubtless detrimental to the realistic rendering of the variants to search for a single person to aim at producing all of these six recordings. Hence, the Spanish accents were produced by Spanish speakers and the French accents by French speakers.

2. Instead of getting speakers to read aloud in a number of different speech varieties the same prepared 'factually neutral' text, some researchers have asked different speakers to speak 'spontaneously' on to audiotape. Reading aloud is, after all, a marked verbal style which is likely to introduce several distinctive prosodic and sequential phono-logical features – perhaps a more evenly modulated stress pattern, pausing at syntactic boundaries, a greater frequency of 'spelling pronunciations', and so on. In an effort to generate and utilize more 'spontaneous' speech, for example, El Dash and Tucker (1975), prepared verbal guises in RP, Egyptian English, US English, Egyptian Arabic, and Classical Arabic, controlling the different speakers of these guises only by the topic of their talk. Huygens and Vaughan (1983), who collected audio-recordings from thirty people for their New Zealand study of attitudes towards the English spoken by high-, middle- and low-status groups among English and Dutch immigrants, and native-born Maoris and pakehas, controlled only for content by asking each speaker to give directions from one part of a city to another.

3. A number of studies have used presentations in naturally occurring (rather than laboratory-type) settings, sometimes face-to-face. For example, in Giles, Baker and Fielding (1975), the

experimenters visited a school at which they presented themselves as being from a local university, and as being concerned about the opinions about psychology among school students. One group of students was addressed in RP, and the other by the same speaker employing a Birmingham guise. In a study by Giles and Farrar (1979), the researcher called at homes on a housing estate, asking residents to complete a questionnaire, which she would collect later that day. The researcher made use of her bi-dialectal competence in RP and Cockney to alternate the guises as she visited each household. Also trying to escape the laboratory setting of so many MGT studies, Bourhis and Giles (1976) used a 'theatre-audience method' to investigate attitudes in Wales (a design subsequently repeated in a Danish setting by Kristiansen, 1997). In their study, pre-recorded announcements were made by the same person over the public-address system in a theatre, during programme intervals over a number of nights, in RP, south-Welsh accented English, or Welsh, asking audiences to participate in a study, and then measuring response rates. In terms of presentation of language varieties, then, all these studies have employed a matching of guises in the sense that a single speaker has delivered the same message in different language varieties.

4. A number of studies have moved away from characteristically 'static' and 'factually neutral' reading passages in order to investigate the effects of accommodative communication behaviour on evaluations, where speakers are converging towards or diverging away from each other's communication styles. These differ from the original MGT, in that they take account of the fact that speakers modify their language in different social situations and with different interlocutors. Ball, Giles, Byrne and Berechree (1984) studied observers' evaluations of interviewees in simulated employment interviews, according to whether interviewees converged towards or diverged from the Australian English accent of their interviewers. (This issue of decontextualized, 'contrived' language use rather than 'natural' language use is taken up again later in this chapter.)

Points 1 to 4 above have concerned some of the variations regarding the *presentation* of language varieties in MGT studies. However, there have also been some variations in terms of the procedures involved in collecting evaluations of these varieties, both in terms of attitude scales, and in terms of alternative measures.

5. In deciding which bipolar adjective scales to use on the questionnaire, researchers have generally made their own decisions about what to include, usually on the basis of those commonly used in earlier studies. In some (albeit relatively few) cases, they have made efforts to elicit adjectives from the respondents themselves (or what is deemed to be a comparable group). The motivation for this is to try to ensure that scaled judgements are made on scales that are meaningful and salient to the respondents, and also that the researchers do not fail to include such meaningful judgements. Paltridge and Giles (1984), for example, conducted an extensive pilot survey asking 249 informants from four different regions of France to list the main positive as well as negative qualities of people from those same four regions, and then adopted the twenty most frequently mentioned traits as their dependent measures in the main experiment. Bourhis et al. (1973), too, selected appropriate dependent measures from a pilot study, in which they asked fifty-three adults in South Wales to list as many words and phrases as they wished which best described the people whose speech would be evaluated in the main study. The eighteen most frequently used adjectives were then selected. Doise, Sinclair and Bourhis (1976) and Price et al. (1983) also used this kind of preliminary procedure.

6. Attitude scales established as bipolar adjective scales have sometimes been replaced or augmented by behavioural measures (and such studies might therefore be termed 'field studies'). Giles et al. (1975), for instance, asked school students to write open-endedly on what they thought psychology was about, and used the mean number of words written as their measure. Giles and Farrar (1979) analysed responses on the subject of the effects of inflation by both calculating communication length (number of words written) and assessing the relative formality of style used in the written responses. In the theatre studies conducted by Bourhis and Giles (1976) and Kristiansen (1997), the number of audience members who responded to the public-address system announcements, taking the trouble to complete questionnaires, was calculated as a proportion of the total ticket sales for the performances (that is, the total number of questionnaires that the audience *could* have filled in). In these studies, the respondents are still not aware of the purpose of the research, so the approach is still indirect, and hence there is still less likelihood that they will respond on the basis of social acceptability. However, the respondents are not asked to record their feelings or opinions directly about language.

Rather, the studies elicit behaviour towards instances of language use, and it is then the researcher's job to infer attitudes from that behaviour. In this last respect (that respondents are not asked to record their attitudes), there is some similarity with societal treatment studies. However, these studies are more obtrusive than societal treatment studies in that they are based upon the elicitation of behaviours.

Commonly claimed successes of the MGT

Before going on to address some of the controversies regarding the MGT, the main successes generally claimed can be summarized as:

1. It is a rigorous and elegant design for investigating people's private attitudes. It is often claimed that direct questioning of respondents about their attitudes is less likely to elicit such private attitudes, and more likely to lead to the expression of attitudes which respondents consider socially acceptable or even socially desirable, as we mentioned in the previous chapter.

2. It has led to a convincing and detailed demonstration of the role of language code and style choice in impression formation.

3. It has generated a very considerable number of studies internationally, especially in bilingual/bi-ethnic, multilingual/multi-ethnic contexts, with a reasonable degree of comparability, allowing for cumulative development of theory.

4. It has led to the identification of the main dimensions along which evaluations are repeatedly made: prestige, social attractiveness, dynamism. It has therefore begun to explain the sociolinguistic ecology of language variation.

5. It has laid the foundations for cross-disciplinary work at the interface of the social psychology of language and sociolinguistics.

Problems with the MGT

We begin this section by considering the problems with the way that the MGT presents speech varieties for evaluation. Afterwards, we consider the gathering and analysis and interpretation of data that is typically associated with the MGT.

The salience problem
The routine of providing judges with the repeated message content of a reading passage presented by a long series of speakers may exaggerate the language contrasts compared to what would otherwise be the case in ordinary discourse, placing excessive emphasis on vocal variations (for example, Lee, 1971). That is, the MGT may systematically make speech/language and speech/language variation much more salient than it otherwise is, outside the experimental environment.

The perception problem
One cannot be sure in most studies how reliably judges have perceived the manipulated variables. For example, Bradac (1990) mentions that it is possible that the manipulated variable 'non-standard accent' was not itself perceived by judges, or was perhaps even misperceived as 'bad grammar'. It is noteworthy that Levin et al. (1994) found that the same texts read in RP and south-east Welsh English were deemed to contain significantly 'fancier words' when read in RP. (See also Ball, Byrne, Giles, Berechree, Griffiths, McDonald and McKendrick (1982) on the 'retroactive speech stereotype effect').

A further aspect of the perception problem is one raised by Preston (1989: 3) and relates to perceptions of dialect areas, which were mentioned in chapter 2. If, say, judges are played audiotaped recordings of Welsh Valleys English and south-west Wales English, and they rate the former voice significantly higher on friendliness but lower on status than the latter, can we be sure that they actually identify each of these as a separate speech-area, and the speakers as representative of them? Preston makes the additional (related) criticism of many MGT studies. Although researchers may have their recorded speech samples 'validated' by a pilot group of judges prior to using the samples in their main study (for example, see Price et al., 1983: 154), they typically do not ask the judges themselves to state where they believe the voice is from, even though there has been increasing attention to careful characterizations of input in MGT research (Preston, 1989: 3). Preston says: 'Though this seems a simple technique to add to attitude surveys, it is rarely done, and language attitude results are made extremely difficult to interpret because the respondents' areal taxonomy and identification of regional provenance of the voice samples are not known' (1989: 3). This issue is revisited in more depth, early in chapter 4, in relation to the dialect-recognition task included in the second of our two studies that we consider later.

The accent-authenticity problem
The 'advantage' of minimizing the effects of some of the more idiosyncratic variations in speech (for example, prosodic and paralinguistic features such as rate and voice quality) may mean that some of the other characteristics which normally co-vary with accent varieties (such as intonational characteristics, or even discourse patterning – so-called 'discourse accent') are also eliminated. This raises issues of the authenticity of these voices/varieties.

The mimicking-authenticity problem
In the seminal MGT study by Lambert et al. (1960), audio-recordings in French and English were made by bilingual speakers, and in some subsequent MGT studies where few (for example, two) accents or dialects have been presented, these too have been presented by bi-dialectal speakers (for example, Giles and Farrar, 1979; Levin et al., 1994). But it seems unlikely that the accuracy of renderings in many studies, particularly where one speaker has produced a large number of different varieties, has been as high. Preston (1996) points to some of the inaccuracies that can occur when people are asked to mimic accents or dialects, for example in his analysis of a Michigan respondent's rendition of a Tennessee newscaster (p. 65). Such inaccuracies may add to problems of reliability. Some studies have included some phonological description of the speech samples (for example, Thakerar, Giles and Cheshire, 1982; Garrett, 1992; Levin et al., 1994), but this is far from the standard practice.

It is possible, of course, for an 'inaccurate' rendition nevertheless to be 'successful' by some criteria, as Preston himself points out (1996: 65). Judges might not be aware of what is *not* incorporated, and might still perceive inaccurately mimicked voices as 'authentic'. There is also a possibility, though, that judges may not be aware of selective representation at a conscious level, but might nevertheless judge the rendition to be 'odd' or 'unconvincing'. The mimicking-authenticity problem certainly warrants more investigation.

The community-authenticity problem
A further point here is that the labels used for the speech varieties in

published reports of studies are sometimes too vague to be meaningful. For example, some studies have referred to 'Welsh English' or 'south-Welsh English', but some more specific or localized label would often be more helpful and more in line with judges' normal labelling conventions. As will be shown in later chapters, there are several perceptually and descriptively differentiated varieties of Welsh English in Wales, even across small distances. Similarly, as we mentioned in chapter 2, and will demonstrate in later chapters, it is important to know the point of data collection, since attitudes are likely to differ amongst different accent/dialect communities.

The style-authenticity problem
In studies the stimulus tapes have generally been prepared by asking speakers to read out a reading passage in the different varieties, but on occasions suggest to judges that they will be listening to spontaneous speech. There are issues of style here, which we referred to briefly above. Labov (1972), for example, asked people to read out reading passages in order to elicit a quite different (more formal) style of language from spontaneous or 'casual' style. The relative formality of the speech-presentation tasks has been largely ignored. Moreover, as we suggested on page 54, 'reading aloud' has its own norms and rhetorical conventions. There are also criticisms concerning whether the use of such decontextualized language to elicit people's attitudes yields findings that can be extended to natural language use, where people are meaningfully and functionally 'doing things' with language, rather than 'merely voicing' utterances (for example, Knops and van Hout, 1988: 8; Potter and Wetherell, 1987; Giles and Coupland, 1991).

The neutrality problem
The notion of a 'factually neutral' text is controversial. It is doubtful, given the ways in which readers and listeners interact with and interpret texts on the basis of pre-existing social schemata (see, for example, Widdowson, 1979: 173ff.), that any text can be regarded as 'factually neutral'. This was clearly illustrated in a study by Giles, N. Coupland, Henwood, Harriman, and J. Coupland (1990), where they found it impossible in a cross-generational study to generate a text that was 'age neutral'. Judges were found to interpret the same extract of text differently – that is, through quite different perceptual frames – according to the speaker's perceived age. For example, the utterance 'I didn't know what to think', when spoken in an elderly guise, was taken

to mean the speaker was 'confused'; whereas when spoken in a younger (early thirties) guise, it was taken to mean that the speaker found the issues complex and was therefore reserving judgement.

Despite all the well-rehearsed advantages and disadvantages that we have been considering in this book, it is important to take a wider view too. These advantages and disadvantages are not untypical of *any* particular methodological paradigm. That is, any particular method will be only partially convincing, and only partially able to meet the usual demands of validity and reliability. Our own position is that we should certainly continue to strive to offset limitations by innovating around the central method. It seems wrong, though, *either* to be uncritical followers of canonical methods in language attitudes *or* to dispense with all attempts to deal with language attitudes systematically through aggregational methods. We set out our own views and priorities in subsequent sections of this book.

The MGT, language attitudes and sociolinguistics

Before moving on to consider the use of semantic-differential attitude-rating scales in language attitudes research (since these are arguably an integral component of MGT studies), and then to discuss the MGT research carried out in Wales, we need to mention broader sociolinguistic issues concerning the nature of dialect and accent, since these, too, impact on the empirical work that we discuss later. The merits and demerits of the MGT have often been debated (for example, Giles and Coupland, 1991). Our own view is that social-evaluation studies will benefit, at least for some purposes, from more ecologically valid source material than the mimicked vocal renditions of linguistic varieties in decontextualized environments that characterize so much matched-guise research. Over and above matters of methodological convenience, the nature of aural stimuli in language attitudes research raises significant theoretical issues, mainly to do with the integrity of accent and dialect varieties and how dialectically-marked speech encodes social meaning (since much MGT work has focused on accent and dialect).

In fact, the descriptive methods of variationist sociolinguistics have themselves contributed to the illusion that socially significant dialect variation can be captured wholly in terms of frequency arrays of discrete sets of phonological, lexical and morpho-syntactic forms. That is, a 'standard' speech variety, for example, an RP accent, within a speech community can be defined as using a particular range of variants with a particular frequency, whereas 'non-standard' speakers in the same community, for example vernacular Cardiff English speakers, will use different features or the same features with a different frequency.

Language attitudes work carried out within the MGT paradigm has tended to work within this same general view of dialect, manipulating 'levels of accentedness', for example, or investigating the relative evaluative potency of 'accent' versus lexical qualities (Giles and Sassoon, 1983; Levin et al., 1994), 'accent' versus grammatical qualities (Petty et al., 1981), etc.

But dialect difference is encountered in less idealized and more complex ways in everyday social situations. Because of the cultural constitution of dialect, speakers of a particular regional or social dialect engage with communicative tasks on a subtly different footing from others. We are accustomed to treating dialect differences as indexing socio-economic class differences, although the experience of class membership shows through in the phenomenology of class-related communication, or 'ways of speaking' (Hymes, 1974; Coupland, 2000), and in ways that are less obvious than through phonological and other quantifiable types of variation. There is a wide range of semantic and pragmatic phenomena on the fringe of dialect which sociolinguistics has not systematically addressed, to do with rhetorical style, stance and implicature. This is why it seems appropriate to view dialects as ideological as well as linguistic entities (Hodge and Kress, 1988; Lee, 1992), and why the study of dialect needs to be coherently linked to current emphases in the analysis of discourse (Macaulay, 1991; Coupland, 2000).

The study of language attitudes has a vital contribution to make to this growing debate. People's responses to dialect are necessarily holistic. They are sensitive to the full range of social meaning that any particular 'dialect performance' generates, with some aspects of the performance likely to be more or less salient in specific judgements in different contexts. However inconvenient the methodological implications may be, it is important for at least some sorts of attitudes research to be based on less-controlled speech data, and to develop ways of accounting for how 'dialect' in the narrow sense interacts with socio-culturally conditioned ways of speaking. In line with this set of priorities, we analyse both teachers' and teenagers' responses to young people in Wales telling spontaneous personal narratives in English. From a broad perspective, the speech samples are a fairly homogeneous set: they were produced for a common purpose and in similar conditions by male school-students of closely similar ages, but from widely different regions of Wales. However, the analyses are 'complicated' by the fact that the speech is unscripted, and therefore differs in rhetorical structure and completeness, and in the details of topics and emphases. This and other research design-features made it less appropriate to employ the standard MGT analytical procedures, and necessary to seek other ways to analyse and interpret the data.

Attitude-rating scales: semantic-differential scales

Typically, as has already been mentioned, judges record their ratings on a number of semantic-differential scales (for example, sincere/insincere, rich/poor). Measurement overlap in these scale ratings is then analysed in order to identify the broader evaluative dimensions that the judges are operating with, and these dimensions are now generally considered to be well established in language attitudes research. Zahn and Hopper (1985) pooled scale adjectives from a large number of speech-evaluation research programmes and used them in a single study involving nearly 600 judges. They found through a factor analysis that each of the scales loaded into one of three differentiated factors, which they labelled 'superiority' (for example, educated/uneducated, rich/poor), 'attractiveness' (for example, friendly/unfriendly, honest/dishonest) and 'dynamism' (for example, energetic/lazy, enthusiastic/hesitant).

This well-documented pattern of evaluative dimensions has meant that many attitudes studies in language and communication have taken their scales from those used in previous studies, whilst others have felt it valuable to supplement them with scales from their own preliminary work with comparable judges (for example, Ball et al., 1984; Nesdale and Rooney, 1996). Other researchers have based all of their scales on those gained spontaneously in such preliminary work to ensure that they are meaningful to the judges. From the pools of items gathered in this way, a number are selected for the main study. Sharp et al. (1973), in their direct-approach survey of language attitudes in Welsh schools, gathered their semantic-differential labels from students, teachers, and students' parents in advance of their main study. In addition, in their study of eight- to twelve-year-olds, Price et al. (1983) used such a procedure, selecting the nine labels most frequently used by their RP and Welsh speakers for their main study. 'Strong', 'selfish', 'good', 'chatty', 'handsome', 'intelligent', 'friendly', 'kind' and 'snobbish' were the traits they arrived at, along with their Welsh translations. Further examples were given of this approach earlier in this chapter (Bourhis et al., 1973; Doise et al., 1976; Paltridge and Giles, 1984).

The pools of items that are gathered in this way, and the process of transforming them into the final set of scale labels, are not generally detailed in such studies (beyond stating usually that selection is based on the most frequently occurring items in the pool). Our experience in the research that we discuss later, though, suggests that this is not necessarily a straightforward process, at least when working with young adults in their mid-teens. The items finally arrived at (where reported) in such studies tend to resemble something more akin to 'tidied-up' adult versions of items. If this is how such items have been arrived at, then there is a risk that the researchers have designed out the evaluations made within adolescent culture and have elicited relatively 'overt' values, in line with the idea that teenagers of this age have developed 'adult-like' attitudes (Day, 1982).

Taking scales used in previous studies can produce additional problems. This practice may induce some circularity in the research process, whereby the well-documented dimensions simply become better documented and so perhaps are assumed to be exhaustive, while others remain out of view. Even though there is a great deal of value in the summary of dimensions by Zahn and Hopper (1985) – for example, comparability across studies – language attitudes research into different populations can not assume that the same set of universal dimensions will always be salient.

In the previous chapter, we noted that open-ended data, for example from focus-group interviews, need not be seen only in terms of a useful preliminary to survey work to ensure the meaningfulness of subsequent survey questionnaires; they can also be seen as useful follow-ups to such data, or indeed as an independent study. The value of preliminary collections of spontaneous items referred to above also need not be limited to providing a basis for semantic-differential labels; they are worthy of investigation in their own right as the *evaluative repertoires* of the groups under study, offering a depth and richness that usefully helps to offset the limitations of scale ratings alone. A more open-ended approach can help in the understanding of not only the different profiles that speakers have, but also the process of evaluation itself and its own cultural constitution.

The limitations of semantic-differential scales have arisen not simply from the way they have been employed in language attitudes work, but connect with the very tradition of this mode of measurement. They have long been used in studies of attitudes in a considerable range of domains, extending far beyond language attitudes: for example, attitudes towards jobs and occupations (Triandis, 1959); attitudes towards academics, and towards the church (Nickols and Shaw, 1964). They are considered to have good reliability and validity (for example, see Osgood et al., 1957). Osgood and his colleagues established as early as the 1950s that the use of such scales with a wide variety of attitude objects produces ratings that correlate into three principal dimensions, referred to as EPA (Osgood et al., 1957: 47–66). Respectively, these are *Evaluation* (for example, good/bad), *Potency* (for example, powerful/powerless) and *Activity* (for example, fast/slow), and they anticipate the three dimensions summarized by Zahn and Hopper in their 1985 study of language attitudes research (respectively, 'attractiveness', 'superiority' and 'dynamism'). Heise (1970: 238) goes as far as to claim that 'the basic goal in a semantic differential study is to get measurements on the EPA dimensions' and that, in order to achieve this, 'the most common procedure is to select scales on the basis of published factor analyses' (p. 239). On the other hand, Heise also mentions that additional dimensions have been found in some studies, albeit accounting for far less variance (p. 236). Our own view is that, for the study of the language attitudes of adolescents in particular, such additional dimensions should also be explored.

However, there are limitations not only in the way that these scales have been selected for semantic-differential studies, but also arguably in the nature of these items in language attitudes research. For a lexical item to be employed on such scales, it must have the qualities of gradeability and (usually) an antonym, for directionality to be expressed. In other words, the two items used for the bipolar scale must be in a paradigmatic relationship of opposites in a paired system, with each member of the pair at opposite ends of a continuum. Some studies, though, employ unidirectional scales that avoid the problem of antonyms – for example, irritating/not at all irritating – but these qualities still need to be gradeable. (The need for gradeability is linked to Osgood et al.'s (1957) claim that this allows for a representation of attitude intensity, though this is not an uncontested claim – see Weksel and Hennes, 1965.) Hence, if, when conducting a preliminary study to collect spontaneous items from a group of judges for later use in the selection of semantic-differential scales, a judge produces a response that has no antonym and/or is not gradable, this has to be discarded. However, as we see later, items of this sort (such as group labels) may well provide insights into the judges' attitudes that semantic-differential scales miss and, indeed, may send out unmistakable impressions of directionality and intensity, too. While the semantic-differential approach (which typifies so much language attitudes research) undoubtedly has many advantages for economy, measurement and comparability, it does nevertheless have limitations.

Apart from issues of antonymy and gradeability, it is also supposed that the evaluative adjectives on these scales are themselves 'semantic primes': that is, that they have the same meaning for all people in all circumstances. (The most extreme instance of this assumption occurs with generalized scales – see Osgood et al., 1957.) However, it can be rash to make such assumptions at times. For example, for teenagers in the UK today, the most common use of the apparently unambiguous word 'sad' is almost certainly as a counter-empathetic response to another person's inadequacy ('He is a sad person' meaning 'He is inadequate') rather than in its 'overt' sense of an empathetic response to a state of event ('He is sad' meaning 'He is melancholy'). With judges of that age-group, one should perhaps be mindful of this if employing this item on a semantic-differential scale.

To sum up this section, the nature of semantic-differential scales and the over-reliance on such scales and dimensions from previously published work may restrict the evaluative picture that emerges from language attitudes research. If they are to be used, there is a strong case for supplementing them with more spontaneous and context-sensitive data. The general point is that we need a complex of methods and of response options that is able to match the inherent complexity of language attitudes, as entertained by different individuals and groups.

MGT research into attitudes towards Welsh English

Principal studies and findings
At the outset of this section, it needs to be emphasized that results from the significant number of matched-guise studies in Wales over the years have not, arguably, led to the emergence of the cumulative body of knowledge one might have anticipated. Overall, the results have been inconclusive, and indeed this is an important motivation for the methodological critique and reappraisal that forms the basis of this book. Giles (1970) was the first MGT study which included a Welsh English accent amongst its guises. He elicited evaluations from 177 secondary-school students in south Wales and in Somerset. Thirteen guises were presented, all of which were accents of English heard in Britain, including both rural and urban British accents, and some foreign (for example, French and German) accents. The judges were asked three questions about each accent they heard: how pleasant they thought the speaker sounded; how comfortable or uncomfortable they would feel if interacting with the speaker; and how much prestige or status was associated with the speaker (Giles, 1970: 215).

The results, though based on interval data using seven-point scales, are set out in rank order, for each of the three questions (p. 218). Although no analysis was conducted to check to see where any significant differences were amongst the ranked varieties, it is nevertheless possible to say that (so-called) 'Welsh English' was the highest scoring British mainland regional accent on all three scales. The matched-guise study was analysed in such a way as not to include the south Wales students' judgements of 'south-Welsh English', or the Somerset students' judgements of the Somerset guise. Hence it gives some insight into how 'Welsh English' is regarded in England (at least, just across the border in Somerset).

Giles (1971a) subsequently investigated the personality traits attributed by judges to speakers of these accents. In relation to RP speakers, 'Welsh English' speakers were downgraded significantly in terms of ambition, intelligence, self-confidence, determination and industriousness. But 'Welsh English' speakers were also seen as less serious, and more humorous, good-natured and talkative than RP speakers. These results reflect the commonly found distinction between 'standard' varieties, scoring more highly on the prestige dimension, and 'non-standard' varieties, scoring more highly on the social attractiveness dimension.

Studies by Bourhis, Giles and Lambert (1975) and Bourhis (1977) both investigated the effects on evaluations of accent shifts during the course of an interaction. That is, how are judgements affected when (so-called) 'Welsh English' speakers move away from or closer to RP in specific situations? In the first of these studies, respondents were told that a Welsh athlete had recently performed well in an international diving competition, and they would hear him being interviewed in two consecutive radio interviews taped after the competition. The interviewer had an RP accent in one interview, and a 'Welsh English' accent in the other. One of the interviews created a 'baseline condition' against which any judgements arising from shifts in accent in the other interview could be measured. This baseline condition was an interview in which both the interviewer and interviewee spoke in a 'mild Welsh English' accent. The second interview had two different outcomes, each of which would be heard by only one group of judges in the evaluation phase of the study. In one version, the athlete began by maintaining his 'mild Welsh English' accent with the RP interviewer, and then shifted his accent towards the interviewer's RP. In the other version, the shift was away from the interviewer towards a 'broader Welsh English' accent, emphasizing intergroup differences and Welsh cultural identity. (The texts were matched for duration, content, grammar and vocabulary.)

The athlete was evaluated more highly on the 'prestige' trait of intelligence when he shifted towards RP than when he did not shift at all (the baseline condition). And he was seen as more intelligent in the baseline condition than when he broadened his accent. But he was rated more highly on the 'social attractiveness' traits of trustworthiness and kindheartedness in the baseline condition than when he shifted to RP, and even more so when he broadened his regional accent.

The findings were replicated in Bourhis (1977), where, this time, two 'south-Welsh' accented 'suspects' were heard supposedly being questioned by an RP-accented policeman, with the suspects accommodating in opposite directions again. An additional finding was that when the suspects broadened their Welsh English, they were deemed to be less guilty and to deserve a milder punishment. It seemed that listeners were prepared to punish the suspect for having betrayed ingroup solidarity, and to reward him for upholding it.

Bourhis et al. (1973), collecting their data in a Valleys community in south-east Wales, presented their respondents with three types of 'Welshmen': an RP speaker, a 'south-Welsh accented' English speaker, and a Welsh-language speaker with a 'south Wales' dialect. These guises were played to three groups of listeners: bilingual Welsh, Welsh learners, and non-Welsh (English) speakers born in Wales. Although the judges differed along other important dimensions such as views on Welsh political autonomy, and the need for their children to learn Welsh, there were no divergences amongst the three groups of judges in their attitudes to the speakers. All groups gave the most favourable ratings on most traits to the Welsh language speaker, but on the 'social attractiveness' scales of trustworthiness, friendliness and sociability, a Welsh accent was sufficient for English speakers to gain ratings as favourable as those of the Welsh speakers. Apart from a high rating on self-confidence, the only traits on which the RP speaker achieved comparatively high ratings relative to 'Welsh English' and Welsh were arrogance, snobbishness, self-confidence and conservatism. The authors suggested that Welsh identity could be asserted through Welsh-accented English where an individual was making an effort to learn the Welsh language.

The Cardiff theatre study conducted by Bourhis and Giles (1976), referred to earlier in this chapter, collected behavioural (degree of co-operation) data rather than the cognitive data collected in the other studies reviewed here. The researchers collected data from Cardiff audiences watching a film in English, when an audio-recorded public announcement requesting help with an audience survey was delivered in RP, 'mild Welsh English', or 'broad Welsh English', and from bi-lingual audiences watching a Welsh-language play, when the announcement was made in RP, 'broad Welsh English', 'mild Welsh English' or Welsh. The film audiences (assumed by the researchers to be monolingual) complied equally in response to 'mild Welsh English' (25 per cent of the audience) and RP (22.5 per cent), but significantly less so when the request was made in 'broad Welsh English' (8.1 per cent). In contrast, the play audiences complied significantly more in response to the Welsh-language request (26 per cent) than to any of the three English requests (broad 8.2 per cent; mild 9.2 per cent; RP 2.5 per cent). These differences in responses are seemingly linked to the immediate context in some way, through the impact of the Welsh play versus the English film, through the different audiences that such performances would attract or through the incongruity of announcements being made in English at a Welsh-medium event. We will return to the importance of context later in this chapter.

Price et al. (1983) also investigated the attitudes towards RP, Welsh and 'Welsh English'. They specify the 'Welsh English' variety in their study as '*west*-Welsh English'. The data was collected in Carmarthenshire in south-west Wales, and their judges were bilingual pre-adolescents, aged 10 to 12 years. Results showed a significant downgrading of the 'Welsh English' speaker on some scales relative to the Welsh speaker and the RP speaker. (No significant differences were found between these latter two speakers.) The 'Welsh English' speaker was seen as more snobbish and less good than the Welsh speaker, and less strong than the RP speaker. (The adjectives for the scales were chosen from a pilot study in which children of a similar age listened to tapes and were asked to produce items they thought appropriate.) The findings in this study also suggest the impact of contextual effects – here perhaps the attitudinal climate of a Welsh-speaking heartland, reflecting, perhaps even at that age, local pressures and politics.

A further finding by Price et al. (1983), as we mentioned in chapter 2, is that the language of testing had some impact on the results. Those given questionnaires in Welsh rated the Welsh English speaker as more selfish than the Welsh and RP speakers. Those responding in English did not make this differentiation, but they did judge the Welsh and RP speakers to be more intelligent than the Welsh English speaker – a distinction not made by those responding in Welsh.

From the above major MGT studies, no consistent picture immediately emerges regarding the evaluative profile of 'Welsh English' in Wales. Overall, Bourhis et al.'s (1973) judges tended to favour Welsh and 'Welsh English' speakers over RP speakers. Bourhis and Giles's (1976) audience watching the English film regarded the RP and 'mild Welsh-accented English' speakers equally favourably, whereas their audience watching the Welsh play downgraded both these speakers in relation to the Welsh speaker. Price et al.'s (1983) judges downgraded the 'Welsh English' speaker compared to the Welsh and RP speakers, and this lack of consistency in findings led to their proposal for studies embracing different subgroups in different regions, which the work included in the subsequent chapters of this book addresses. At this point, however, it is worth considering what factors might contribute to these highly variable results.

Regional linguistic features in Wales
To begin with, it is notable that the studies were not all conducted in the same parts of Wales. For example, Bourhis and Giles's (1976) theatre study was conducted in the urban centre of Cardiff, whereas Price et al.'s (1983) data was collected in relatively rural Carmarthen in the

south-west. Inevitably, neither of these data sources can be considered representative of Wales as a whole. One might at the very least anticipate the linguistic and cultural distinctiveness of urban and rural, bilingual and monolingual, and north and south Wales to be reflected in attitudinal differences.

Although we lack detailed linguistic surveys of contemporary usage for all the main regions of Wales, it is apparent that substantial community-based differences in vernacular forms of English exist across the country. (See Coupland 1990 for a collection of illustrative descriptions, Coupland, 1988, for detail on Cardiff English, and Coupland, forthcoming, for worked analyses of some of the features listed below. Descriptive evidence from traditional dialectological surveys of 'conservative' older speakers can be found in Parry, 1999 and Penhallurick, 1991. Thomas (1973) provides an integrative overview.) Socio-phonetic differences between the major dialects of Welsh English can be established at different levels of generality.

First, it is clear that many, and probably all, English-speaking communities in Wales take part in highly generalized patterns of deviation from Received Pronunciation in respect of social accent/ dialect features, such as so-called 'H-dropping' (variable absence of voiced onset /h/ to syllable-initial 'h' words, such as 'have', 'had', 'heavy') and 'G-dropping' (variable use of alveolar /n/ as opposed to velar /ŋ/ nasals in verb compounds with '-ing' and nominal compounds with '-thing', such as 'running' and 'swimming', 'something' and 'nothing'). These social dialect forms are not regionally distinctive of Welsh versus other British English varieties, even though close analysis might show interesting differences in the frequencies of use of these forms across Welsh communities, and between Wales and England varieties.

Second, there is a set of features which, as a rough generalization, goes some way towards distinguishing the English of many or most Welsh communities from non-Welsh communities. (Although the existence of this set seems to give credence to the concept of 'Welsh English', a raft of other features, see below, undermines this.) These features include variation in the lexical set with the 'wedge' vowel (ʌ), which has [ʌ] in RP but values closer to the central schwa vowel [ə] in most of Wales (in stressed-syllable words like 'brothers', 'lovely', 'bunch'). Similarly, most Welsh English vernacular varieties have variable (iw) in words of the 'you', 'news', 'institution' set, realized as [juː] in RP but [ɪw] in Wales (with a prominent first element of the glide, contrasting with the RP-type glide to prominent /u:/). Other candidates for pan-Welsh English features are (ɔ:) which has [ɔə] in RP but [uə] or [ɪwə] in Wales (in words of the set 'poor', 'sure'), and short (a) varying between [æ] in RP and less close forms [a] or [ɑ] (in the short /a/ lexical set, for example, 'gran', 'back', 'man', etc.). The absence of RP-type reduction of unstressed vowels to schwa, for example maintaining [o] in the middle syllable of 'photograph', is another. Sporadic use of Welsh-language lexis in English discourse might again be a pan-Wales characteristic, although we would expect this to show regional and social variation consistent with the highly variable pattern of Welsh-language usage across Wales.

Thirdly, and most importantly, however, many phonetic and some morphological and lexical features are diagnostic of significant structured regional and social differences *within* Wales. For example, (ou) in words of the lexical set 'hello', 'home', 'nose', and then in a second set including 'low' 'widow' and 'know', shows complex regional differences. In contemporary Cardiff speech (and 'Cardiff' can usually be taken to typify the wider conurbation, including Newport, Penarth and Barry), especially among younger speakers, realizations of this variable in both lexical sets are typically diphthongs, as they are in RP. But RP has central onset for the glide [əu], while Cardiff speakers have the backed and open onset form [ou]. In Valleys and south-west Wales vernacular English, however, monophthongal [o:] is common in the 'hello', 'home', 'nose' set of words, while diphthongs are used in the 'low' 'widow' and 'know' set (giving an additional phonemic contrast between 'knows' and 'nose' in those regions). North-west Wales is different again, with the regular possibility of monophthongs across both sets of words, so that 'knows' and 'nose' can both have the monophthongal form [o:]. North-east Wales, under the influence of the Liverpool conurbation, has different meanings for (ou) variants. While centralized onset forms are heard to be decidedly 'posh' in most of Wales, because they suggest RP which usually itself suggests 'English', in the north-east it is identified to be a feature of vernacular Liverpool speech and is therefore heard as 'non-standard' or 'local'.

The variable (ei) is somewhat similar, in that the diphthong [ei] and the monophthong [e:] are variant forms in words of the set 'name', 'later', 'game', and of the set 'hey', 'day', 'anyway'. Once again, though, Cardiff and the north-east have only the diphthongal variant in both sets, while the monophthong is a variable local feature in the Valleys and in the south-west in the lexical set 'name', 'later', 'game', but not in the set 'hey', 'day', 'anyway'. Again, the north-west dialects allow monophthongs in both sets. The set of words with (ai), such as 'died', 'time', 'find', 'bye', very commonly have centralized schwa-type onset to the glide [əi] in many parts of Wales, although there is a feature in Cardiff that gives backed and more open onsets, [ɔi]. Cardiff and its conurbation are linguistically distinctive and 'un-Welsh' in many other ways too. The long open back vowel (a:) has forms ranging between [a:] and the broadest local form [æ:] in words of the set 'are', 'charcoal', 'barbecue', 'starving', sometimes also having distinctive nasalization. Popular written representations of this pronunciation stereotype sometimes capture the vernacular form as 'Kairdiff' (and indeed these appear in some of our data). Fronted and raised qualities of (a:) of the type [æ:] are also found in the Liverpool-like north-east, but also in the north-west of Wales, though with different social meanings there. In Cardiff and the north-east they seem to connote working-class, urban, non-Welsh affiliation; in the north-west they connote rurality and 'Welshness'.

Realizations of orthographic 't' between vowels, especially across word boundaries as in 'lot of', 'got to', 'but I', and 'about Evans', are commonly voiced taps [t̬] in Cardiff and are particularly frequent. Mid-Wales, away from the western coast, shows influences from the west-of-England accent, and is rhotic (having audible /r/ after vowels where it is marked in the written form, as in both syllables of 'farmer' and 'darker'). Most other regions of Wales are non-rhotic, except for south Pembrokeshire in the south-west and, residually, in Gower English. At the same time, varieties of English that are heavily under the influence of the Welsh language have a different form of rhotic pronunciation, often with the trilled /r/. North Wales English tends to have a tense glottal vocal setting (of the sort that also characterizes Liverpool speech). Under the influence of north-Wales Welsh, north-west Wales English also has tensing of lax /z/ consonants, for example in plurals, as in [hɔːsɪs] or [hɔrsɪs] for RP [hɔːsɪz].

Morphological present-tense verb agreement forms such as 'I goes' and 'they likes' are again common in and close to Cardiff. These are also heard in many regions in the south and west of England but not usually elsewhere in Wales. The compound adverbs 'by here' and 'by there' are common in many parts of Wales, but they are phonologically reduced in the Valleys and the south-west, though not in Cardiff. Cardiff alone has the compound question form 'where's it to?', although 'where's it by?' has a wider distribution in Wales. The address tag 'mun' is quite widely distributed, although its phonetic form can be [man] rather than [mən] in Cardiff, and Valleys speakers also use [bət] (a short form of 'butty' meaning 'friend') in similar contexts. In fact, many regions of Wales have their distinctive lexical/discourse stereotypes, including the so-called 'Bangor aye', where 'aye?' is an utterance-final tag seeking confirmation that a listener has understood or agrees with the speaker. North Wales speakers also use 'yeah?' for this function, while a high-rising terminal intonation pattern with equivalent meaning seems to be mainly restricted to Cardiff.

This informal summary of linguistic variation in English used across Wales is, we hope, sufficient to demonstrate the importance of treating Wales as not one but several speech communities, at least as regards the distribution of linguistic forms. The challenge to language attitudes research in Wales is to assess the extent to which community-level *perceptual* factors endorse or undermine the community structure evidenced in linguistic distributions.

Labels used by the researchers, such as 'south-Welsh English' (Giles, 1970) and 'west-Wales English (Price et al., 1983) do not objectively capture the varying degrees and qualities of anglicization (historical and contemporary) of varieties of English in Wales, differences in class structuring of urban and rural communities in Wales (Williams, 1987), or the variable symbolic associations between the Welsh regions, their speech (actual or stereotyped) and notions of 'authentic Welshness'. In studies where actual speech samples (that is, verbal guises of various sorts) are played to judges, it is clearly possible to give an accurate description or characterization of them (though this has typically not been done). More precision in identifying *which* Welsh Englishes are being evaluated is likely to show differences among them in terms of their evaluative profiles along the established dimensions of status, social attractiveness and dynamism. The relatively favourable findings for 'south-Welsh English' (which one might assume to include Cardiff) in Giles (1970) may differ markedly from attitudes towards Cardiff English, whose 'uniquely strangled vowels' (*Radio Times*, 25 August 1984) may well evoke evaluative reactions similar to those towards Cockney or Birmingham English vernaculars (Coupland, 1988: 98).

Authenticity
It is likely, too, that regional varieties of Welsh English will be seen as projecting different degrees of 'authentic Welshness'. Such a dimension has not been investigated in any systematic manner in previous

research, although it is addressed in incidental terms in some studies (for example, Bourhis et al., 1973). Yet it seems likely to be an important dimension of English and other colonial languages in post-colonial settings. The issue is whether communities, like Wales, that have adopted English as a majority code are viewed as authentically able to symbolize national identity through English, where, when and to what extent.

Outside the research that focuses specifically on language attitudes, there is other literature that points to a differentiated distribution of Welshness across Wales. In chapter 2, we mentioned Williams's (1985) perceptual study of culture regions in Wales, in which schoolchildren in Wales identified on a map which towns they felt were mainly in Welsh-speaking areas.

Edwards (1991) puts forward a two-dialect model of English in Wales: a southern variety, which is in some ways related to the speech of the English west Midlands and the south-west of England, and on which the influence of Welsh is mainly substratal; and a northern variety, which is to some extent influenced by the speech of north-west England, and on which the Welsh language is very much a living influence because of the comparatively high proportion of Welsh/English bilinguals.

Balsom (1985: 1) proposes a 'three-Wales' model, relevant to socio-political groupings, to interpret Welsh cultural geography (see figure 3.1), arguing that Wales has three distinct and identifiable socio-linguistic groups. The model is based upon a combination of data from the 1981 census, and the Welsh election survey of 1979 (in Balsom's view, a low point in Welsh self-assertion). Balsom's (1985: 6ff.) three main regions are: (1) *Y Fro Gymraeg*: the Welsh heartland, Welsh-speaking and Welsh-identifying, almost totally Welsh-born, mainly working class, and largely occupying the north and west of Wales; (2) *Welsh Wales*: non-Welsh-speaking, but Welsh-identifying, almost totally Welsh born, and predominantly working-class, and largely occupying the traditional south-Wales area; and (3) *British Wales*: non-Welsh speaking, relatively more British-identifying, more middle-class than working-class, dominating the remainder of Wales.

On the other hand, the sociolinguistic distributions we described in the previous section suggest that two- or three-zone models *under*-specify the extent of potentially salient English dialect communities in Wales. As we see in the studies to follow, a more plausible geolinguistic structure identifies at least two north-Wales zones – the more anglicized

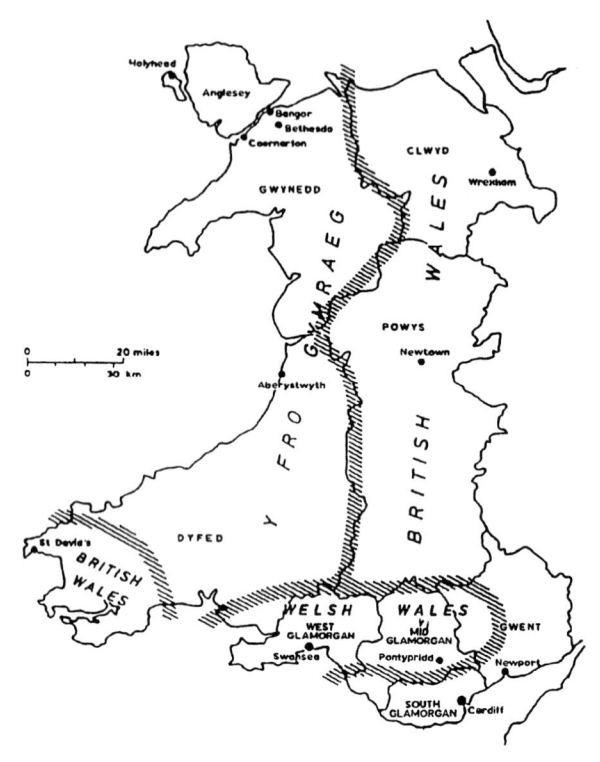

Figure 3.1: Language and identity in Wales, based on the 'three-Wales' model (Balsom, 1985)

east and the more Welsh-speaking west, a mid-Wales zone, and probably three zones in the south – the Cardiff conurbation, the Valleys, and the rural south-west.

Age
The age of respondents is also of importance, with some evidence of minority- and majority-group children becoming aware of the social significance of language variation by the age of ten or eleven (see the review in Day, 1982). There is also some evidence that elderly speakers are less prone to differentiate evaluatively among non-standard varieties on some factors (Paltridge and Giles, 1984). Ages of judges have certainly differed amongst the earlier studies in Wales. Giles (1970) selected judges of two age-groups: mean ages 12 years 3 months, and 17 years 4 months. These two groups differed in their perceptions of status

differences, with the older group evaluating RP more positively for prestige than the younger group, and the younger group showing more accent-loyalty in their evaluations of 'an accent identical to your own'. These findings are not supportive of the conclusion mentioned above that ten or eleven is the age of 'maturity'. Price et al.'s (1983) judges were even younger, with ages ranging from ten to twelve years (mean age 11 years 6 months). Bourhis et al.'s (1973) judges were adults (range twenty-one to fifty-five), and Bourhis and Giles's (1976) judges were also adults (no ages provided).

Social-group membership of judges
Social-group membership of judges can also have attitudinal effects (Giles and Coupland, 1991). Bourhis et al. (1973) describe their judges as 'lower middle-class'. Bourhis and Giles describe theirs as 'middle class'. Price et al. (1983) use (but do not clarify) a term from Williams (1979) in describing their pre-adolescent judges as coming from a 'high-order culture area'. One should not be reassured though by this pattern of using middle-class respondents. Coupland (1990), for example, sees the middle class in Wales as being subdivisible into quite different ideological groups. A pan-UK RP-oriented group certainly needs to be contrasted with a rising middle-class group of Welsh speakers who are an important force pressing for political and cultural initiatives in support of the Welsh language, for example occupying roles in the mass media, politics and Welsh cultural life. Indeed, the theatre study by Bourhis and Giles (1976) arguably gives a clear reflection of such a division. Their 'lower-middle-class' bilingual and monolingual audiences react in a uniform and perhaps predictable way to the broad-accented English, probably displaying the familiar middle-class negative reaction to socially stigmatized speech varieties in relatively formal settings. But they differ markedly from each other in their reactions to RP. Only 2.5 per cent of the bilingual audience cooperate with the RP request, whereas 22.5 per cent of the monolinguals comply. Amongst the bilinguals, both the mild and broad variants gained little compliance compared to the Welsh request. Amongst the monolinguals, the mild Welsh-accented English request gained the most cooperation, more even than RP. Group identities, it appears, are realized linguistically through quite different means for these groups. Conceivably, too, despite the young age of Price et al.'s (1983) respondents, the significantly different answers they received according to whether they issued their questionnaire in Welsh or in English may

have been tapping into the very same social divisions within the middle class that Bourhis and Giles (1976) encountered.

Situational influences
Situational factors are also likely to have attitudinal effects. These can be broadly differentiated into effects, firstly, from the immediate situation, and secondly, from the larger sociopolitical background in which language attitudes may develop. One much-cited instance of the former is the study by Carranza and Ryan (1975), where they found that bilingual Anglo-American and Mexican-American students all preferred English in a school context, but Mexican-American students showed a slight preference for Spanish in the home setting, especially on traits relating to solidarity or social attractiveness values. Attitudes to language are thus seen to be attitudes to the functions normally allocated to that language, or dialect, or style. This was conceivably a contributor to the differing attitudes towards RP, for example, among the English film and Welsh play audiences in Bourhis and Giles's (1976) theatre study.

The larger sociocultural background of a speech community may also have an impact. Earlier in this chapter, we referred to different ideological values in different areas of Wales (for example, bilingual versus monolingual, urban versus rural) reflecting local pressures and politics. There may also be temporal and cultural change factors involved. For example, the 1970s in Wales has been seen as a revivalist period for the Welsh language and Welsh identity (Giles, 1990). The present era, with the establishment of the National Assembly for Wales, is another. Giles, Bourhis and Taylor (1977) put forward a framework for assessing the impact of such background sociocultural factors in contact situations in terms of components of ethnolinguistic vitality: demographic strength, institutional support, social status of members of the linguistic group. The higher the vitality of the group, the more probable it is that there will be a preference for ingroup languages and varieties. The assessment of the strength and impact of such components requires some investigation of the social and political forces operating within the history of a nation (Genesee and Bourhis, 1982, 1988).

Taking stock

Having looked at the strengths and weaknesses of the MGT as a research method, summarized the MGT work in Wales, and given a preliminary review of the sociolinguistics of Wales, there are particular points to notice which form an important backdrop to the research we look at in the remainder of the book.

In terms of building a clearer picture of language attitudes in Wales, the research we have reviewed so far reveals a need to:

1. construct profiles of community attitudes towards a number of different varieties of Welsh English, where the range of salient communities is at this stage an open empirical question;
2. define these profiles in terms relevant to community members;
3. investigate whether such profiles differ significantly according to the geographical localities of respondents;
4. investigate whether such profiles differ according to whether judges are bilingual Welsh and English speakers, or whether they speak English but not Welsh;
5. investigate whether such profiles differ according to the age of the judges (specifically, adults versus young adolescents), or at least gain coherence by looking at specific social and demographic groups (school teenagers and teachers).

In terms of methodological concerns, in addition to the disadvantages of employing the MGT set out earlier in this chapter, it is also arguable that too much reliance on a single research method can produce skewed results. Hence, the work that is the focus of the following chapters has been designed to explore alternatives in the collection and analysis of data, in part to address some of the criticisms of the MGT. In particular, it considers the following:

1. Presentation of dialects/accents
The use of 'factually neutral' reading passages, read out by the same person in different accents, and then played to judges on audiotape has always been contentious. Earlier in this chapter, an argument was made for more ecologically valid material to be used. In a further response to such doubts, however, there have been studies in which two different presentations have been employed and the results compared. Giles (1970) presented his accents to half of the judges through the use of the MGT, and so used an indirect approach. To the other half of the judges, they were presented *conceptually*, as a simple written list of accents, and so used a direct approach. Rank correlations of mean accent ratings deriving from each of these modes were high (+0.88 for

status, +0.87 for communicative content, and +0.79 for aesthetic qualities). Giles compared his results from the 1970 (MGT) study with those from his later (1971a) study in which he used thirteen genuine accents (by using the voices of thirteen different speakers), and found a rank-order correlation for status of +0.94. The intention with these correlations was to demonstrate the value of the MGT, but given the persistence of the questions about the validity of such contrived presentations, it is equally valid to argue the other way: if the correlations are so good in this context and both approaches seemingly tap the privately held attitudes the researcher aims to access, then there would appear to be no necessary advantage to using these other (direct) modes of presentation rather than the MGT. As we mentioned in chapter 1, indirect methods are likely to be of more value in certain research settings than in others. The difficulty, of course, is that we need first to be sure that there is no benefit from using indirect methods, and in so many instances it may not be easy to ascertain this. As Giles's work has shown, it can be advantageous to use both approaches and compare outcomes.

2. Scales and dimensions
Although the scales and dimensions used in language attitudes studies now seem well established, particularly since Zahn and Hopper's (1985) synthesis paper, it nevertheless seems important to elicit the descriptive and evaluative terms used by the judges themselves, at least to supplement those usually included, and particularly in, say, intergenerational or cross-cultural research. In part, this is to ensure that there is no simple imposing of categories that are less central than ones not included. In addition, it will help to ensure that the terms used are ones that make sense to judges – in other words, to ensure that appropriate questions are being asked.

There is a further issue regarding scales and dimensions that seems to have been lost in so much of the MGT research of the past thirty years. Even if the 'right' questions are being asked, it is important to try to ascertain the relative importance of these questions to the judges. It is straightforward to ask informants to rate accents for status and for dynamism, for example, but this in itself does not show which of these is more important to them, in the same way that we can judge an acquaintance to be kind *and* short-tempered, and feel that their kindness more than compensates for their short-temperedness. It is noteworthy that such data have seldom been sought in language attitudes studies. Interestingly, such data *were* collected in the seminal MGT study by Lambert et al. (1960).

In addition, there is much value in supplementing quantitative scales-data with at least short open-ended items, asking judges to elaborate on their judgements. This is not a weakness in the MGT per se, but an illuminating corollary to what has been the dominant mode of data collection, and one which could facilitate more powerful interpretations of quantitative results.

3. Perceptual data

The criticisms of the MGT made by Preston (1989) relate to whether the judges responding to audio-taped speech are able to identify where the speaker is from (an issue independently and more recently highlighted by Nesdale and Rooney, 1996), and to judges' beliefs as to the geographical distribution of the speech they hear. Such additional data, Preston maintains, will remove some of the difficulty of interpreting the results of language attitudes studies. As will be seen later, speech-style *recognition* deserves to be seen as an issue in its own right.

In short, although there is a great deal of pre-existing data on language attitudes in Wales, much of which has been considered above, the empirical work that we consider in the remainder of this book is intended to be much more socioculturally focused, and to be much more open to methodological exploration.

4

An integrated programme of language attitudes research in Wales

In this chapter we cover details of the procedures, materials and respondents involved in two sets of studies, along with some background discussion to provide a rationale. In both studies, language attitudinal data were collected from schools all over Wales. We employed a number of different data-collection methods, both in the ways that dialect communities were presented to respondents for evaluation, and in the types of qualitative and quantitative responses that were required of them.

The first set of studies – the questionnaire phase – is a survey of teachers' attitudes. The questionnaire in this study contained a range of tasks, including a map-filling and labelling task based on the recent methodological developments in perceptual dialectology mentioned in chapter 2, and sets of semantic-differential attitude-rating scales linked to conceptually presented dialect communities, a mode of presentation that we referred to in chapter 3. The second study – the narratives phase of the research – is also an attitudinal investigation of teachers, but this study embraces a further and contrastive focus on a large sample of students aged fifteen. In fact, a questionnaire was used in this narratives study too, gathering both quantitative and qualitative data, in addition to some focus-group discussions. In the narratives study, in contrast to the questionnaire study, dialects were presented to respondents through audio-recorded excerpts of teenagers from schools all over Wales, telling stories in their local dialects about things that had happened to them. This presentation mode lacks the highly controlled 'rigour' of the MGT, and allows many of the 'interfering' effects the MGT is designed to eliminate, but it addresses many of the ecological validity and authenticity issues we set out earlier. On the narratives questionnaire, there were two tasks to be completed apart from the scales. One was a question asking respondents to identify the dialect of each storyteller they heard. The other task required respondents to write down their immediate impressions of each of the speakers. The qualitative data provide deeper insights into the processes of identity-building amongst the teenagers, and a richer evaluative picture of the dialect communities and narrative performances than scales alone can access.

In chapter 1, we gave an introduction to attitudes and the methodological problems involved in studying them. But before setting out the details of how both our studies were conducted, some additional background is needed to contextualize two aspects of the narratives study not strictly concerned with the methodological issues dealt with in earlier chapters. Firstly, we give further explanation of the selection of teachers and young adolescents as respondents, and set out some of the relevant research background. Secondly, we provide more background for the dialect recognition task than we gave when we briefly introduced the recognition issue in chapter 3.

Teachers and young teenage students as informants

Teachers

Teachers and students have been sources of data in a considerable number of language attitudes studies. In part, though, this has been a result of the sometimes relatively easy access researchers have had to them, and the advantage at times of being able to generate a great deal of data in a short space of time in such school settings. The same advantages have also led to many studies being based on convenience samples of university students. However, some studies have had a specific research focus on teachers as gatekeepers (see Erickson, 1975), whose judgements are likely to have considerable impact on students' life opportunities. Hence the degree to which their judgements of students might be influenced by students' speech features, and teachers' attitudes to standard and non-standard language varieties generally, is an important research issue, particularly given the status-stressing environment of schools, and the commonly found drive towards prescriptivism and an ideology of linguistic 'correctness'.

A good number of teacher-focused language attitude studies have taken the form of surveys. For example, in the UK, there have been studies by Giles (1971b) investigating teachers' attitudes towards accent usage and change, by Chandler, Robinson and Noyes (1988) and Garrett and Austin (1993) on trainee teachers' attitudes to non-standard, 'erroneous' language use, and by Mitchell and Hooper (1991) on language teachers' beliefs about language and language teaching. Elsewhere, Winford's (1975) survey studied trainee teachers' attitudes towards Creole speech in Trinidad, and Davies (2000) surveyed teachers' attitudes to regional dialect use in Germany. Other studies have been designed with experimental properties in order to research any possible causal links between students' speech-style and teachers' assessment of their schoolwork: for example, Seligman et al. (1972) in Canada, Choy and Dodd (1976) in Hawaii, and Granger, Mathews, Quay and Verner (1977) in the USA.

It will suffice here to give brief details of two of these studies in order to gauge the potential for students' speech to impact on others' assessments of them. Granger et al. presented teachers with differing combinations of pictures of schoolchildren and school students' speech-samples. When the teachers were then asked to rate the speech performance of the students, race and class were found to be the significant variables affecting their assessments, and black speakers as a group were rated lower than white speakers. Seligman et al. showed teachers a range of combinations of audio-taped voices of students, pictures of students and pieces of schoolwork. When the teachers then assessed the students, speech style was found to be an important cue.

Our own series of studies, that are reported in the following chapters, do not have as their main goal to attempt with rigorous experimental design to estimate the extent to which teachers' assessment of students is influenced by the students' dialects. In so far as they involve data from teachers, they are primarily investigations of the evaluative profiles that teachers attribute to the main Welsh English dialect communities across Wales, and to speakers of these dialects. However, they do contain items that could arguably link dialect and speech performance to teachers' estimates of school performance: for example by asking the teachers whether they think the audio-taped teenage speakers they listen to are *good at school*. Two developmental issues arise. The first of them is to establish to what extent language attitudes have developed by what is usually referred to as 'adolescence'. The second is to consider how attitudes impact on various aspects of development (for example, identity building) during this stage of life.

Language awareness and attitudes in young people
In chapter 3, we provided a brief summary of the significance of age in language attitudes research, and of how in some studies (for example, Price et al., 1983), some respondents were as young as ten. To what extent, then, can we be sure that language attitudes have developed to any stable configuration at such an age, or even by the age of the teenage respondents in the narratives study?

Research into children's ability to distinguish their own language from that spoken by others points to such awareness having developed around the ages of five or six years (Aboud, 1976), if not by 3.6 to 4 years (Mercer, 1975). There is some lack of accord in the findings regarding the development of language attitudes. Labov (1965), for example, claimed that children did not become aware of the social significance of their dialect until early adolescence. However, there is evidence in other studies that children are already making judgements about varieties before they begin primary education (see review in Day, 1982). One pattern which emerges from such studies (for example, Rosenthal, 1974; Cremona and Bates, 1977; Day, 1980) is one where minority students enter school with either neutral attitudes or a preference for their own speech code, and then acquire the attitudes of the dominant culture as they grow older. But there is an exception to this pattern in the work of Schneiderman (1976), who found that not all minority students acquire favourable attitudes towards the majority language, possibly because they perceive their own speech as a valued symbol of ingroup identity and pride (Giles et al., 1983).

Labov's claim that adolescence is the key period for attitudinal development should not be pushed aside, however. Language attitudes are seemingly not fully developed by puberty. Through adolescence, attitudes towards majority varieties may become far more positive. For example, as we mentioned in chapter 2, during adolescence, there is a general tendency for Welsh bilingual children to shift towards a more positive attitude towards English and a less positive attitude towards Welsh or to bilingualism itself. Giles (1970), too, found some significant differences between his 12- and 17-year-old judges in their evaluations of accented speakers. Or there may even be a more marked attitudinal reversal during adolescence, involving a swing away from the attitudes of the dominant culture towards those of the minority ingroup. Hence, Lambert, Giles and Picard (1975) found that, while 10-year-olds in St John's Valley, Maine, USA, were rejecting French ethnicity and language in favour of English assimilation, high-school and college students were gradually placing European and local French on a par with English.

For our present purposes, there are two broad conclusions to be drawn from this complex set of developmental studies. Firstly, although there is evidence that children have become socialized into appreciating some aspects of the perceived socio-economic correlates of speech varieties by the age of about eleven or twelve, it is also clear that young adulthood can be an interesting developmental period from a language-attitudes perspective. Secondly, these findings on attitudinal development in such young people need to be kept in perspective, since much of the work is mainly concerned with the evaluative distinctions made between the prestige variety in the judge's own context and the judge's own non-standard variety (or some other variety which they are able to place in a broad undifferentiated 'non-standard' category). This is of course only a first step towards an awareness of the differentiated social meanings of a whole range of non-standard varieties (compare with children and adolescent groups in Kristiansen, forthcoming). It is this latter degree of awareness that facilitates the experimentation, changes and reorientations referred to in the next section, and which is the basis of the research in our narratives study.

Evaluative reactions and identity building in adolescence

In the growing research interest in adolescence from the human communication perspective (for example, Eckert, 1989; Bradford Brown, Mory and Kinney, 1994; Catan, Dennison, and Coleman, 1996; Drury, Catan, Dennison and Brody, 1998; Williams and Garrett, 2002), along with the interest in the mid-teens in language-attitudes research in Wales, it is frequently emphasized that this is a period of rapid change and development. Physical changes are occurring alongside changes in self-concept, and there is a move away from family identity towards peer-group identity (Baker, 1992), especially amongst working-class teenagers (Eckert, 1989). Entry into secondary school (at the age of eleven in the UK) leads to some abrupt and major transformations in peer relationships. Youngsters come into direct contact with a much larger population of peers, on account of both school size and the move away from the self-contained classrooms of primary school to the daily routine of moving from class to class for different subject lessons. Moreover, adults' overseeing of peer relationships diminishes, and youngsters have to negotiate this new and radically enlarged peer terrain relatively independently. Research has shown quite clearly that more time is spent with other members of peer groups as children move into early adolescence, and that less time is spent with the family. As adolescents progress through the teenage years, they are actively engaged in 'progressive identity formation' (Waterman, 1982), and their peer groups become increasingly important as a 'vehicle for social comparison' (Heaven, 1994: 95), providing a niche for identity exploration, functioning as a source of companionship and social support, and protecting from adult authority (Heaven, 1994: 79). The price of group membership is peer pressure to experiment with new roles and behaviour, a process which is implicit in identity formation (P. Newman and B. Newman, 1988). And at early adolescence, there is a greater willingness than before to conform to such pressure (for example, V. Bixenstine, DeCorte and B. Bixenstine, 1976).

As regards language, Bradford Brown et al. (1994) maintain that teenagers' images of identities available to them are formed and refined not simply through observation of peer groups, but also through evaluative conversations about peer groups and identities with their friends. Hence, evaluative language, and in particular the lexical typologies of adolescents, are an important part of this process of locating niches and establishing identities. Rampton (1995) has demonstrated how teenagers experiment through language with these alternative identities that are available to them. His work focuses specifically on stylistic 'crossing', in which, for example, young people of Anglo descent might use English-based Caribbean Creole, or kids of Asian descent might use stylized Asian voices to present themselves as less competent in spoken English than in fact they are. Language is shown to provide a means through which adolescents try out various identities to explore how others react, and how these identities impact on social relations with others.

Adolescents' metalinguistic awareness can be viewed as important for a theory of human cultural-development: that is, 'knowing' cultural alternatives, exploring them evaluatively, on the way to (re)defining self- and group-identities. Such cultural alternatives are, partly, established sociolinguistically. Belonging to (or being perceived to belong to) a particular group of peers at school, or aligning oneself with a regional community, or projecting a professional identity, etc., relates partly to a way of talking, and partly perhaps to a thought style and set of attitudes that goes with it, or is indexed by it. Hence, evaluation of language variation has several potential functions. For example, it is where it is possible to engage with and in a range of cultural identities, to role-play them and try them out (as illustrated in Rampton's work), to help clarify the alternative identities that are available in the social system (perhaps accessed through interpersonal contact, perhaps presented through the media), to boost the identity or identities one currently adopts and/or to establish the difficulty or ease with which one might switch to another. Hence, evaluating one's peers is part of evaluating oneself. Comment about language variation, too, is where social evaluations are made, for example, among peers, as illustrated in the work reviewed by Bradford Brown et al. (1994). It is this latter function of evaluative comment on language use that is a primary focus in our narratives study, particularly in our 'keywords' data.

This emphasis on peer evaluation also makes it important to point out that, where adolescent respondents have featured in earlier matched-guise studies, such studies have for the most part involved teenagers in evaluating adult speakers rather than other teenagers. In our narratives study, teenagers evaluate speakers of their own age, who are telling narratives in their dialects to their peers. The aim here is to study the teenagers' evaluations that were firmly embedded in young people's own activities contained in these narratives, as well as relating to sociolinguistic dialect variation.

Dialect recognition

The significance of dialect recognition
In the research traditions of dialectology and variationist sociolinguistics on the one hand, and the social psychology of language attitudes on the other, there has been a tendency to presume that people regularly and fairly accurately recognize localized dialect varieties, as part of their sociolinguistic competence as speech community members. In Labovian community surveys, for example, the question of how consistently community members, let alone outsiders, identify the varieties in question as regionally or socially localized forms is rarely asked. Yet one might expect that low levels of dialect recognition would necessarily limit people's ability to position themselves psychologically within, or in opposition to, local community norms. A dialect is often presumed to confer a sense of social identity. But the extent to which people map social or geographical information on to dialect forms that they hear around them, or for that matter that they use themselves,

would appear to be an important intervening variable. Furthermore, work on dialect recognition by Preston (1993: 188ff.) provides evidence that non-linguists may be far more sensitive to dialect boundaries than dialect surveys are, and may identify and be influenced by boundaries that linguists have not yet discovered.

As we mentioned in the previous chapter, in relation to the language attitudes research tradition in which respondents are presented with voice samples which they are then asked to rate on a range of scales, Preston (1989: 3; 1993: 193ff.) is critical of the failure to include a request to respondents to 'tell me where you think this voice is from'. In some studies, prior to the main data-collection, voice samples are 'validated' by asking other groups of respondents (assumed to be comparable with the later respondents) to rate them in various ways, including for their geographical origins. The rationale for conducting this procedure in advance of the main study is that it enables the researcher not to draw attention to this variable in the main study itself, thereby (at least arguably) diminishing the likelihood that the respondents judge the language variety rather than the speaker. However, designing recognition out of the main study arguably tends to draw attention away from the theoretical significance and potential social-psychological complexity of dialect recognition. Our narratives study includes a recognition item to be completed by the teachers and the mid-teenagers. So there is a significant preliminary issue to address before giving details of the study itself: what is the relationship between language awareness (and, whatever processes are subsumed in 'recognition', they must include awareness) and language attitudes?

Awareness, recognition and attitudes
There is a theoretical argument that the ability to recognize what language or variety one is listening to makes no difference to attitudes, or at least that recognition is not a necessary condition for social evaluation. The argument is that the *sounds* of the language or variety, rather than where it is anchored geographically or socially, are what trigger off the evaluative reactions in listeners: that is, that people respond to the *inherent value* of the language. The inherent-value hypothesis (see Giles and Powesland, 1975) is not totally lacking in supporting evidence. For example, Brown, Strong and Rencher (1975) audio-recorded French Canadian speakers from a variety of social-class backgrounds and presented the speech samples to a group of Anglo-American students. Although the students had no knowledge of

French and so could not recognize the varieties, they were able to differentiate broadly between the speakers in terms of social class. It is certainly plausible that there are sufficiently general correlations between phonetic/prosodic realizations and broad socio-demographic categories to allow interpretations of this sort to be made, however partially or 'inaccurately'. In any event, one might expect listeners to *transfer* aspects of their sociolinguistic appreciation of dialects they know to dialects they do not know, and this could generate reliable patterns of evaluation.

Generally, though, the received position argues that judgements are based not upon inherent value, but upon *imposed social norms*, or social connotations. To take an example, Giles, Bourhis and Davies (1979) played an audio-recording of various forms of Quebec French to people in Wales and to French Canadian listeners. In contrast to the French Canadians, the attitudes recorded by the Welsh respondents did not differentiate the varieties on measures of prestige and aesthetic qualities. (See also Giles, Bourhis, Trudgill and Lewis (1974) for a similar study with Greek dialects.) If social connotations are filtering through into attitudes, then arguably attitudes and recognition should go hand in hand. But it is already clear that what is here being called 'recognition' can be a relatively complex process. What has been called the 'inherent' value of a feature or a style is necessarily an evaluation made in the light of particular sociolinguistic understandings and experiences. 'Recognizing' a dialect is inseparable from that same cluster of affective and evaluative processes, and it is in these terms that our narratives study has addressed it. We should expect interesting patterns to emerge in what informants do and do not 'recognize' correctly as the dialects of their local communities, and also to see interesting patterns of 'error' or 'false recognition'.

The questionnaire survey of teachers in Wales: maps, labels and scales

Participants
From a comprehensive list of state secondary schools throughout Wales, seventy-one secondary schools all over Wales were selected, and their headteachers contacted by mail, with follow-up telephone contact. The headteachers were invited to encourage their teaching staff to participate in the questionnaire study, and to reply with an estimate of the number of questionnaires their staff would complete. They were

A PROGRAMME OF LANGUAGE ATTITUDES RESEARCH 91

informed that questionnaires were available in English or in Welsh, and that a stamped addressed envelope would be provided to cover the costs of returning the completed questionnaires. They were also informed that a further study (the narratives study) was planned, and were asked to consider whether they would be prepared to participate in that one too. Thirty-two of the seventy-one headteachers agreed to their schools taking part in the first study, and they returned 129 questionnaires.

Although self-selected, the database represents a wide geographical spread in terms of teachers' places of employment, albeit with mid-Wales (even allowing for the fact that it is a less densely populated area of Wales than most others) somewhat less represented. Of the respondents, 51.9 per cent were female and 46.5 per cent male (1.6 per

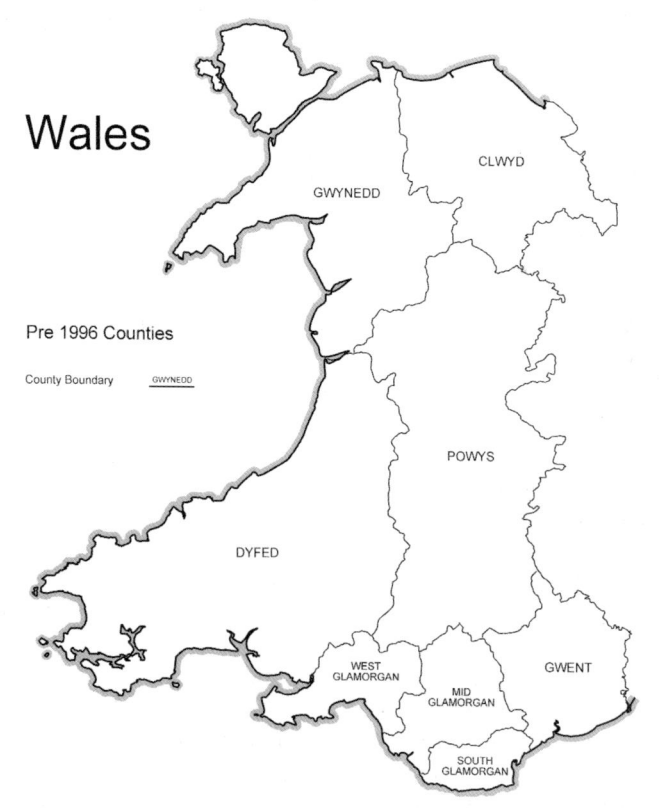

Figure 4.1: Map of Wales showing county boundaries at the time of data collection

cent omitted to disclose their sex). Ages ranged from 22 to 63 years, with a mean of 40.8 years. The teachers in the sample had lived in Wales from 4 to 63 years, with a mean of 32.1 years; 45 per cent had lived in Wales all their lives. Schools in the counties of (as they were called at that time) Dyfed, Powys, Gwent and the Glamorgans provided 65.5 per cent of the teachers, and the remainder were located in the northern counties of Gwynedd and Clwyd (see figure 4.1 for a map of Wales showing county boundaries as they were at the time of data collection). The range of school subjects taught by the teachers was also very wide. Although 24.3 per cent omitted to state their teaching subjects, 31.6 per cent taught English, 19.1 per cent taught maths and science, 11 per cent taught languages, 6.6 per cent were teachers of art, drama and music, and the small remainder taught a variety of other subjects, such as business, technology and physical education. Almost half, 46.9 per cent, reported that they spoke Welsh 'as a first or equal language' or 'quite well', and 53.1 per cent said they spoke it 'only a little' or 'not at all'.

Materials
A questionnaire was designed containing several tasks. In the first task, respondents saw a map of Wales with no information marked on it, apart from principal towns and cities. Piloting of the questionnaire with students from north and south Wales established that, when asked to outline (by drawing lines on the map) the geographical areas that, according to their own experience, represented the main regions or zones within Wales that are associated with particular dialects of English, informants could regularly identify up to eight areas. Even though some could identify more than this, eight seemed a realistically manageable number for the purposes of anticipated analytical procedures, and one that did not limit most respondents' responses unduly. Hence, in this main study too, the teachers were asked to outline a maximum of eight such areas. The second task asked respondents to provide, for each of the areas they had marked on the map, a label that they would themselves normally use for identifying it. They were then asked to take each of their labelled areas in turn and to characterize it by writing briefly about how each accent/dialect type strikes them when they hear it spoken. The compound term 'accent/dialect' was used on the questionnaire. Although there are important distinctions to be made between the two terms on the part of linguists (with 'dialect' subsuming 'accent'), the teachers could reasonably be seen as non-

linguists, and non-linguists do not regularly make a significant distinction between 'accent' and 'dialect'.

Having provided their own perceptions of dialect distribution in Wales and their own labels and characterizations of them, the next section of the questionnaire was of a more traditional design. In this second part, respondents were given the names of particular Welsh English accent/dialect communities, and were then provided with a number of pre-labelled seven-point scales to complete for each one. The scales were unilinear, bounded by 'very' (1) at one end, and 'not at all' (7) at the other. The pre-labelled scales were presented in random order, and were labelled as follows:

(a) well-spoken
(b) prestigious-sounding
(c) likeable-sounding
(d) pleasant-sounding
(e) dynamic-sounding
(f) lively-sounding
(g) truly Welsh-sounding
(h) how well will this accent serve the overall interests of school-leavers?

An additional open-ended question was included at the end of the questionnaire (that is, when judges had completed all of the scaled responses for all of the communities). This question asked: 'Identify one Welsh accent of English that you think has a very wide social acceptability over others for life in general in Wales. Describe its social advantages and how you think it is regarded outside Wales.'

In this second part of the questionnaire, then, accents/dialects were presented conceptually and in random order for respondents to rate on scales. The conceptual presentations were of six specifically designated community accents/dialects of English in Wales. In addition, for further comparison, a Standard British English 'control' variety was included. In order better to ensure that the judges understood what was meant, rather than refer to this variety as 'Standard British English', it was referred to as 'the English associated with south-east England (e.g. Cambridge)'. We selected *Cambridge* as the most appropriate tag after much deliberation, feeling that there was a great risk that *London* might easily be associated with cockney rather than Standard British English, but that the risk of similar confusion would be much less with

Figure 4.2: Map of Wales showing the locations of the 'place-tags' in the questionnaire, and of English urban centres close to the border with Wales

Cambridge. From the piloting of the questionnaire, it seemed that respondents did indeed associate *Cambridge* with the Standard (presumably orientating to the city's 'Oxbridge' status and not to its working class vernacular dialect). With the six community accents/ dialects within Wales (set out below), names of specific places were also included as focusing terms. Figure 4.2 shows where these specific places are located in Wales, along with English cities that are not far from the border with Wales, some of which we mention later. The intention with such 'tagging' was to increase the likelihood that judges would share a common understanding of what was meant by 'mid-Wales', etc., and to ensure validity and reliability. The respondents were asked to give scaled responses to:

- the English associated with south-east England (e.g. Cambridge);
- the English associated with north-west Wales (e.g. Bangor);
- the English associated with urban south-east Wales (e.g. Cardiff);
- the English associated with south-west Wales (e.g. Carmarthen);

- the English associated with the south Wales Valleys (e.g. Merthyr Tydfil);
- the English associated with mid-Wales (e.g. Newtown);
- the English associated with north-east Wales (e.g. Wrexham).

These communities were selected as the focus for this phase of the study in order to guarantee a reasonable geographical spread of communities in Wales, and also to match (even if only approximately) the broad pattern of differentiation that is apparent from descriptive dialectological research reviewed in chapter 3 and in Coupland (1990). Since in this and the coming chapters we make reference to a number of

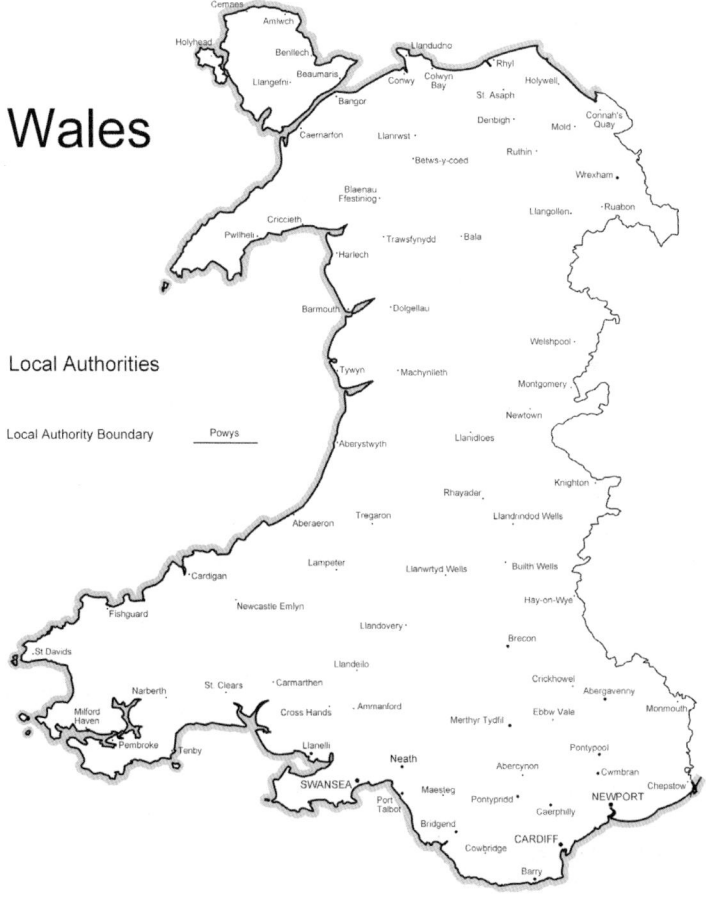

Figure 4.3: Map of Wales showing main towns and cities

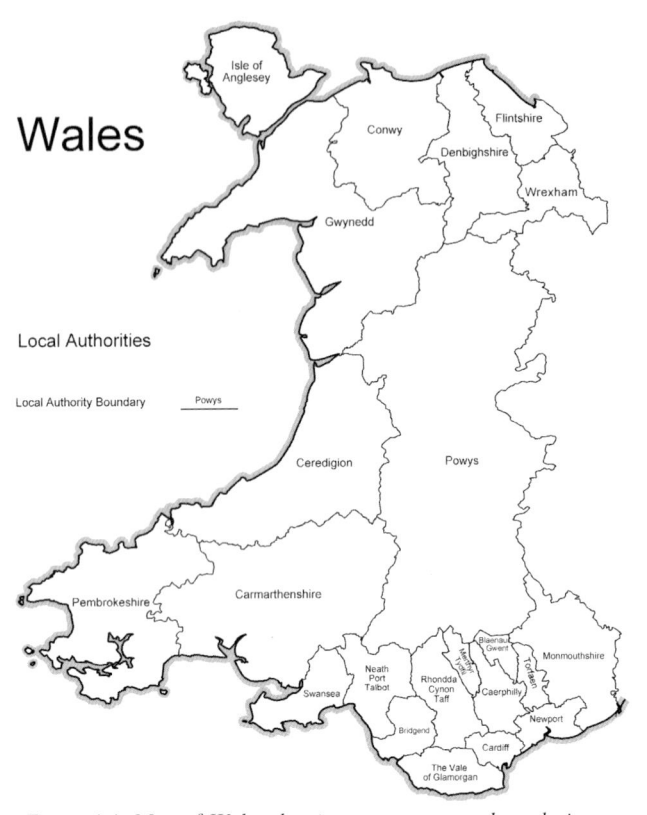

Figure 4.4: Map of Wales showing current county boundaries

other towns and cities in Wales, and a number of regions, we provide two maps at this point for continual reference for readers who are less familiar with Wales. Towns and cities are shown in figure 4.3. The current local-authority boundaries (at the time of writing) are shown in figure 4.4. It may be helpful for us to provide brief sketches of the main socio-cultural characteristics of the six Welsh areas.

1. The Cardiff conurbation: Cardiff is the capital city of Wales. The region established itself as an industrial urban centre during the nineteenth century, and is historically very anglicized. Compared to other parts of Wales in recent years, Cardiff has been prospering from a great deal of inward investment, and is economically more buoyant than the other regions. The English language variety in this area has been characterized in many studies (for example, Coupland, 1988;

Mees, 1983; Windsor Lewis, 1990). In recent years, Cardiff has seen significant growth in its numbers of Welsh speakers, especially up to age sixteen, reflecting the growth of compulsory Welsh in secondary schools. However, Welsh is still making only a limited impact on English as a community language in the capital city.

2. The south-east Wales Valleys: this was, from the nineteenth century until the 1980s, a heavy industrial zone producing coal and steel, but with the rapid closure of these industries it now suffers high levels of unemployment and social deprivation. This area has another broadly distinguishable regional variety of English (for descriptions of localities impinging on this region, see Connolly, 1990; Hughes and Trudgill, 1979; Tench, 1990).

3. The south-west: a rural, agricultural and traditionally Welsh-speaking 'heartland', now somewhat fragmenting in terms of its Welsh-language speakers, according to the 1991 census data (Aitchison and Carter, 1994). The English variety here is more subject to influence from the Welsh language than the previous two regions (see Parry, 1990).

4. Mid-Wales: a predominantly agricultural zone occupying the centre of Wales on a north–south axis, but taken to exclude western coastal areas, which tend to be incorporated into the south-west zone. Compared to the 'heartlands' of the north-west and south-west, this area is largely non-Welsh-speaking, particularly its areas away from the west coast. Sociolinguistic or dialectological studies of this region are entirely lacking, but the eastern mid-Wales English dialect in some respects aligns with the features of the 'upper south-west' dialect area of England (Trudgill, 1990: 63).

5. The north-east: a comparatively urban industrial zone, and, like mid-Wales, quite strongly anglicized in contrast to the north-west and south-west regions. The English dialect of the north-east is strongly influenced by the English of the nearby Liverpool conurbation.

6. The north west: a predominantly rural and agricultural zone, strongly associated with sheep-farming and slate-quarrying, the latter having declined considerably over recent decades. The region is a key part of the Welsh-language heartland, *Y Fro Gymraeg*, where Welsh language influence on English remains very strong.

Drawing limits to the design of this study, many smaller but potentially salient accent/dialect zones of Welsh English have been excluded (for example, south Pembrokeshire and Gower). Furthermore, the study cannot reflect the considerable descriptive variation within any of the designated communities, whether regionally based or from normal patterns of internal differentiation within British speech communities (Trudgill, 1978). Our prime goal is to capture a broad sweep of teachers' evaluations of varieties of Welsh English, relative to a high-prestige English English variety. Moreover, our decision to work with these six Welsh communities is supported by the pilot data from the earlier (perceptual map) part of the questionnaire.

At the end of the questionnaire, a section asked for biographical data from each respondent. These data included age, sex, main teaching subjects, self-reported ability to speak Welsh on a scale of 'as first or equal language' to 'not at all', self-reported accent of English, number of years and details of places in Wales lived in.

Two versions of the questionnaire were prepared, varying the order in which the seven accent/dialect communities were presented. Each of these was then prepared in English and in Welsh. Since the questionnaires were prepared with the object of posting them to schools for completion, clear instructions were included on them for each of the tasks.

Teenagers' and teachers' evaluations of narrative performances

Preparation of audio-recorded materials

We collected a large database of audio-recorded narratives by school students aged fifteen to sixteen throughout Wales. To achieve this, in addition to schools from the questionnaire study which had indicated a willingness to participate in further work, forty state secondary schools were selected and contacted from the comprehensive list. Their selection was based on the criteria of regional spread and lack of proximity to the borders between the six focal regions. The schools were invited to participate in a study of regional variation in Welsh English. To these schools were added a private school in Cheltenham in England, as a source of potential RP speakers, to function as a 'control' outgroup to the regional Welsh speakers of English. Fourteen schools agreed to participate, and these covered each of the six regions identified and described in the earlier study.

In each of the fourteen schools, audio-recordings were made of approximately fourteen 15-year-olds, males and females, telling personal anecdotes which they judged newsworthy in some way in front of their peers in a classroom setting. They were told that the researcher was interested in collecting 'stories that young people your age tell'. This general request was supplemented with the following prompt:

> All people are storytellers. You come to school every day and tell your mates about things that have happened to you. This is what I want you to do today. Think of something that has happened to you or someone you know and tell us about it. For example, a funny or embarrassing incident, a frightening story, accident or danger, or a time you got into trouble with your parents.

The request clearly encouraged the speakers to produce interesting and somehow involving narratives. But given that the students self-selected into the task, and that they then needed to survive the event in front of their peers, it seemed reasonable to assume that a degree of predicted newsworthiness was also an internally motivated requirement. There was generally no difficulty in eliciting a supply of volunteered narratives. The majority are based around (actual or fictitious) events with a mildly anti-establishment character, often involving personal and physical threats or accidents. In all, 179 narratives were collected from schools throughout Wales.

For the purposes of the evaluative study, two narratives were then selected from each of the six Welsh regions. The six specific Welsh communities represented were *Cardiff*, *Newtown* (mid-Wales, *Mid*), *Carmarthen* (south-west Wales, *SW*), *Merthyr Tydfil* (south-east Wales Valleys, *Valleys*), *Mold* (north-east Wales, *NE*), and *Blaenau Ffestiniog* (north-west Wales, *NW*). The selection criteria were that the speakers should be representative of their particular dialect-communities (confirmed by detailed phonetic descriptions produced by ourselves and by independent phoneticians), and that the narratives were reasonably successful (in the sense of being well received by their audiences). Obscenities and particular regionally identifying references were also avoided. In addition and for comparison, personal narratives of an identical sort were tape-recorded from two RP-accented 15-year-old school students from the private school in Cheltenham, where there was a high concentration of RP speakers. To restrict the complexity of the eventual study design, it seemed best to focus on either male or female speakers, and since the majority of storytelling volunteers were males, male storytellers were selected for the judgement phase of the research.

For the responses study, a coherent sequence of around fifty seconds was excerpted from each of the fourteen narratives. The brevity of the excerpts is an inevitable requirement of the listening task to follow, in order to reduce possible fatigue effects. Even with only two representative dialect examples from each of the six communities, plus two RP speakers, each group of listeners had to hear and respond to fourteen narrative extracts. To offset order effects, two audiotapes were prepared, allowing the narratives to be heard in a different sequence by each half of the sets of students and teachers.

Narratives
Below are transcriptions of the fourteen short narratives that we presented. They are included below, rather than in an appendix, because the reader will need to be familiar with them to follow much of the subsequent discussion of results. Bracketed numbers in the texts indicate pauses, timed in seconds (2.0). A brief pause is marked as (.). Unintelligible items are marked as (( )). We use 'cos' for the conventionally reduced form of 'because'. Punctuation is omitted because it typically misrepresents the grammatical and functional character of spontaneous talk. Incomplete words are included, such as 'al' as a non-completed form of 'albums'. Each narrative is listed under the coded reference to the speaker (*Cardiff1*, *NE2*, etc.). This code contains the dialect category of the speaker (Cardiff dialect, north-east Wales dialect, etc.), followed by a randomly allocated number from 1 to 14. The speakers will from now on be referred to by this convention.

Cardiff1
um (.) went on ho I went on holiday (.) to stay at my uncle's (2.0) cos he he's got a (.) he used to have a house in Spain until he came home and my cousin and my aunt used to live over there as well (2.0) so we stayed over there (1.0) an um it was about the (.) second week cos we were over there for two weeks (.) and my cousin (.) cos at that time he couldn't really get a job over there (.) used to sell lighters for all to all the English bars cos there's all English bars along the beaches there's two beaches like (1.0) so we were coming back from selling all these lighters (1.0) and half way along then I said oh (.) Craig I think I'm gonna be sick (1.0) cos I really felt sick cos we'd been we'd been out in the sun all day and I really wasn't used to it (1.0) so (.) got back then (.) he said oh don't worry we'll get back in time

NE2 (Mold)
I went to (.) tip it was the second time I'd ever been (.) was a couple of

weeks ago (.) and um first time I (.) went I just walked straight in cos you had to be eighteen to get in and we got inside (.) and about half an hour after we got in they announced that MTV were gonna arrive nobody knew they were gonna be there an they all turned up and um (.) well I didn't know anyway (*laughs*) and they turned up and they started throwing t-shirts out and everything most of the big fellas there were already drunk (.) and I was just grabbing these t-shirts (.) and I was fighting the for them off people (.) six seven foot (.) easily and I was really amazed by this it was great (*laughs*) and it gave me a real big ego boost that did (2.0) and um got several autographs one off a band which I (.) been listening to and I've got a couple of their al got one of their albums I was rather chuffed with that

RP3
and we were finishing off some (.) boxes alright they were something like that and there's a belt-sander which has now been sort of stopped use (.) stopped the use of and uh I was just sanding something down and I was really tired and my fingers slipped off the box (.) and actually hit the belt-sander just the ends of my fingers luckily it didn't hit I took it away in time (.) I I didn't think much had happened I thought I'd just sort of scraped the top (.) and um I I didn't feel that bad so I just sort of run it under some water (.) some cold water to try and to try and stop it bleeding but (.) uh it sort of about after two or three minutes I (.) I started feeling really bad I sort of felt really sick (.) so I told the teacher in charge of it (.) and he said oh well if you're feeling sick you'd better go go and sit outside and he said it's quite nasty

SW4 (Carmarthen)
I got a friend called [name] oh he's just massive I just got to say he's just massive (.) and he plays rugby with us (.) and he plays prop but oh one d time we were playing up at [place] (.) and he had to come on in the second half to substitute for a small chap (.) he came on the small chap pulled his jersey off (.) and then [name] literally attempted to put the jersey on (.) yeah he just got it on his (.) his (.) two arms and he tried to put his head in but he just couldn't get through (.) I was everybody was howling (.) his everything was wobbling his chest his belly his back his legs his oh it was disgusting and he's got oh ay I just everybody calls him Michelin man he's got to be he's got so many rolls of fat so disgusting (1.0) and then (sigh) he came on (.) and he oh he can't run at all he's so unfit and it's a bit sad to tell you the truth

Valleys5
one night it was raining heavily and as he was coming back (1.0) um (1.0) the farmers were fetching in in I fetching in the sheep cos of the thunder and lightning and that (.) and he didn't see em so as he come round the corner (.) as he swerved to miss em he hi he hit the lam he hit three lamp-posts bounced off (.) one hit another as he come off that one (.) um he w went head first into the third (.) and a a as as that happened (1.0) he went flying out through the window (.) th through the windscreen (.) we (.) when he went through the windscreen his foot had become left foot had become trapped in in the (.) in between the pedals so as he went through it tore his foot off (.) and (2.0) where if he had had his seatbelt on he would have been dead (.) completely otherwise (.) cos when when he had hit the engine (.) with the force come back and (.) when a when he when the fire brigade come um my father was laying on the floor and the engine was where he wa where the passenger and the driver's seat was

Mid6 (Newtown)
I was mucking out the shed I was and (1.0) in the (.) tractor (.) and I got one load in the front fork mm and (.) and I went in and I went into the mixen and what you do you just lift up the muck and put it on the top (1.0) so you dig in to a bit of the mixen and get a bit more in the front fork and lift it up into the top (.) and instead of when I put it into the mixen instead of the front end coming up with the muck the back w end wheels came up (.) cos there wasn't enough weight in the back so the back end came up (.) but the wheels still going round (.) but the front fork only goes so far up so the wheels stopped after a while (.) and the back wheels are (.) above the front ones (.) and the bonnet was on the front (.) so it was swaying about a bit like this and I (.) just about managed to get off half way up (1.0) so then dad came along after and stopped the tractor and put it down and I just (1.0) there's me standing there getting really worried (*laughs*) what am I going to do now (1.0) could have been dangerous

NW7 (Blaenau Ffestiniog)
um (.) I know this bloke (.) and he's well known of because (.) he's acting a bit weird (.) um there (.) quite a lot of stories going round about him (.) but (.) um (.) I think the best ones are (.) the one where he (.) went to buy a new helmet for his bike (.) and to see if this helmet worked and was unbreakable he found a brick (.) and threw the brick up in the air (.) and tried to make it land on top of the helmet but as the brick came down he put his hand on top of his head (.) and the brick landed on his hand and broke all his fingers

Valleys8
I was ah me and my friend we decided ah go for a walk one day and there's this tunnel by his house (.) and it's like all sewage going into it there's like a walkway (.) in it so we had some torches and we went up it (1.0) and there's a like a bank s down there so we walked it it's about half mile long (.) and when we came out the end the it's like um workmen machines pumping (.) stuff out and pumping stuff in I don't know what (.) and um (.) you know we were just sort of mucking around with all if that see what they were doing and (2.0) my friend (.) he decided to turn it on to see what it done (.) so he turned it on on and and it was pumping a bit and he turned it off (.) and then he turned it on again and the pipe was starting to come off and it was squirting up in the air (.) like a a sprinkler

NE9 (Mold)
then I so er (.) decided to cool down and go downstairs and have a meal in the restaurant and er (.) my feet were a bit tired and er (.) it was pretty pretty warm (.) and erm I felt this tickling in my feet and I thought it was just cos I'd been walking quite a bit and that but um (.) so I ignored it for a while and we ordered our food and (.) I I as I I finally go got tired of it and so I asked my mum if er (.) if she if she could feel the same thing and she said yeah and so did my dad so did my sister so we were getting a bit worried and just (.) slowly peered under the table and there was just a huge swarm of cockroaches they were just going everywhere all over the floor it was disgusting like

NW10 (Blaenau Ffestiniog)
he's done some pretty stupid things um (( )) as well he (.) stole a gate from the fire brigade place (.) and um cut the gate up and used the bars to um build a go-kart with a welder (.) and stuck a motorcycle engine on it and he got in some pretty deep trouble for that (1.0) um (.) he also about three years ago no about two years ago (.) he was o he was on a motorbike that he had built himself (.) and um he he was doing a wheelie and the throttle cable s um stuck it wouldn't go back down so he was still going on this massive wheelie and he didn't have a clutch or anything on it (.) and um he collided with a car and somersaulted over that car and over a police car that was um (.) behind that car landed behind the police car and um well the motorcycle you know was just a scrambler it wasn't a road bike or anything (.) and um his um kneecap came out of his leg

Cardiff11
there was one time when (.) we were all playing pool on the pool-table (.) and I saw you know I saw the latch on the thing so I thought oh I know if I put my hand down this pool-table hole you know and I can tief a few

games like (.) you know keep the latch up (.) and (.) puts my hand down you know ten minutes later I realise I couldn't get it back out (1.0) (*laughing*) so I thought oh no (.) I got my hand stuck down a pool-table (.) you know so had to go and find the caretaker and he was he was like about three hours eventually until they found the caretaker you know I had to stand in this one place and one hand stuck in the pool-table you know and one hand trying to eat my tea and my food and stuff (.) and (.) you know come across and he said oh he said how are we gonna get your hand out then (.) and he goes oh (.) well there's only one thing we can do like you know (.) I said what's that he said we'll have to saw the whole pool-table in half and I said how you going to do that well he said you know go to the thing goes out to the garden shed like in the back and brings out this massive chainsaw

RP12
so (.) after that (.) we went (.) ah (.) round to the big wheel (.) and er (.) it was spinning merrily round and then the the bloke decided to stop the wheel and get everyone off (.) and er (*laughs*) a little car fell off it (.) I dunno how high they were (.) God knows how they didn't sort of get squashed I suppose they weren't very high (1.0) um (.) I don't know (.) five metres up in the air or something when it (*laughing*) fell off (.) and they sort of rolled about the floor a bit stunned (.) stood up (.) looked at this guy and he quickly sort of put this put this little chair back on and they walked off (.) and the bloke pretended as nothing had happened and (.) we were all standing on there (.) totally amazed absolutely flabbergasted I dunno how on it could have happened (.) should have been shut down really I suppose

SW13 (Carmarthen)
I remember it was about two years ago (.) and ah we were on (( )) at home (.) and er (2.0) well my father told me and my brother then to take the motorbike (.) and the trailer behind and knock a few posts down to hold to hold the gates open (.) and er (1.0) well after finishing then my brother told me oh let's go up the field to see how the how the contractors are going along (.) and uh we went up the top field as fast as we could on the motorbike a doing about forty forty-five miles an hour (.) and we were following the hedge all the way round and the machine was right at the far corner of the field and uh (.) I stopped the bike and asked the boys what's wrong and they said that they had a blockage and so forth (.) and I talked to them for a while and my brother come over and said that we'd lost the trailer (1.0) and we looked around and (.) I saw the motorbike there with only the hitch behind (.) and the trailer was up in the hedge with the wheels (.) well'

Mid14 (Newtown)
I was sleeping in bed and um (.) well I heard this clicking noise cos bats click and (.) we knew there was these bats outside (.) oh and they sometimes fly into the house or there were some in my brother's bedroom and I thought there were some in mine cos I heard them clicking (.) and I shouted my dad and he said (.) oh don't be silly there's no bats in this house cos the windows were shut and um (.) they must have flew in in the day or something like that I don't know but I didn't think they flew in the day (.) and they came in (.) and um (.) I turned on the light and I couldn't see nothing and my dad couldn't see anything a so I went back to sleep heard clicking again (.) and I turned on the light and I could see the the flying round in the (.) in the landing (.) and I shouted my dad and a he came in and knocked it and it must have he must have just chucked it out or something (.) and then I went back to sleep I thought they were all gone and then we heard another clicking noise (.) and I thought nothing of it as cos I thought it was out it must've been they were kind of heard him out from outside

Speakers
All the speakers were fifteen years old. Only four of the speakers spoke Welsh – *SW4*, *NW7*, *NW10* and *SW13*. Both the Cardiff speakers lived in Cardiff. The *NE* speakers lived near Mold. The *RP* speakers were from England – *RP3* lived in Cheltenham, whereas *RP12*'s home was in Devon. Both *SW* speakers lived in Carmarthen. Both the *Valleys* speakers lived in Merthyr Tydfil. *Mid6* lived near Newtown and *Mid14* in Newtown. The two *NW* speakers both lived in Blaenau Ffestiniog in north-west Wales.

Preparation of questionnaire
We prepared a speaker-evaluation questionnaire containing a separate page of items to be completed for each voice heard. The questionnaire contained seven judgement scales, to be completed after each of the speakers/narratives was heard. The labels for the scales were selected after extensive pilot work, in which a mixed-gender and mixed-ability sample of thirty-five mid-teenagers in a Cardiff secondary school was asked to listen to the stimulus tape and write down, open-endedly, their thoughts about and reactions to the speakers. These written evaluations were discussed and elaborated in a classroom setting. The procedure provided a set of frequently used evaluative labels that were particularly pertinent and meaningful for this group of listeners. All seven resulting questions were formulated to be answered on a unidirectional

five-point scale, where 1 = 'not at all', and 5 = 'very much'. The questions were:

1. Overall, do YOU LIKE this speaker?
2. Do you think this speaker does WELL AT SCHOOL (e.g. gets high marks in exams)?
3. How much LIKE YOU do you think this speaker is?
4. Do you think you could MAKE FRIENDS with this speaker?
5. How WELSH do you think this speaker sounds?
6. Do you think this speaker is a GOOD LAUGH?
7. How INTERESTING does this STORY sound?

Several of these scales (*you like*, *like you*, *make friends*, *good laugh*, and *interesting story*) were intended to relate to Zahn and Hopper's (1985) social attractiveness dimension. On the other hand, the *interesting story* scale, which is event-focused, rather than speaker-focused, is particularly relevant to present interests in accounting for non-dialect-based as well as dialect-based responses. The *good at school* scale indirectly reflects the status dimension (Zahn and Hopper's superiority dimension), to the extent that this is salient in judgements of these young people. The *how Welsh* scale reflects an ethnicity criterion, but more specifically an 'authentic-ethnicity' criterion, which, as will be seen later, emerged very strongly in the questionnaire study as a salient evaluative dimension of Welsh English dialect communities.

During the pilot study, a rich stock of evaluative terms was elicited from the teenagers from which the labels for the scales were drawn. The stock of terms gathered in this way gave some crucial insight into the sociocultural world inhabited by these adolescents, and warranted further study. For this reason, instead of this procedure merely forming a preliminary to the main study, an item was included in the questionnaire to elicit more of them. Hence, each page of the questionnaire began with an open-ended instruction (before the scales-completion task): 'Write down your three first impressions when you listen to this speaker.' This allowed spontaneous cognitive and emotional responses free of the restrictions imposed by forced choice. These data are hereafter referred to as 'keywords'.

The final task on the questionnaire asked the listeners to write down where they thought the speaker lived (following Preston, 1989: 3; 1993: 193ff.). For this recognition item, respondents had to choose from seven answers (the six Welsh English dialect communities, plus

'England') along with a further two: a 'don't know', and an open-ended option for other responses.

Respondents: students
The evaluation phase of the study involved returning to each of the six regions to collect school-students' responses. The risk that students would recognize individual speakers precluded using the same schools that provided the initial audio-recordings. However, the schools in the evaluation phase needed to be matched as far as possible with those from which the narratives had been collected. Teachers assisted in the selection of schools that made a reasonable match. In the more rural locations, where few secondary schools exist, there were some difficulties in finding good matches nearby. Hence, in mid-Wales, we included a school in Builth Wells as a match for the Newtown school, even though the schools were about forty-five miles apart. A summary description of each of these schools follows below.

To avoid any effects due to differences in scholastic ability or achievement, mixed-ability groups were achieved in all the schools, either by drawing students from a number of classes, or, where numbers were smaller, by taking all the students from a whole year. All the schools were co-educational and, in each school, these male and female judges were all from year ten (fifteen years old).

Respondents: teachers
Evaluational data were also collected from a group of forty-seven teachers. These data were collected in different locations from the students' data. The teachers' ages ranged from 30 to 79 years (mean age 47.7); 68.1 per cent were female and 31.9 per cent were male. They taught in a wide range of educational contexts: 21.3 per cent at primary schools, 34 per cent at secondary schools, 12.8 per cent in higher education, while 23.4 per cent were supply (that is, casually employed) teachers. They taught a range of subjects: 27.7 per cent taught arts and humanities subjects, 8.5 per cent were social-science teachers, 14.9 per cent were physical-science teachers, and 42.5 per cent described themselves as general teachers. A large proportion, 44.7 per cent, had lived in Wales all their lives. Non-Welsh speakers made up 51.1 per cent, while 15 per cent were bilingual with fluent Welsh. Over 87 per cent described their own accents as 'regional', and 12.8 per cent described their accents as 'RP', (which would be a reasonably representative prediction for such a professional group in the UK, given

the estimate in Hughes and Trudgill (1979: 3) that probably only 3 per cent of the wider population are RP speakers).

Due to difficulties of gathering good numbers of teachers together on any single occasion, the sample of teachers was drawn from schools in the south-east of Wales. However, it seemed reasonable to make evaluational comparisons with the more widely spread student sample, since teachers are more likely to have moved localities within Wales during their lives than are teenage schoolstudents. Support for such a comparison is also found in overlapping findings in the questionnaire study. Those findings are set out in the next chapter.

Additional information on the schools and students where data were collected
SW: Carmarthen. The judges in this school came from mixed backgrounds. Some were rural and others came from the (nearby) Gwendraeth valley, a light industrial area. Many of the students were Welsh learners rather than Welsh first-language speakers. The group was mixed ability, drawn from all classes.

Valleys: Merthyr Tydfil. This school was situated in an area of high unemployment. All the students were local. This was a single mixed-ability class.

NE: Mold. The students were pooled from a number of classes, and were mixed ability. They were all local. The catchment area of the school was quite wide, with some students coming from traditional 'Old Mold' villages, and others coming from as far away as Connah's Quay. The school appeared to be a typical 'mixed-bag' comprehensive with widespread parental unemployment.

Cardiff. This was a school in a working-class area of Cardiff. The class contained a small number of Bengali children who were English second-language speakers, and was mixed ability. All informants were again local.

NW: Bethesda. All the students were Welsh first-language, local, and the groups were mixed ability, being pooled from all classes. Bethesda grew up around slate-quarrying, and suffers high unemployment since the closure of most of these quarries over recent years.

Mid: Builth Wells. The teenagers in this school were the entire year-ten class, so mixed ability. They were all English first-language, and lived in and close to Builth Wells itself.

Procedure
Overall, a total of 169 mixed-ability year-ten students, male and female, listened to the selected audio-recorded story extracts, and each filled in a questionnaire to evaluate each speaker in turn. These data-collection sessions took place over approximately fifty minutes of normal lesson time. Teachers were not present during these data-collection sessions.

The questionnaire was the same for the teachers as for the students, and they appeared to have no difficulty in responding to them as meaningful evaluative dimensions. The basis of interest in collecting these comparable data from the teachers was that they would (predictably) respond to these items from a perspective that was different from that of the students.

Focus-group interviews were also conducted with these school students during the same visits. Each group comprised (maximum) eight students. The excerpts were played to them, with a break after each one for the students to respond to the questions: 'what do you think of the speaker?' and 'what do you think when you listen to this person's story?' These interviews were intended partly as a validity check, and partly to enrich our understanding of how social judgements are articulated in the students' own terms.

Summary of data collected

Questionnaire study: teachers
1. Teachers' perceptual maps, with labelling and characterizations of their perceived dialect communities.
2. Evaluative responses on semantic-differential scales to the six conceptually presented Welsh–English dialect regions.
3. Open-ended item asking which variety had wide social acceptability, what its social advantages are, and how it is regarded outside Wales.

Narratives study: teenagers and teachers
1. Keywords from students: that is, immediate spontaneous emotional and cognitive responses.

2. Recognition: where they think the speaker is from.
3. Evaluative responses on unidirectional semantic-differential scales to each of the fourteen voices/narrative extracts.
4. Student focus-group data.

The results and discussion of data analyses from the two studies described in this chapter are divided over the next five chapters. Chapters 5 and 6 set out the analysis and discussion of the questionnaire study, and chapters 7 to 9 set out those for the narratives study.

5

Mapping and labelling

The data in the questionnaire study are essentially in three parts: firstly, the perceptual maps and labelling; secondly, the scaled responses to conceptualized Welsh English dialect communities; and thirdly, the open-ended item on social advantages. In this chapter, we analyse and discuss these data in that same order, and then consider the most interesting lines of interpretation relating to these three methodological strands. These are, of course, very different sorts of data. Even if we can place them all under the 'direct-approach' heading, they nevertheless differ considerably in the ways by which they elicit language attitudes.

Perceptual maps and labelling data

Our main goal in this part of the study is to investigate the general patterning of teachers' social evaluations in terms of specific categories of geolinguistic labels. The nature of the data means that a great deal of preliminary processing was required. The steps involved in this preparatory processing of the data were:

1. To see what sorts of zones the respondents identified on the maps.
2. To categorize their labelling of zones into label-sets.
3. To carry out a content analysis on the characterizations given by the respondents to each of the dialect zones they identified.

The categories that emerged during this processing are of considerable interest in themselves. So to a large extent, for this part of the study, there is no worthwhile distinction to be made at times between the categories arising during this prior process of data analysis, and the findings as a whole from this section of the questionnaire.

The identification of dialect zones in the mapping task

Respondents generally identified the maximum (eight) number of zones that they were asked to (the mean number was 7.72), although comments volunteered by a few teachers suggest that some could have identified more than eight. The most important aspect of this basic finding is that it confirmed expectations that teachers would be sensitive to quite substantial regional variation within what is often referred to in the sociolinguistic and language attitudes literature as 'Welsh English'.

The teachers employed territory labels that drew on a wide range of classificatory dimensions or principles. They included specific town/city names (presumably as perceived centres of accent/dialect zones), versions of county names, compass-point designated zones (that is, zones specified in terms of northern, southern, eastern and western Wales, separately or in combination), zones marked as central/peripheral within Wales (for example, mid-Wales and the Welsh borders), named regions that have a currency in popular rather than administrative domains (for example, the Valleys, Llŷn), zones defined as urban versus rural, and zones defined by their Welshness/Englishness. The open-endedness of the requirement to label each of the numbered areas by means of the 'label you yourself normally use to identify each of your numbered accents/dialects' allowed informants to coin labels that were to varying degrees geographical or linguistic designations, and indeed in very many instances they managed to combine both facets.

An informal examination of all the labels suggests that some Welsh towns and cities have much stronger geolinguistic salience than others: Cardiff, Merthyr (Tydfil), and Swansea appear to be most strongly salient as geolinguistic centres, with Carmarthen, Cardigan, Bangor and Caernarfon also featuring regularly. Some of these (for example, Cardiff, Bangor, Carmarthen) are places that were used to 'tag' the dialect communities in the scales part of the study (see chapter 4). But this is unlikely to have led to respondents recycling them as labels, since the labels part of the questionnaire study was completed *prior to* the scales task. Interestingly, a substantial number of towns/cities marked on the questionnaire map are never picked out as centres (for example, Builth Wells, Aberystwyth). It is also of interest that Liverpool does appear to function as a highly salient reference centre for discussions of variation in Welsh English (even though it lies outside geopolitical Wales).

Of the officially designated counties at the time of the data gathering, only Dyfed (south-west Wales) is selected as having any geolinguistic salience, and then only rarely. The older county names are used more frequently, particularly Pembrokeshire (most frequently its southern area) and Carmarthenshire. (Since then, many of these older county names have now been reinstated, see figure 4.4.) But labels representing the south Wales Valleys are very strongly represented. It appears that south, north and mid are the most strongly salient of the possible labels from the compass-point and central/periphery sets. When 'west' features in designating zones, it is more commonly with reference to the south-west than to western parts of the whole of Wales, or of the mid- or northern regions. Frequencies in the use of specific labels add further detail to these generalizations.

Sets of labels invoked

In our analysis, we placed into groups the various zone-labels that teachers invoked and adjectival descriptors that they used in characterizing these labels. The verbatim labels used by teachers in the sample fall fairly unambiguously into nine sets (sets A to I in table 5.1). In most instances, the labels themselves designate specific geographical areas (for example, 'Cardiff', 'Liverpool', 'rural mid-Wales'). In a smaller number of cases, it was necessary to consider the placement of the dialect zone on a respondent's map before assigning that label to a set (for example, 'city harsh' is grouped with the *Cardiff* set because the label was applied to a zone roughly coterminous with the city of Cardiff). Label sets H and I (*English* and *Welsh*) are of course very non-specific in themselves, although a substantial proportion of respondents chose to identify dialect zones in these terms (about 20 per cent of the sample, in each case). But the very diffuseness of these sets is itself interesting; a point that will be further discussed later.

Assigning individual labels to the *English* and *Welsh* sets was necessarily more problematic than with other sets. The designation 'anglicized Welsh', for example, might appear to owe allegiance to both the *English* and *Welsh* categories, although it seemed best to infer that, in context, 'anglicized' constituted the 'new' information within this phrase rather than 'Welsh' (which is very probably a 'given' element). Similarly, 'Welsh spoken English' was taken to signal the Welshness of the zone rather than any form of perceived Englishness. On the other hand, the label 'English as a second language' was taken to be an attempt to designate the non-Englishness, and so the Welshness, of a zone. 'Little England' is a label that is commonly used when referring to south Pembrokeshire, so there is an obvious area of overlap between sets G and H in this regard.

Table 5.1: Label-sets for Welsh English regions invoked by teachers

SET A: CARDIFF	Items included in each subset
Cardiff	*Cardiffian*
Caardiff	*Kaerdiff, Cediff, Kairdiff and other pseudo-phonetic realizations*
City/Town	*City harsh, Towny, Metropolitan, Urban, Industrial, S. Wales industrial*

SET B: VALLEYS	
Valleys	*S. Wales Valleys, Glamorgan Valleys*
Rhondda	*Y Rhondda, Rhondda boyo*
Merthyr	*S. Wales Merthyr, Merthyrism*
Swansea	*Swansea and Neath/Valley, Swansea Valleys, Swansea Jack, Swansea Jac-Valleys*

SET C: NORTH WALES	
North Wales	*N.Walian, N. Wales Welsh, N. Wales Llŷn*
Gogledd	*Gog, Gogs, North Wales Gogledd, North Wales Gogs, Gogland*

SET D: MID-WALES/BORDERS	
Mid-Wales	*Rural mid-Wales, mid-Wales Borders, Urban mid-Wales*
Central Wales	*Central east, Centre east*

MAPPING AND LABELLING

SET E: SOUTH-WEST WALES

West Walian	*West Wales and Lleyn, W. Wales Carmarthen, Soft west Walian*
Carmarthen	*Carms/Cardi, North Carmarthen, Old County of Carmarthen*
Cardigan	*Cardi*
Dyfed	*Dyfed/Powys, Rural Dyfed*

SET F: LIVERPOOL

Liverpool	*Liverpudlian, Welsh Liverpudlian, Clwyd Liverpudlian, Liverpool influence, Liverpool/Manchester, Like Liverpool, Nasal Liverpool*
Scouse	*Scouse Welsh, Liverpool Scouse influence, Coastal Scouse*
Merseyside	*Merseyside influence*

SET G: PEMBROKESHIRE

Pembrokeshire	*South Pembrokeshire, South Pembrokeshire ugh!, Pembroke/ Cornish, Pembs slightly anglicized, Old Pembrokeshire, Bottom Pembrokeshire*

SET H: ENGLISH

English	*English English, English/Bristol, English/Pembs, Very English, Basic English, Old English, English sounding, English type*
Little England	*Little England south Welsh*
Anglicized	*Anglicized Welsh, Quite anglicized, Anglicized monotone, Anglicized Border*

SET I: WELSH

Welsh	*Welshy, The Welsh, Welsh spoken English, Soft Welsh, Very Welsh, First language Welsh speakers, English as a second language, Medium Welsh accent, Very fast clipped Welsh, Welsh speaking, Cultured Welsh*

Table 5.1 lists the individual labels that were invoked by teachers in the sample and shows how they were assigned to label-sets. In the individual sections below, we discuss the frequencies with which groups of comments were associated with labelled areas.

Welsh-speaking respondents and those from northern schools were, not surprisingly, less likely to identify and label an area 'north' than either those who did not speak Welsh or those who were from southern schools (chi square = 9.10, df = 2, p<0.01, and chi square = 22.63, df = 1, p<0.01 respectively). This contrasts with the comparative absence of use of the label 'south' by northern respondents. This is a feature which will be further discussed in the narratives study in chapter 8. Respondents who spoke Welsh and those from northern schools were more likely to split the northern areas of Wales into a number of smaller categories such as Anglesey, Gwynedd, Bangor 'aye', Clwyd and/or Colwyn Bay/Flint. But there were no other differences between these subgroups in their labelling of areas.

The territorial span of folklinguistic dialect-zones

It is important to emphasize the abstract nature of the label-sets investigated here. The nature of the task means that any one instance of mapping out an accent/dialect zone requires an attempt to reduce an open-ended set of individual subcultural experiences (over time and space, perhaps mediated by radio, television or second-hand reports), and/or an assemblage of stereotyped beliefs about dialect usage, to a geographically bounded zone. That the teachers were prepared to attempt this task implies that there is indeed a viable regional basis to their perceptions, although it would be wholly implausible to suggest that actual dialect variation can be adequately captured within a two-dimensional map. (This assumption did seem to be given substance in traditional dialectology, but it is strongly refuted within contemporary sociolinguistics: see, for example, Chambers and Trudgill, 1980.) Then, when respondents attribute a label to any mapped zone, they further consolidate their categorization. As was evident in this study, they often do this by choosing labels evoking both geographical and linguistic characteristics.

The procedure for collapsing individual labellings into sets is essentially a linguistic procedure, based on the forms of the particular labels chosen. To that extent, the label-sets ignore the predictably varying ranges of territory referred to in respondents' individual uses of labels. Technical means are presumably not yet known for the representation of this perceptual space-variation in physical space, but it is informative to describe the general patterns.

Some label-sets are relatively sharp and others are relatively diffuse, meaning that they vary in the extent to which they are precisely controlled geographically, and consistently so. Most obviously, the *Cardiff* and *Liverpool* sets are sharply focused by being centred on major conurbations that all teachers can reliably identify. The *Valleys* and *Pembrokeshire* sets are reasonably sharply focused, though each subsumes some variation. For example, *Valleys* subsumes Swansea, Merthyr Tydfil, and the Rhondda and Newport valleys, while *Pembrokeshire* encompasses an area from Fishguard to Carmarthen (infrequently beyond Carmarthen) or as little as the tip of Pembrokeshire, limited to include St David's, Haverfordwest and Tenby.

South-west Wales is an intermediate set centring around Carmarthen, but sometimes including Cardigan, and even extending as far up the western coast as Aberystwyth and Machynlleth. Occasionally, Pembroke is included within the west or south-west Wales label. *Mid-Wales/Borders* and *North Wales*, on the other hand, are diffuse sets, and labels within each of them relate to quite wide-ranging territories. For example, the label Mid-Wales is more likely to include the mid-west coastal regions, whereas 'Borders' is more likely to refer to an area east of Rhayader and bounded on the north by Oswestry and on the south by Brecon.

The *Welsh* and *English* sets are highly diffuse. Within the *English* set, three areas are typically referred to: the north-east (for example, Wrexham/Merseyside, coastal Clwyd Scouse), the far south-west (Pembroke) and the borders (Shropshire, Newport/Gwent). In fact, in characterizing this label-set, respondents mentioned specific areas of England with which they associated the 'English' accents/dialects of Wales. They included 'Worcester', 'Liverpool', 'Somerset', 'Bristol', 'Manchester' and 'Birmingham', as well as 'Cornish' and 'Little England beyond Wales' (that is, Pembrokeshire). The *Welsh* set includes the western coast of Wales (except Pembrokeshire), Dyfed, and parts of mid-Wales and the Valleys.

There is some interesting variation in the use of English, Welsh or mixed forms in the teachers' labels themselves. Although the task is framed as an English-language task for the great majority of teachers (who opted to answer in English), they sometimes invoke Welsh spellings – for example, 'Jac' for 'Jack', 'Cardi' as the Welsh nominal for a Cardigan person, and 'Gog' for a north Walian person (in Welsh *gogledd* means 'north').

Evaluative potential of dialect-zone labels

As Preston found in his research, and as our comments above suggest, the labels chosen to represent dialect zones in this study in many instances themselves encode social evaluations. Some of them are explicitly evaluative ('City harsh'; 'cultured Welsh'). Others reflect various regional and cultural stereotypes and prototypes. 'Rhondda boyo' suggests that the Rhondda Valley is a prototypically Welsh zone, because 'boyo' is itself a pan-Welsh, class-laden, somewhat derogatory designation. 'Swansea Jack' is a conventional prototype caricaturing the urban south-west coastal male. A 'Cardi', and the Cardigan/ Ceredigion region itself through that term, opens up another culturally familiar discourse of the far-west-Walian, usually implying rural life and thrift. Similarly, 'Bangor-aye' (the perceived frequent use of utterance-final *aye* that we mentioned in our section on regional factors, in chapter 3) and 'Kaerdiff' (fronted and raised realizations of the long /a:/ vowel in Cardiff English) trigger sociolinguistic stereotypes that are already well-established within the regional mythology of Wales.

There is creativity in the labellings, too, however. 'Gogland' would appear to be an innovative coining from the familiar 'Gog' (see above) to suggest a consolidated northern territory, inhabited by an unfamiliar race, the 'Gogs'. 'Merthyrism' succeeds in transforming a town name into a phenomenon, even perhaps a culturally significant social process. 'Ooarshropshire' as a label for mid-Wales speech draws on a familiar pastiche of rhotic south-west (of England) rural dialects (oo-ar).

The attributed characteristics of label-sets

To investigate the general patterning of teachers' social evaluations of specific categories of geolinguistic labels, a content analytic procedure was followed to group descriptions, as follows: 30 per cent of the questionnaires were randomly chosen from the total, and the major descriptive themes that surfaced within the full range of label descriptions were identified. These themes were cumulatively organized into

MAPPING AND LABELLING

main and subordinate categories. Subsequently, a further 30 per cent of the questionnaires were examined to determine whether or not the categories were an adequate description of the data. Descriptions that appeared very infrequently were not coded. This process resulted in the following coding categories, which subsume virtually all the descriptive characteristics of the dialect areas identified by respondents in the study.

1. Linguistic form

Attempted characterizations of the sounds produced by speakers of the various perceived accents/dialects. Examples include 'open', 'full', 'rounded', 'clipped', 'biting', 'nasal'. Although some of these rather conventional characterizations of speech styles – a mixture of non-technical and potentially technical descriptive phonetic forms – have clearly positive or negative evaluative force, subcategorization of the whole set was not attempted. One reason is the ambiguity of descriptions like 'open', 'rounded' as technical and non-technical terms, when it is uncertain whether they are intended to be heard as part of a (largely) objective discourse of phonetic analysis or in some more obviously evaluative sense.

2. Affective

From the lexicon of affect, implying a range of emotional consequences for the individual evaluator. For ease of coding, the category can be divided into two broad subtypes:

(a) Affective positive, in two senses: comforting (for example, 'warm', 'homely', 'soft', 'gentle', 'comforting'); and high positive arousal (for example, 'fun', 'excitable', 'dramatic', 'expressive').

(b) Affective negative, in two senses: high negative arousal (for example, 'irritating', 'annoying', 'grating'); and discomforting (for example, 'cold', 'harsh', 'hard', 'heavy', 'guttural', 'throaty').

3. Status and social norms

Comments about levels of education and social status associated with certain accents:

(a) Uncultured: for example, 'uneducated', 'uncouth', 'common'.
(b) Cultured: for example, 'posh', 'affluent', 'educated'.

4. Geo-social belonging

Again, two subcategories cover the range of items used:

(a) *Welsh*, including sociolinguistic stereotypes of Welsh people: for example, 'second-language English speakers', 'Gogs'.
(b) *Not Welsh*: for example, 'anglicized', 'Liverpudlian', 'Merseyside', 'Scouse', 'English'.

5. *Rural versus urban.*

Frequencies in the attribution of characteristics to label-sets

A frequency count of the full set of questionnaires made it possible to assess the dominant traits attributed by the teachers to particular dialect-communities (coded as label-sets). The frequency results are summarized in table 5.2.

Set A: Valleys
The 'Valleys' of the south and south-east of Wales occupy a crucial place in the political history and popular cultural mythology of Wales as a whole. As we suggested earlier, they are strongly associated with the now-decimated mining industry and Welsh working-class culture. Not surprisingly, therefore, some version of the 'Valleys' is the most frequently identified and labelled English accent/dialect area of Wales (63.8 per cent) in teachers' responses. Of the respondents who identify and label a zone within this set, 18 per cent comment on the linguistic form of Valleys English, although no predominating linguistic stereotype is discernible within them. Examples include 'stressed', and 'closed' or 'elongated' (of vowel forms).

Valleys English is typically described in positive terms (29 per cent). Such descriptions commonly comprise comments about its being 'friendly', 'warm' and 'soft', but also *lively* and *strong*. A few descriptions incorporate some negative connotations, but there is no particular pattern to these comments. The instances are 'pushy', 'unpleasant', 'female sometimes shrill', 'harsh/heavy/rough', 'lazy', 'dull' and 'slovenly'.

Welshness is quite frequently mentioned in descriptions of Valleys speech (31 per cent). This association takes highly stereotypical forms, calling on images of community, mining, and choirs. Examples are:

'Full of clichés about how Welsh people speak.'
'What foreigners expect Welsh English to sound like.'

MAPPING AND LABELLING

Table 5.2: Frequencies of categorized comments by sets of labelled areas (numbers of instances mentioned, with rounded percentages in bold italics below)

	VLY	CDF	NW	Mid	SW	LIV	PEM	ENG	WSH	Total
Linguistic form	14	26	22	4	3	6	2	1	1	=79
	18	*34*	*34*	*7*	*6*	*13*	*4*	*4*	*4*	
Affective	22	4	3	12	15	3	4	4	10	=77
positive	*29*	*5*	*5*	*21*	*32*	*7*	*9*	*15*	*39*	
Affective	9	33	19	7	3	5	5	1	1	=83
negative	*12*	*43*	*30*	*13*	*6*	*11*	*11*	*4*	*4*	
Welsh	24	1	15	7	14	1	1	0	11	=74
	31	*1*	*23*	*13*	*29*	*2*	*2*		*42*	
Not Welsh	3	5	8	14	4	35	31	14	2	=116
	4	*7*	*13*	*25*	*8*	*76*	*69*	*54*	*8*	
Cultured	0	2	0	3	1	0	2	2	2	=12
		3		*5*	*2*		*4*	*8*	*8*	
Uncultured	4	2	0	0	0	1	0	1	0	=8
	5	*3*				*2*		*4*		
Rural	0	0	1	3	2	0	5	0	0	=11
			2	*5*	*4*		*11*			
Urban	0	4	0	0	0	0	0	0	0	=4
		5								
Total comments	76	77	68	50	42	51	50	23	27	=464

Key: VLY = Set A: Valleys
CDF = Set B: Cardiff
NW = Set C: North Wales
Mid = Set D: Mid-Wales/Borders
SW = Set E: South-West Wales
LIV = Set F: Liverpool
PEM = Set G: Pembrokeshire
ENG = Set H: English
WSH = Set I: Welsh

'Cliché media films like *How Green was my Valley*.'
'Welsh accent, "foreign" image of boyo, beer and rugby.'

There are very few comments within the cultured/uncultured categories generally, although the few respondents who use this dimension imply that Valleys accents sound uncultured and uneducated (5 per cent). Examples are: 'workman', 'uneducated', 'uncouth', 'working class without higher education', 'common', 'lazy', 'down to earth'.

Set B: Cardiff
Cardiff is the centre of by far the largest conurbation in Wales. *Cardiff*

is a second very commonly identified and labelled area (by 58.8 per cent of all respondents). Along with the *North Wales* set (below), Cardiff attracts the highest percentage (34 per cent) of comments to do with linguistic form. For Cardiff, the large majority of those invoking distinctive features of pronunciation focus on vowel features (for example, as 'stretched' and/or 'flattened'). Consistent with this trend, 14 per cent of respondents use the label 'Caerdiff' (or another pseudo-phonetic variation such as 'Ceydiff', 'Carediff') in designating this area, highlighting the raised and fronted long /a:/ variable mentioned earlier.

Affective characterizations of Cardiff are very predominantly from the negative and discomforting categories (43 per cent), the most frequently used adjectives being 'hard', 'harsh' and 'ugly'. Also, 9 per cent of the comments are negative on a high-arousal dimension, such as 'irritating' and 'annoying'. In fact, overall, there are very few positive comments, and those who do mention positive qualities tend to use negative descriptions as well.

Set C: North Wales
Some variant of 'north Wales' or 'Gogledd' is a label used by 50.4 per cent of the sample. As noted earlier, north Wales is a diffuse, multiply-centred perceptual area, and evaluations vary depending on whether or not respondents include north-east Wales as well as north-west Wales in their labelled zone. For example, 12 per cent of those associating this set with 'Welsh' mention 'strong'/'broad' Welsh or 'Welsh first language' and this corresponds with their focus on north-west Wales. On the other hand, 13 per cent of the sample mention Merseyside or Liverpool, due to their focus on north-east Wales.

This important qualification aside, 34 per cent of those who demarcate north Wales produce a linguistic-form characterization, and nearly 50 per cent of these describe the accent as 'nasal', 8 per cent mentioning 'guttural'. There are few positive affective evaluations of the *North Wales* set. In fact, *North Wales* is the only label-set other than *Cardiff* to attract a very clear preponderance of negative over positive affective evaluations (though *Cardiff* is the more extreme case). 'Unpleasant', 'annoying', 'harsh', and 'painful' are common descriptors. Some responses transcend the coding scheme through their vivid pejorative comments. For example, all of the following comments refer to north-west Wales:

'Slow, makes speakers seem mentally deficient.'
'Sounds as if they have a bad cold.'
'Sounds as if vomit is welling in the throat.'

North Welsh accents/dialects are described as 'Welsh' by 23 per cent of the respondents, and by 13 per cent as 'not Welsh'. When the accent/dialect is described as 'Welsh', respondents are most frequently referring to north-west Wales. Overall, 20 per cent of the labels used to denote north Wales use the form 'Gog'. Three of the fifteen descriptions coded as *Welsh* also include 'Gog' in the label description. Others include:

'Strongly influenced by Welsh.'
'Welsh as a first language.'
'Would be happier speaking Welsh.'
'Welsh order to words.'

All of the comments referring to north Wales which were classified as 'not Welsh' associate this accent/dialect with Liverpool, and thus are referring to north-east Wales.

Set D: Mid-Wales/Borders
Even though this area was identified and labelled by 47.1 per cent of respondents, it is hugely diverse and diffuse. No doubt because of this, there are few distinctive patterns among the descriptive terms used to characterize it. Unlike all label-sets discussed so far, there are very few references to linguistic form. Positive affective evaluations (for example, 'soft', 'gentle', 'pleasant') are made by 21 per cent of respondents, and 13 per cent make comments coded as negative (including 'bland', 'plain', 'nondescript'). The set is thought of as somewhat more non-Welsh (25 per cent) than Welsh (13 per cent), but within the set, 'Welshness' is exclusively associated with the specific label *Mid-Wales* in relation to which comments such as 'very Welsh', and 'pleasant Welsh' were recorded. At the same time, *Mid-Wales* is also described on occasions as 'standard English with a Welsh accent', 'English feel' and 'can be more English than Welsh'.

When labels within the set specifically designated the Welsh *Borders* (usually corresponding to an area constituting half of mid-Wales, from Brecon to Welshpool) and, to a lesser extent *Central*, they are described as 'not Welsh'. Respondents note the influence of English regions, such as Hereford, Gloucester, Shropshire and the (English) Midlands here.

Again, there are very few comments concerning 'cultured/uncultured'. Such comments as do occur were 'middle class' and 'well-spoken'. As in the sets *North Wales*, *South-West Wales* and *Pembrokeshire*, there is a slight recognition that *Mid-Wales/Borders* is a rural accent/dialect (5 per cent). Besides 'country' and 'rural', respondents mention 'rustic', 'rich', 'farmer', 'hippy', 'yokel'.

Set E: South-West Wales
Just over 40 per cent of the sample identified an area that was grouped within the *South-West Wales* set. This set, along with *Valleys* and *Welsh*, attracted the most positive affective evaluations (32 per cent compared with 29 per cent for *Valleys* and 39 per cent for *Welsh*) with 'soft', 'pleasant', 'melodious' being common descriptors. If the label-set *Welsh* is ignored, which predictably (if tautologically) attracted the most frequent evaluations as being 'Welsh', then *South-West Wales* (29 per cent) joins *Valleys* (31 per cent) as being deemed the most *Welsh* label-set within the data, and more so than *North Wales* (23 per cent). The Welshness attributed to *South-West Wales* may be distinct from that attributed to Valleys, suggested by frequency of comments to do with authenticity. One respondent describes the *South-West Wales* zone as the 'heartland accent', and another as 'the true accent of Wales'. Others refer to 'inherent, acute Welsh' and 'extreme Welsh', and the influence of the Welsh language is also referred to:

'English spoken with difficulty.'
'High percentage of Welsh speakers.'
'Strongly influenced by Welsh.'

Set F: Liverpool
A large urban centre in the north-west of England, Liverpool adjoins north Wales, which lies south and west of Liverpool across the river Mersey. Of the sample, 38 per cent identified and labelled a zone within the *Liverpool/Merseyside/Scouse* set. The set is evaluatively swamped by being characterized as highly un-Welsh (76 per cent), and more so than *Pembrokeshire* with its 69 per cent. Few other characteristics were recorded, although the zone attracted a modest frequency of comments as to its linguistic form (13 per cent); most respondents who comment within that category note a 'nasal' quality. There are few entries within the affective evaluative categories. One of the five comments recorded describes the *Liverpool* set as 'unattractive', 'ugly', 'grating'.

It is possible that respondents felt it inappropriate to provide affective evaluations of accent/dialect zones in this set because its non-Welshness placed it beyond the apparent remit of the questionnaire. (The same may be the case with the *Pembrokeshire* and *English* label-sets.) In their characterizations of these labels, most respondents merely recorded the fact that they were 'Scouse', 'Merseyside', or 'Liverpudlian', and hardly as Welsh at all. Comments such as 'back end of Liverpool softened with Welsh' do nevertheless express implicit evaluations that might have been expressed more openly under other circumstances.

Set G: Pembrokeshire
Pembrokeshire is the county label for the most south-westerly region of Wales, lying within what was the county of Dyfed at the time of data collection. In terms of employment, Pembrokeshire is associated primarily with tourism, through the beauty of its countryside and beaches. Its popular image as being relatively 'un-Welsh' reflects its distinctive history as well as its attraction to English and other tourists in summer months. In the data, 33.9 per cent of respondents located a zone within this set. Similar to the Liverpool set, the Pembrokeshire set is associated with non-Welshness and little else. Negative affective evaluations (11 per cent) show no particular pattern among attributions such as *shrill, bland, husky, odd*; positive evaluations (9 per cent) include *soft, delightful, relaxing*.

The frequent designations include 'English' and 'anglicized', but two instances, 'Somerset' and 'Cornish' show awareness of the rhoticity of the south-Pembrokeshire accent. The comment 'does not sound as if the people live in Wales' might be read as alienating the community from authentic Welshness, and one respondent suggests repatriative ethnic-cleansing, no doubt in jest: 'send them back to England'. There are five comments (11 per cent) which classify this set as rural.

Set H: English
Labels within the *English* set were invoked by 19.8 per cent of the sample. The manifest non-Welshness (54 per cent) of this diffuse set seems to preclude the use of all other potentially evaluative dimensions. Affective descriptions are somewhat less positive than for the *Welsh* set. Four positive comments are made, including 'soft' and 'pleasant', but in three of these cases the label 'English' is being applied to Pembrokeshire.

The fact that an 'English' label-set is needed to account exhaustively for the zones that teachers attribute to accent/dialect areas within Wales is in itself evidence of a perceptual trend to define some aspects of Wales in English terms. But it should also be remembered that English-ness is a highly salient dimension for characterizing zones that are not themselves labelled in this way (see table 5.2). As we pointed out in chapter 3, the historical anglicization of Wales (Williams, 1990) has left its imprint on the perceived and actual dialectology of Wales. Wales is itself perceptually mapped, in accent/dialect terms, as a territory with 'pools' of Welshness of variable 'depth'. This is in fact the metaphor used in Aitchison and Carter in their (1994) discussion of the demography of the Welsh language following the 1991 census.

Set I: Welsh
In the data, 19 per cent of respondents identified an area with a term from the *Welsh* label-set. It has already been observed how several zones (and in particular the Valleys, Liverpool, Pembrokeshire, and south-west Wales) do tend to be evaluated along a perceived dimension of Welshness/non-Welshness. Therefore it is not surprising that 'Welsh' and 'English' become available to some respondents (about a fifth in either case) as labels for the accent/dialect sets themselves. From a wider perspective, it is nevertheless an interesting testament to the potential for Welsh people to 'ingroup' and 'outgroup' themselves and their compatriots along the dimension that, one might have assumed, defines the whole group ('the Welsh') in the first place. The issue here is the much-discussed variable ethnicity or 'regionalism' that is endemic within the very concept of Welshness, as reflected in our earlier discussion of the 'two-Wales' and 'three-Wales' models in chapter 3.

There is only one reference to linguistic form within this set, and that relates to Bangor: the appending of 'ai' (a variant written representation of 'aye') to the end of each utterance. However, respondents are clearly orienting to different regions within the set, but still regions which can each claim the status of 'heartland' areas. Hence, in noting the Welshness of zones within the set, respondents make repeated reference to 'native Welsh speakers', 'Welsh-speaking area', 'Welsh first language', and so on. The most common zone referred to under this rubric is south-west Wales, excepting Pembrokeshire, extending east and north of Pembrokeshire to include Carmarthen and Llanelli, sometimes as far north as Machynlleth or Dolgellau (taking in the coastal regions of Cardigan/Ceredigion, Aberaeron and Aberystwyth etc.), but not extending east beyond Llandrindod Wells. Another common zone is an area on the north-west of Wales, north of Machynlleth and west of Bala and Llandudno. There are also some designations of the south-Wales Valleys through the label-set *Welsh*. Taken together, the set produced the most positive affective evaluations in the data as a whole, with 'pleasant' and 'soft' being typical.

The results of this part of the study will be discussed together with the results from the scales data in the next chapter. Here, we just sum up these findings briefly. At the global level, it is noteworthy that references to urban/rural associations are extremely sparse. The same is found in the case of prestige (cultured/uncultured). Most of the labels refer to linguistic features, affective qualities, and associations with Welshness and non-Welshness. In other words, the teachers express the similarities and differences they perceive amongst the dialect zones in terms of these three broad categories.

Where linguistic features are pointed to the most (*Cardiff* and *North Wales*), it is noticeable that the dialect zones are also associated with the highest levels of negative affect. There tends to be much less attention to linguistic form where there is positive affect (for example, *South-West* and *Mid-Wales*), as if linguistic features become more salient where there is negative affect, and serve to illustrate it. There seems to be less association between linguistic forms and Welshness/non-Welshness. For example, *Liverpool* and *Pembrokeshire* attract a high proportion of non-Welsh characterizations, but little attention to linguistic features. On the other hand, *Cardiff*, which is also high on non-Welshness, is high on linguistic form as well.

There is also less association between affect and Welshness. *North Wales* is high on both. *Cardiff* is high on negative affect, but low on Welshness. The two zones perceived to be the most non-Welsh are *Pembrokeshire* and *Liverpool*, both of them with affective profiles quite evenly balanced between positive and negative. There are two zonal profiles that are particularly conspicuous. The *Cardiff* zone is the most disliked of all (in terms of negative affective comments) and one of the least Welsh. In this sense, it is the most negative of these Welsh zones. The *South-West* is viewed in particularly positive terms affectively, and is also perceived as strongly Welsh, a profile to be kept in mind when considering the other results in the questionnaire study, as well as those in the narratives study.

6

Attitude scales and 'social advantage' items

We now turn to the analysis and interpretation of the scales data, where respondents used rating scales on the questionnaire to indicate their attitudes to the six conceptually presented Welsh English dialect communities, along with RP. Data from all 129 questionnaires were coded and entered, but minor items of missing or incomplete data reduced this to 80 cases. Where questionnaires were incomplete, respondents most commonly said they felt unable to make specific evaluations because they were unfamiliar with specific communities. Preliminary analysis found no differences between overall profiles of responses with missing data and those with complete data.

Independent variables

No significant differences for gender were found among respondents. Differences emerged between teachers who completed questionnaires in Welsh (14.7 per cent) and those who completed them in English, but these mirrored those found for self-reported Welsh versus non-Welsh speakers in the sample. For further analysis, therefore, the sample was split between respondents reporting that they spoke Welsh 'only a little' or 'not at all' versus those reporting that they spoke Welsh 'as a first or equal language' and 'quite well'. The sample was also classified into 'southern' versus 'northern' teachers, defined by area of employment (in the southern counties of Dyfed, Powys, Gwent and the Glamorgans, or the northern counties of Gwynedd and Clwyd – see figure 4.1). These two classifications were then treated as independent variables in our analysis.

A MANOVA was performed – 7 (accent/dialect communities) by 2 (north/south) by 2 (non-/Welsh-speaking respondents). A MANOVA is a statistical model for testing the effects of more than one independent variable, where each of these variables has two or more levels. In the MANOVA used here, the two latter dimensions were between-subjects variables, each with two levels, and the first was a within-subjects variable with seven levels. Analysis can reveal *main effects* and *interaction effects*. The former is where analysis of the levels of one variable shows significant effects, and the latter is where effects are due to a combination of variables. Interaction effects are then analysed further through follow-up tests of means (for example, in this study, Scheffe tests).

For ease of reference, the seven accent/dialect areas are hereafter referred to as the independent variable 'community', and the seven sub-areas as *Valleys, NE, Cardiff, SW, Mid, NW* and *Cambridge (RP)*.

Dependent variables

Reliability analysis using Cronbach's alpha indicated that the eight scales comfortably captured the three principal dimensions that have consistently emerged in the long tradition of language attitudes research (Zahn and Hopper, 1985). Specifically, the speakers' perceived status (alpha 0.87) comprised 'well-spoken', 'prestigious-sounding', and 'how well will this accent serve the overall interests of school-leavers?' Perceived likeability/solidarity (alpha 0.84) incorporated 'likeable-sounding' and 'pleasant-sounding'. Perceived dynamism (alpha 0.82) consisted of 'dynamic-sounding' and 'lively-sounding'. The 'authenticity' judgement in the form of the 'truly Welsh-sounding' question which, as argued earlier, is particularly relevant in the context of this research, did not correlate well with the other scales, and because it has not been isolated as a recurring factor in previous studies, we treated it as a separate dimension in our analysis. Hereafter, these dependent variables are referred to by the labels 'prestigious', 'pleasant', 'dynamic' and 'truly Welsh-sounding'.

No association was found between non-Welsh-speaking and area of employment. Multivariate analysis of variance showed a significant main effect only in the case of accent/dialect community. There were no main effects for non-Welsh-speaking, or for area of employment. Hence, we can conclude that the regional varieties are viewed differently from each other by all respondents combined. Univariate tests showed a significant effect at the p<0.01 level for all four dependent measures: prestigious, dynamic, pleasant and truly Welsh-sounding. This means that the varieties are differentiated from each other on all the attitudinal dimensions.

Main effects: community profiles

Table 6.1: Means and *(standard deviations)* of teachers' judgements of the accent/dialect communities

	Prestigious	Pleasant	Dynamic	Truly Welsh
NW	4.47	4.25	4.42	2.52
	(1.2)	*(1.3)*	*(1.6)*	*(1.2)*
Cardiff	4.72	4.75	3.97	4.87
	(1.2)	*(1.4)*	*(1.3)*	*(1.7)*
SW	3.77	2.63	3.68	2.10
	(1.1)	*(1.1)*	*(1.2)*	*(1.4)*
Valleys	5.03	3.25	3.63	2.43
	(1.2)	*(1.6)*	*(1.4)*	*(1.6)*
Mid	3.92	3.33	4.25	4.41
	(1.2)	*(1.2)*	*(1.2)*	*(1.7)*
NE	4.82	4.78	4.58	4.86
	(1.1)	*(1.3)*	*(1.3)*	*(1.9)*
RP	2.32	4.08	4.09	6.66
	(1.2)	*(1.1)*	*(1.3)*	*(1.2)*

In table 6.1, we summarize the general findings regarding main effects. *Post hoc* analyses indicate that RP is viewed as the most prestigious variety overall, but that SW is viewed as more prestigious than the other Welsh communities. Valleys is attributed the least prestige, though not significantly less than Cardiff, NE and NW. This overall pattern suggests that the more stereotypically 'rural' communities within Wales attract more prestige than the more 'urban' ones, but still far less so than a stereotyped high-status English English community. This finding echoes the findings in many earlier language attitudes studies (see, for example, van Bezooijen, 1994: 253).

All communities are rated towards the low-dynamism end of the scale, but Valleys and SW are viewed as significantly more dynamic than NE, Mid and NW. These dynamism results, based on the two scales *dynamic* and *lively*, are not straightforward to interpret without some open-ended data alongside. There are some clues in the reference to the Valleys dialect as 'lively' and 'strong' in the characterizations reported in the previous chapter, and as 'ebullient' in the results for the *social advantage* item below, and perhaps in the reference to the SW avoiding the 'guttural moroseness of the north'. SW is also judged significantly more pleasant than all the other communities, being the only one to feature in the top half of the scalar space, although Valleys is ranked at the halfway point. Amongst the other rankings, RP is seen as significantly more pleasant than Cardiff and NE. Finally, the greatest variability in evaluations occurs with 'truly Welsh': a dimension that seems to be a very strong discriminator for the respondents. As with the findings from the characterizations in chapter 5, SW, NW and Valleys are clearly viewed as the most truly Welsh-sounding, quite distinct from NE, Cardiff and Mid.

Among the Welsh communities, then, SW has evaluative advantages on all dimensions, and this again is in line with the findings in chapter 5. NE and Cardiff (the urban, eastern Wales communities) have low attributed prestige and are deemed far less pleasant and far less Welsh. NW is low in prestige and pleasantness, though it is considered a truly Welsh-sounding community. Valleys has a mixed characterization: truly Welsh-sounding, relatively dynamic, and pleasant, but very low in prestige. Mid emerges as a community which is non-Welsh-sounding but has no other strongly stereotyped associations: lacking in dynamism but still prestigious and pleasant relative to other communities within Wales. RP produced mixed judgements: highly prestigious, but ranked amongst several Welsh communities in terms of pleasantness and dynamism.

Interaction effects

Multivariate interactions were significant at the $p<0.01$ level for non-Welsh-speaking and community, and also for teachers' area of employment (north versus south) and community. Means and standard deviations are displayed in tables 6.2 and 6.3 respectively.

Welsh/non-Welsh speakers

Compared with Welsh speakers, non-Welsh speakers significantly downgraded Cardiff on prestige and pleasantness, NW on pleasantness and dynamism, and NE on all three. In addition, non-Welsh speakers judged RP as more dynamic than did Welsh speakers, who in turn judged SW and Valleys as more dynamic than RP.

Table 6.2: Means and *(standard deviations)* for Welsh versus non-Welsh speakers

	Valleys	*NE*	*SE*	*SW*	*Mid*	*NW*	*RP*
Prestigious							
Welsh	5.15	4.43	4.42	3.74	3.84	4.61	2.27
(n=38)	*(1.4)*	*(1.2)*	*(1.2)*	*(1.1)*	*(1.3)*	*(1.2)*	*(1.0)*
Non-Welsh	4.92	5.18	5.0	3.79	3.99	4.34	2.37
(n=42)	*(1.1)*	*(1.1)*	*(1.2)*	*(1.1)*	*(1.1)*	*(1.3)*	*(1.4)*
Dynamic							
Welsh	3.66	4.32	3.71	3.56	4.08	4.06	4.49
	(1.4)	*(1.2)*	*(1.2)*	*(1.1)*	*(1.1)*	*(1.6)*	*(1.1)*
Non-Welsh	3.61	4.82	4.20	3.78	4.40	4.74	3.72
	(1.4)	*(1.4)*	*(1.4)*	*(1.3)*	*(1.3)*	*(1.6)*	*(1.5)*
Pleasant							
Welsh	3.27	4.45	4.32	2.41	3.50	3.96	4.21
	(1.8)	*(1.3)*	*(1.6)*	*(0.9)*	*(1.3)*	*(1.2)*	*(1.1)*
Non-Welsh	3.24	5.08	5.14	2.83	3.18	4.51	3.96
	(1.4)	*(1.3)*	*(1.2)*	*(1.4)*	*(1.2)*	*(1.5)*	*(1.1)*
Truly Welsh							
Welsh	2.66	5.13	4.91	1.70	4.61	2.43	6.68
	(1.7)	*(1.8)*	*(1.6)*	*(1.4)*	*(1.8)*	*(1.3)*	*(1.1)*
Non-Welsh	2.23	4.62	4.83	2.33	4.22	2.61	6.64
	(1.6)	*(2.0)*	*(1.9)*	*(1.5)*	*(1.7)*	*(1.1)*	*(1.3)*

It would appear that the stigma that attaches to the English of the generally heavily anglicized communities of NE and Cardiff is particularly strong in the judgements of non-Welsh speakers. With judgements of prestige, perhaps Welsh speakers are orientating to the limited but in some ways Welsh language-facets of Cardiff and NE's social presence. Alternatively, and we think more likely, it might be that the non-Welsh speakers are more sensitive to the stigma carried through the one language they rely on in their everyday lives. Another possibility is that these groups operate with different notions of the territorial scope of prestige. The social comparisons of the non-Welsh speakers may stretch further afield, embracing a wider range of varieties of English: if comparisons are restricted to the local area, prestige is high, whereas if extended to a larger (for example, national or international) context, it is relatively lower. This is not the conventional sociolinguistic distinction between 'overt prestige' (public endorsement of a cultural norm of correctness) and 'covert prestige' (private endorsement of local community ingroup values), but a suggestion that there are layers of overt prestige. Similarly, one might speculate whether the Welsh speakers are more content to anchor their perceptions of dynamism, too, in the ingroup bilingual context. As a result of issues of identity, the groups could be operating with different norms of dynamism. If there is an element of threat involved in English speakers' downgrading of Welsh English varieties, then speakers who are also able to project their identities through Welsh may feel less prone to that threat.

North/south teachers

Compared to northern teachers, southern teachers saw Valleys and Cardiff as significantly less prestigious, and, along with Mid, less 'truly Welsh-sounding'. They also saw Valleys as less pleasant than did northerners, and more strongly promoted SW and NW as sounding more authentically Welsh.

Familiarity effects may explain these north–south differences. More negative prestige assessments are made by respondents living within the Cardiff and north-east communities. As teachers, respondents may be less affected by feelings of language loyalty than have been found in other studies (for example, Giles, 1970). Teachers more familiar with, say, Cardiff's sociolinguistic stigma will predictably give it lower prestige. Similarly, with pleasantness, northerners may be less familiar with and so more influenced by the rosy picture sometimes painted of the Valleys in, for example, traditional films (see the responses to the open-ended social advantage question). Furthermore, against the northern backdrop of grey slate-quarry towns, the coalmining connotation of Valleys may be fairly weak for northerners, but its 'green valley' association very strong. Southerners, however, may be more familiar with other nearby places and make these the main basis for comparison: for example, SW.

Table 6.3: Means and *(standard deviations)* by area of employment of teachers (north versus south)

	Valleys	NE	SE	SW	Mid	NW	RP
Prestigious							
Southern	5.46	4.92	5.06	3.80	3.92	4.61	2.08
(n=57)	*(1.1)*	*(1.0)*	*(1.1)*	*(1.1)*	*(1.1)*	*(1.1)*	*(0.8)*
Northern	4.61	4.70	4.42	3.73	3.86	4.34	2.56
(n=23)	*(1.4)*	*(1.1)*	*(1.2)*	*(1.1)*	*(1.2)*	*(1.4)*	*(1.5)*
Dynamic							
Southern	4.14	4.63	4.03	3.78	4.36	4.64	3.97
	(1.4)	*(1.3)*	*(1.3)*	*(1.2)*	*(1.2)*	*(1.6)*	*(1.4)*
Northern	3.41	4.44	3.47	3.68	3.99	4.32	4.29
	(1.4)	*(1.2)*	*(1.3)*	*(1.3)*	*(1.1)*	*(1.6)*	*(1.3)*
Pleasant							
Southern	3.79	4.96	4.58	2.51	3.58	4.43	4.15
	(1.6)	*(1.4)*	*(1.2)*	*(1.2)*	*(1.2)*	*(1.2)*	*(1.0)*
Northern	2.72	4.58	4.88	2.73	3.10	4.03	4.02
	(1.5)	*(1.3)*	*(1.4)*	*(1.1)*	*(1.3)*	*(1.6)*	*(1.2)*
Truly Welsh							
Southern	2.98	4.96	5.23	1.61	4.79	2.21	6.91
	(1.7)	*(1.9)*	*(1.5)*	*(0.7)*	*(1.3)*	*(1.6)*	*(0.6)*
Northern	1.92	4.80	4.51	2.43	4.04	2.82	6.41
	(1.2)	*(1.7)*	*(1.8)*	*(1.3)*	*(1.9)*	*(1.8)*	*(1.8)*

With 'truly Welsh-sounding', too, in their promotion of SW and NW, southerners perhaps reflect how SW is taken to represent so-called 'south-west Wales' as a heartland territory in the south, and may also be less prone to the north Wales negative stereotype of Bangor speech (with 'Bangor-aye' as its iconic feature). The northern perspectives of Valleys, Cardiff and Mid may be due to less familiarity with these communities and/or the associated sociolinguistic stereotypes.

The social advantage item

Forty-four of the respondents did not answer this item. There are of course several possible reasons why any one respondent did not answer it: for example, they could not identify one accent/dialect in answer to this question, or they were unwilling to do so, or, since this was always the last task on the questionnaires and was open-ended, there may have been fatigue effects.

There were three components to this item. The first was: 'Identify one Welsh accent of English that you think has very wide social acceptability over others for life in general in Wales.' The second was: 'Describe its social advantages.' And the third was: 'How do you think it is regarded outside Wales?' Because teachers were not confined to the community labels that were provided for the attitude-rating scales, their responses to the first component were much more varied, and we group them under general headings, such as 'south Wales Valleys', 'south-west Wales', 'Cardiff or south-eastern cities', 'mid-Wales or borders', 'Pembrokeshire', 'north-east Wales', 'north-west Wales', 'BBC or educated Welsh' and 'others'. For the second and third components of this item, comments were grouped under the dominant themes which emerged from the responses.

Component 1: social acceptability of the regional dialects
The accent most frequently named as widely acceptable was that associated with 'south-west Wales' (25.9 per cent), followed by 'south Wales Valleys' (20 per cent) and 'mid-Wales' (20 per cent). 'Cardiff and the south-eastern cities' were mentioned by 15.3 per cent of the sample. Only one person mentioned 'north Wales'. That the accent should be 'educated' or approximate to a 'BBC accent' was stated by 4.7 per cent and four of these respondents added this as a precondition to the social acceptability of south-west Wales English. In components 2 and 3 below, the first two of these – south-west Wales and south Wales Valleys – are taken up. Note that these two dialect communities, while rated positively for Welshness, dynamism, and social attractiveness (pleasantness), were graded quite differently from each other on prestige in the attitude-rating scales. Teachers might link prestige very strongly with notions of social acceptability.

Component 2: social advantages
Commenting on what social advantages their chosen accent conferred, the advantage most identified with a south-west Wales accent was

sometimes put negatively – its avoidance of specific advantages, conferring ethnic identity but 'not too strongly'. For example:

> (If educated) it avoids the north–south prejudice. It avoids the sometimes shrill 'sing-song' of the south and the sometimes guttural moroseness of the north, it effects a compromise.
>
> It's Welsh but not too idiosyncratic and doesn't have the class overtones of other south Wales accents – gives a definite Welsh identity but not too Welsh.

There was frequent mention of the association of south-west Wales English with education and success. For example:

> It sounds cultured.
>
> Top jobs when allied with an ability to speak Welsh – S4C, BBC Wales, etc.

For the accents associated with the south Wales Valleys, there was no clear consensus. Comments centred around three main themes. Firstly, familiarity and friendliness:

> Warm, friendly, and therefore [the] person [is] accepted.
>
> Easy to listen to, relaxed and reassuring – warm therefore gives a feeling of trust.

Secondly, articulate and confident spokesperson.

> The natural ebullience of the valleys and confidence.
>
> (Educated) tradition of oratory.
>
> Neil Kinnock – some authority. [Neil Kinnock is a former leader of the British Labour Party, and his voice and political persona are associated with left-wing Valleys politics.]

Thirdly, strong (including strongly stereotyped) Welsh identity:

> Unfortunate echoes of *How Green was my Valley*, local-boy-makes-good-in-university-type thing.
>
> People associate it with Welsh 'culture', i.e. the stereotypical view presented by the media of the singing Welsh miner.

Component 3: how regarded outside Wales

Respondents were also asked how they thought their chosen accent was judged *outside* Wales. South-west Wales accents were said to be viewed positively outside Wales by most respondents. For example:

> The majority of people I've spoken to regard it as very pleasant and stereotypically Welsh.

> Quite highly, like the cultured Scot.

However, others thought that a south-west Wales accent is viewed negatively outside Wales, with several referring to low status.

> Welsh accents are looked down upon by various areas, e.g. south-east England.

> From the sticks.

The dominant theme for the perceptions of south Wales Valleys accents outside Wales, on the other hand, was high-profile media figures and stereotypes.

> Reasonably attractive – especially when the accent reminds them of famous Welsh figures in public life.

> As the language of singing colliers. ['colliers' = miners]

> Inferior to standard English and susceptible to stereotyping.

Questionnaire study findings: an overview

The data clearly demonstrate the multidimensional nature of accent/dialect stereotypes and generally confirm the salience of Zahn and Hopper's (1985) three dimensions. However, they also show what we are calling authenticity to be a highly salient dimension of attitudes to English in Wales, and this is doubtless a dimension that needs to investigated in other similar sociolinguistic settings where local versus 'standard' varieties of a colonizing language are available for the expression of quite contradictory allegiances.

Community profiles

Alongside this multidimensionality to evaluative judgements, the Welsh English dialect communities emerge as having quite distinctive evaluative profiles. Hence, some of the inconclusiveness of findings from earlier studies that we mentioned in chapter 3 can be attributed to the regional variation in dialects. The study has, then, demonstrated the caution needed with simple designations such as 'Welsh English' or 'south Wales English', and doubtless further discriminations would need to be made in respect of still more precise territorial designations.

Beyond this, some degree of the earlier inconclusiveness may also be understood in terms of the social location of the judging groups. The rating-scales results provide modest evidence of systematic variation in social judgements according to whether the teachers work in northern versus southern Wales, and whether they are predominantly monolingual versus bilingual. For example, familiarity/unfamiliarity effects were found, whereby, as we argued earlier, south Wales teachers are more prone to downgrade the prestige of the generally stigmatized urban Welsh English of the Cardiff region than were those in the north. Similarly, perceptions of the authenticity of some Welsh varieties were qualified by area of employment of the teachers. Such regionally coloured qualities of ethnicity and social status deserve further and more precise investigation, and are further addressed in the narratives study.

The open-ended characterizations and the 'social acceptability' data suggest that judgements of Welsh community accents are themselves sometimes mediated in the more direct sense of deriving from social images of Wales and Welshness reproduced through films and television, for example, via well-known political figures. Although beyond the scope of the studies we report on in this book, it is clear that further work is needed on the mass media's role in constructing, modifying or focusing speech stereotypes. It may be that familiarity effects, such as those seen above, are powerful enough to operate as a counter to mediated social images.

The traditional quantitative paradigm of language attitudes research seeks to contrast speakers, groups or communities along particular evaluative dimensions (usually those just mentioned above). In chapter 3, we mentioned that in most such studies, there has been little assessment of how these dimensions compare in importance to the judges, and hence of the significance of specific differences found in, say, accent ratings. The labels study, by contrast, is arguably well-suited to assessing *which* evaluative dimensions are salient for judging particular communities. Table 5.2 suggests, for example, that affective qualities are important to the teachers in this study. South-west Wales, the Valleys, and perceptually Welsh communities of the country are favoured, whereas Cardiff and north-west Wales English are disfavoured, and these results conform to those findings from the scales data. The English speech of Cardiff and north Wales, however, has perceptual salience through stereotyped linguistic forms as much as by negative affect. It seems reasonable to say that the negativity of these zones' sociolinguistic stereotypes is strongly mediated by their folk-linguistic qualities.

Welshness and affect
The perceptual and evaluative salience of a Welsh/non-Welsh dimension needs to be emphasized. Not only did teachers invoke labels for some of their perceptual zones from within this range, but they used the Welsh/non-Welsh dimension more than any other in characterizing the full set of their labels. Osmond (1985: xix) asks whether Welshness is a graded dimension rather than a category, and the evidence of this study is clearly that it is graded. Attributed Welshness is a productive resource for sociolinguistic stereotyping. It is highly salient for characterizing the urban north-east of Wales, and Pembrokeshire in the extreme south-west as 'un-Welsh'; and, on the other hand, for identifying 'Welsh', 'true' or 'deep' Wales, designating the Valleys, south-west Wales (Dyfed) and north Wales (minus the north-east).

Even if evaluated Welshness is associated with positive affective evaluations in the cases of south-west Wales and the Valleys (and in the case of the Welsh label-set itself), this is not an inevitable association. A zone can be seen as relatively Welsh but relatively negative in affect (north Wales), very un-Welsh and only mildly negative in affect (Liverpool), very un-Welsh but still relatively positive in affect (the designated English label-set), or rather un-Welsh and relatively positive in affect (mid-Wales/Borders). The most negatively evaluated zone, Cardiff, is thought to be only mildly un-Welsh (perhaps in this case because it is after all the Welsh capital city).

Perceived zones of Welshness
The findings modestly support claims made from quite different sources about Welsh regionalism and subcultural identity. The concept of 'the Welsh heartland', '*Y Fro Gymraeg*' (in figure 3.1), is endorsed by the teachers' subjective labelling of north Wales, south-west Wales and perceptually Welsh zones as separate from others. But it is important to be clear that the respondents are constructing a 'heartland' territory on

the basis of their perceptions of *English language* use. Teachers do perceive 'authentic' or 'heartland' Wales to be symbolized through patterns of English language usage, overlaid on the more conventional assumption that *Y Fro Gymraeg* is defined as high-density *Welsh language* use. Also, teachers clearly prefer to subdivide *Y Fro Gymraeg* into more specific communities, basically northern and southern, which have respectively more negative and more positive evaluative profiles.

The concept of 'Welsh Wales' within the 'three-Wales' model (figure 3.1) is supported to the extent that teachers distinguish Valleys as a discretely labelled sociolinguistic domain. However, the evaluative profiles of the Valleys and south-west Wales (Pembrokeshire, Cardigan/Ceredigion and Carmarthenshire) zones are in fact very similar in the data, but different from the north Wales zone (which we have already noted is much more negatively stereotyped). The notion of 'British Wales' is perceptually real for the respondents, to the extent that Pembrokeshire, Cardiff, Mid/Borders and Liverpool are indeed segregated from the other zones by geographical boundaries very similar to those plotted in figure 3.1. But it is again the differentiation *within* this area that is most striking in the data. Not only is this territory divided into labelled zones, but there are also great differences in perceived non-Welshness across the zones. The claimed 'Britishness' of Pembrokeshire and the Liverpool-influenced zone may be reflected in these zones' strongly perceived non-Welshness, but the mid/border zone is far more mildly non-Welsh, and Welshness seems not to be a salient dimension in perceptions of the Cardiff zone. The data therefore suggest that the notion of 'British Wales' should be treated with some scepticism.

There is perhaps a tendency with perceptual maps to interpret them as we do with most maps, as descriptive representations of how things are, or, in this case, of how people's perceptions are at this time. Maps can take on a static reified 'snapshot' nature, and so conceal from us, or lead us to overlook, the dynamics that are at work tugging at the map in different directions, and trying to redraw the boundaries and contours in line with sectional interests and aspirations. Yet there is some evidence that the contours of Welshness in the maps of Wales that this study is constructing do represent ongoing identificational struggles in Wales. The contours of Welshness we have revealed in the attitudinal-mapping task do appear to reflect – and with a remarkable degree of consistency – *political* contours, wherever competing notions of Welsh identity take shape as salient oppositions in national political aspirations and ambitions. The evidence for this is most striking in figure 6.1.

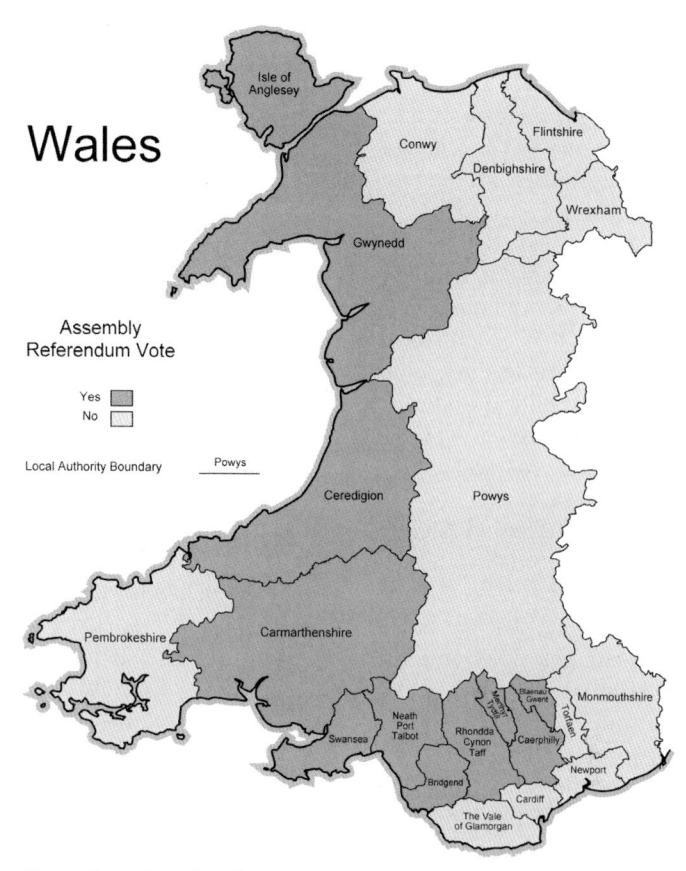

Figure 6.1: Map of Wales showing regional voting patterns in the 1997 referendum for a Welsh assembly

This map depicts the results of the referendum for a Welsh Assembly in 1997, and shows how the voting patterns differ across the various Welsh local authorities. The distribution of support for and opposition to the establishment of a Welsh Assembly is a close reflection of the perceptual map of Welshness evolving from our research. Yet this particular referendum map hides the gradeability of Welsh identity; majorities and minorities varied considerably across Wales, which arguably bring it even closer to the distributions of Welshness set out above. Relatively strong majorities in favour of an Assembly were to be found in the areas referred to as south-west (65 per cent for and 35 per cent against in Carmarthenshire), north-west (64 per cent for and 36 per cent against in Gwynedd), and Valleys (58 per cent for and 42 per cent against in Rhondda Cynon Taff), with far less support for a Welsh Assembly found in most of the south-east coastal and border areas (37 per cent for and 63 per cent against in Newport; 32 per cent for and 68 per cent against in Monmouthshire). The regionality is both north-south and east-west.

In the open-ended questionnaire data, there were glimpses of some of the stereotypes held of and by the various dialect communities. We will see more such glimpses in the narratives study, in the data from the teenagers. Such labels provide some insights into the intergroup dynamics and struggle that may ultimately fashion new Welsh identities at a time of new political opportunities in Wales, with the possibility of links of some kind between attitudes (here, regarding Welshness) and behaviour (here, political affiliation and voting).

Differentation of dialects: linguists and non-linguists
It is of general methodological interest that the perceptual dialectological approach to dialect and stereotype mapping should have produced results that are broadly comparable to, but *far more differentiated than*, the descriptive (English) dialectological map of Wales as it has been established so far. We have just mentioned that, with regard to Welshness, the teachers have quite regular perceptions of rather precisely delimited accent/dialect zones of English in Wales. The seven zones that they recognize (ignoring the zones labelled *English* and *Welsh* in tables 5.1 and 5.2) certainly confirm the broad division into southern and northern dialects, as characterized by Edwards (1991), as having perceptual salience. But the teachers also responded to a clear differentiation of Valleys and Cardiff dialect types within the southeast, and Pembrokeshire and south-west. The teachers are also aware of an important difference within north Wales English, distinguishing a zone under the influence of the Liverpool conurbation from so-called north Wales speech. Again, mid-Wales/borders has its own (albeit lower) perceptual salience for them. Our initial review of English dialect differences across these territories indeed suggested that linguistic features are available as resources to index divisions of this sort, but the perceptual approach configures the geolinguistic map more convincingly than dialect descriptions are able to at this stage.

The question is not whether descriptive studies can capture patterns of objective differentiation, to which these perceived differences presumably relate. But descriptive studies of varying sorts can proceed on the assumption that community members (if teachers do in fact prove to be representative of other groups) do themselves have differentiated representations of English dialect variation in Wales. Language use and linguistic change may well pattern in ways that correspond to these perceptual maps.

Standardness

The study has produced ambiguous findings concerning the debate about 'standard English'. Overall, in their scaled responses, teachers show allegiance to the non-Welsh variety (tagged 'Cambridge'), attributing to it a level of prestige far above any Welsh English variety. Since the prestige dimension subsumed the scale 'would serve the interests of school-leavers', the teachers appear to endorse the social value of a high-prestige non-Welsh sounding variety for their students' social advancement. At the same time, the familiar corollary of a high-prestige 'standard' attracting moderate-to-low levels of perceived pleasantness and dynamism again emerges in the data. If 'Standard English English', or RP, is in fact considered 'standard' in Wales, it is only the voice of perceived competence, not of social attractiveness or dynamism.

Indeed, a candidate for the title 'standard Welsh English' has emerged – the variety associated with Carmarthen in the south-west, which one respondent (presumably with some linguistic training) actually characterizes as the *Welsh version of RP*. It does not reach the level of prestige attributed to RP, but it is relatively prestigious and has a superior *overall* evaluative profile to that usually found for RP. It is deemed the most pleasant of the varieties, reasonably dynamic, and the most truly Welsh. Its social connotations perhaps relate to its heartland situation, in a non-urbanized, non-industrial landscape. The findings confirm the conclusion reached by Edwards and Jacobsen (1987) in their study of evaluative reactions in Canada to Canadian and US varieties of English:

> in contexts possessing regional standards, these varieties have greater all-round favourability than standard varieties typically possess in settings in which more clear-cut distinctions can be made between standard and other, non-standard forms. The explanation for this presumably relates to the fact that regional standards are at once regional and standard, and so may be expected to elicit both status *and* solidarity reactions. (p. 378)

Sociolinguistic definitions of standardness remain contradictory and occasionally tautological (Coupland, 1990, 2000; J. Milroy and

L. Milroy, 1985). However, there is much agreement in the literature that a 'standard' needs subjective, and hence evaluative, definition. Language attitudes researchers in Denmark have recently argued that there is now more than one standard Danish. Kristiansen (2001) has pointed to one standard operating in schools and another in the media, while Ladegaard (2001) has identified a number of regional standards. The teachers in our study certainly seem willing to authenticate southwest Wales's claim to represent a viable regional standard for English in Wales. With a caveat of 'moderation', they recognize the symbolic potential for this variety inside, and sometimes outside, Wales.

Teachers' perceptions of prestige
The data from this study need to be contextualized with data from other sources. It needs to be recognized that the sociolinguistic perceptions of teachers may not in fact be fully representative of other groups. Most obviously, teachers may have more accurate representations of geolinguistic variation than other groups, in terms of their perceptual isoglosses corresponding to descriptive dialectological ones.

The relatively low return-rates from the questionnaires that were distributed might in part be because the study touched on a sensitive issue for teachers, against the background of contemporary debates about the UK national schools' curriculum, and particularly about the role of standard English within it. On the other hand, teachers who did participate in the study were prepared to articulate their stereotyped judgements, negative as well as positive, with apparent freedom and considerable consistency. An unexpected finding was that, in their descriptive comments about perceived varieties, teachers made very little use of the status/class dimensions that were coded under the cultured/uncultured opposition (see table 5.2). Status is one of the most firmly established evaluative dimensions in language attitudes research generally (along with social attractiveness and, in many cases, perceived dynamism).

At the same time, it is already evident from these data that teachers do command a richly differentiated set of sociolinguistic stereotypes which are likely to be deployed in various ways in their professional work. The finding in the labels data that teachers express their stereotyped judgements almost exclusively in relation to perceived Welshness, dimensions of affect, and linguistic form, rather than prestige, might indeed give reassurance to educationists concerned about the effects of teachers having low expectations of some students and about self-fulfilling prophecies in the classroom. There is no overt evidence of potentially punitive judgements in the data, beyond the obvious fact that teachers command a familiar repertoire of terms to express their liking and disliking of varieties – 'soft', 'gentle', 'comforting', 'irritating', 'annoying', 'grating', 'harsh', 'hard', 'heavy', 'guttural', etc. They are certainly prey to and reproducers of stereotypes, but (in the labels data) specifically *not* of those dimensions of stereotypes that associate variety-use with class or status.

In chapter 4, however, we referred to earlier research conducted in other settings, showing how teachers' evaluations of students can be influenced by the students' speech. On these grounds, there is reason to speculate on these findings in the labels data. The infrequent reference to prestige in the teachers' open-ended characterizations needs to be set in the context of the same teachers' differentiation of the prestige of the dialect communities on the rating scales. There are at least two possible interpretations of this difference, and both of these relate to the kinds of research methodological issues that are part of our agenda in this book.

Firstly, we argued earlier in this chapter that, even if respondents are prepared to rate a speaker on a particular trait when asked to, we cannot estimate from that alone the comparative degree of importance they attach to that trait. The respondent may significantly differentiate speakers on, say, friendliness, but make little distinction amongst the same speakers on traits of dynamism. If the respondent attaches far more importance to friendliness than to dynamism, there will be much to choose between the speakers, whereas if the respondent's prime interest is in their dynamism, there will be little to choose between them. So, although the teachers were prepared to differentiate the dialect communities on the prestige dimension when they were given a prestige scale to complete, it cannot simply be taken for granted that prestige is an important factor for them. In the labelling and characterization task, however (which was completed prior to the scales task), no pre-selected dimensions were given to them. Instead, they thought of and wrote down their own judgements. Arguably, in this task, they wrote what was most salient and important to them. Hence, it could be reasonable to conclude from this that prestige really is *not* an important dimension to them in their judgement of different dialect-speakers.

A second interpretation of the different prestige-findings in the labels and scales tasks is based on the claim by, for example, Henerson et al. (1987: 89) that data from semantic differential scales reflect people's general impressions rather than thought-out opinions. Where more time is available for 'thinking through' (that is, for information processing), there is some evidence of a greater risk of a social desirability bias in responses (Cargile, 2002). Our second interpretation also relates to Lambert's (1967) view that the use of semantic-differential scales in conjunction with the MGT is more likely to elicit people's privately held views and be less susceptible to social-desirability bias than direct-questionnaire procedures (see also Lambert, Anisfeld and Yeni-Komshian, 1965). Given that some studies have found strong correlations between results from semantic-differential scales used with matched-guise presentations on the one hand, and conceptual presentations on the other (for example, Giles, 1970; Ball, 1983), the differing prestige-findings from the labels and scales tasks might be seen to reflect two different dimensions, contexts, or levels of knowledge. Preston (1989: 4) would view the former as the teachers' overt knowledge, whereas the latter might be regarded as less overt, and so perhaps more likely to be working beneath the surface, and giving rise to the sort of discriminatory effects in the classroom seen in the earlier studies that we mentioned in chapter 4. Thus the absence of evaluative comments about prestige in the labels and characterizations may, in this interpretation, signal a professional taboo at work, preventing teachers from embarking on talk about language varieties in terms of comparative prestige, and perhaps even acting as a barrier to their own conscious awareness. To address these important issues, research exploring teachers' more covert attitudes, and the mobilization of attitudes in work-settings, is required.

Closing comments

The overall impression that emerges from these data is certainly one of clear and regular patterning of social evaluations over sociolinguistic space. These patterns, though, are subject to increasing specification and qualification as more and more contextual considerations are added to the evaluative mix. At the most local level (in the open-ended data), individual teachers voice idiosyncratic responses which are themselves internally complex, qualified and variable. However, these properties are very much in the nature of language attitudes, just as in the case of language variation. It is this that motivates the use of a variety of methods, in order to address questions at different levels of delicacy and detail.

In chapters 7 to 9, attention now moves on to the narratives study, where actual dialect 'performances' rather than conceptualized communities are being judged. This arguably further enriches the evaluative mix, involving 'real' people doing 'real' things with dialect, however contentious these terms might be. Such regular and quite safely interpretable patterning as we have reported in these last two chapters, if it is found at all, might be expected to be quite different. On the other hand, in line with our general argument in this book, it might also be expected to fill out other corners of the complex picture of language attitudes in Wales. In the final chapter, we will provide a summary discussion of both studies in relation to the research questions that we set out at the start of this book.

7

The narratives study: performances, responses and evaluations

This and the next two chapters deal with the data from the narratives study, in which audio-recorded episodes from fourteen teenagers' narrative performances in their local Welsh English dialects were evaluated by teenagers in other schools in the same regions, and by teachers. In this chapter, we analyse and discuss the quantitative data from the seven attitude-rating scales, looking first at descriptive statistics, and then at findings from forms of statistical analysis not conventionally employed in language attitudes research. In the next chapter, we deal with the 'keywords' data, and in chapter 9 we look at the dialect-recognition responses. We make references and comparisons, as appropriate, to the questionnaire-study findings reported in the last two chapters.

Our two sets of studies differ in particular in the way that dialect communities are presented to respondents. Whereas, in the questionnaire study, these were presented conceptually for the scales-completion task, audio-recordings were employed in the narratives study. And it will be recalled from chapter 4 that, unlike recordings used in MGT studies, those used in our narratives study are of spontaneous, situated dialect 'performances', with teenagers from the same dialect community telling similar stories in the same dialect.

Narratives as performance

We intend the term 'performance' in a technical sense, distinguished, for example, from more general terms such as 'talk', 'speech' or 'language behaviour'. We mean to imply that, within the constraints of the classroom situation, the storytelling activities that we recorded for later evaluation were 'performance events'. In the spirit of Bauman's (1992: 46; see also Bauman, 1977, 1996; Bauman and Briggs, 1990) analysis of performance as a specifiable genre or set of genres, we can say that the narratives were 'scheduled', 'coordinated' and 'intense' communicative events. Although they were relatively informal events, with only modest amounts of time made available to students to plan their stories, the storytellings positioned the speakers for short periods of time as 'performers', and their co-students as 'audience members'. The stories, and particularly the ones that proved to be most successful and interesting, had the effect of focusing and highlighting selected aspects of the young people's personal experiences and offering them up for evaluation. In one sense it is more natural to evaluate narratives than other types of talk, precisely because they are designed to 'work' as small-scale performance events.

This perspective proves to be useful in our discussion of findings from different sorts of evaluation tasks later in this chapter, when aspects of the relationships between speakers and judges have to be interpreted. As we see below, social evaluation of the various stories involved much more than reacting to the stereotyped meanings of speakers' dialects. It included reacting to the content and quality of their storytelling performances and to the identities – real or fictionalized – that storytellers were able to construct for themselves as protagonists in their narratives.

We are also able to unravel some of the normative expectations that young people appear to hold for storytelling by their peers. We do this by looking at extracts from a sub-sample of the focus-group discussions that we conducted, where groups of young people from different regions of Wales listened to the narratives and were prompted open-endedly to discuss their reactions to the speakers and stories that they heard. We suggest that the task of telling personal stories to age-peers is done against the background of specific normative *demands*, which are made apparent in the follow-up discussions.

First, though, we discuss the more formal responses made to the fourteen narratives through the questionnaire instrument, by students and teachers. We begin with a brief look at the descriptive quantitative data (that is, the mean scores on the attitude scales) from the students and the teachers, and we then move on to more in-depth discussion of the findings from the use of multidimensional scaling and cluster analysis (explained below) on these data.

Students' overall evaluations

Since preliminary quantitative analysis of young people's scaled responses to the fourteen narratives revealed no significant effect for gender, evaluations from males and females are considered together below.

Table 7.1: Overall means for Welsh teenagers' evaluations of regional speakers

Speaker	Do you like	Good at school	Like you	Make friends	How Welsh	Good laugh	Interesting story
Cardiff1	2.43	2.62	1.88	2.39	2.83	2.34	1.87
Cardiff11	3.20	2.44	2.53	3.12	2.88	3.75	3.69
NE2	2.74	3.01	2.22	2.79	1.88	2.97	2.87
NE9	2.86	2.48	2.26	2.77	1.60	3.24	2.71
NW7	2.09	2.09	1.53	1.95	3.44	2.27	2.52
NW10	2.72	2.67	2.22	2.74	3.41	2.97	3.28
SW4	2.67	2.52	2.01	2.67	4.47	3.17	2.60
SW13	2.14	2.38	1.65	2.15	3.91	2.16	1.89
Valleys5	2.23	2.35	1.67	2.14	4.01	2.16	2.58
Valleys8	2.01	2.40	1.46	2.11	3.76	2.16	1.79
Mid6	2.13	3.11	1.71	2.19	2.29	1.99	1.89
Mid14	2.03	3.00	1.66	2.07	2.14	1.98	1.86
RP3	2.04	3.49	1.73	1.93	1.56	1.70	1.78
RP12	2.01	3.56	1.70	1.98	1.51	1.88	1.99

Table 7.1 shows the mean values for all 169 students' responses to the fourteen extracts on the seven evaluative scales. Speakers are listed down the left side of the table. Following the convention established in chapter 4, the regional origin of each speaker is listed, followed by the speaker's randomly allocated identifying number (1 to 14).

Even from these descriptive data, several major trends are apparent. First, taking 3 as the mid-point assessment on the five-point scale, the judgements of the teenagers are better seen as differing in *degrees of negativity* rather than positivity. Indeed, on the *like you* scale, even the highest-rated speaker does not reach the mid-point. Second, some speakers/narratives attract relatively favourable evaluative profiles along a number of scales that would appear to make up the affiliative/ attraction dimension. Cardiff11 (the pool-table story) is ranked the highest on the *you like, like you, make friends* and *good laugh* scales, and has the highest score for *interesting story*. Other speakers with relatively high affiliative profiles are NE9 (the cockroaches in the restaurant story), SW4 (the Michelin-man story), and NW10 (the home-made go-kart and motorbike story). Thirdly, a few extracts attract distinctively low ratings on these same scales, particularly the two RP speakers, RP3 (the belt-sander story) and RP12 (the 'big-wheel' story). The lowest rating on each of the *you like*, *make friends*, *good laugh* and *interesting story* scales is achieved by one or other of RP3 and RP12, with RP3 being the lower-rated overall. Of the speakers from the Welsh regions, Valleys8 (the sewage-pump story) and Mid14 (the bats story) have quite consistently low ratings on affiliative scales.

Fourthly, the *good at school* ratings pattern very differently from the social-attractiveness scales, since RP3 and RP12 are rated highest on this scale. The only speakers from within Wales to reach mid-point on *good at school* are Mid6 (the tractor story) and Mid14, neither of whom is deemed socially attractive, and NE2 (the nightclub and MTV story), who is awarded moderate social attractiveness. Fifthly, students' assessments of *how Welsh* speakers are show far greater variability than other dimensions. SW4 is judged the most Welsh of all fourteen speakers, with Valleys5 (the father in the car-accident story) also rated high. Welshness is in fact the only scale which almost perfectly pairs speakers from particular Welsh communities in an overall rank order, suggesting that perceived regional provenance tends to override other variables for this question. And the rank ordering (for teachers as well as students, in fact, as will be seen in table 7.2 below) is closely in line with the results of the earlier study, a point we return to in chapter 9.

Correlations among the students' responses to the seven questions almost all reach statistical significance, perhaps owing to the large number of individual students' judgements. However, the variable size of individual correlations lends support to the above interpretation that *good at school* and *how Welsh* pattern less well with the other (affiliative) scales than the latter do amongst themselves. For example, the coefficients for *how Welsh* are 0.26 (*you like*), 0.33 (*good at school*), 0.17 (*like you*), 0.24 (*make friends*), 0.39 (*good laugh*), and 0.28 (*interesting story*).

Teachers' overall evaluations

Table 7.2 shows that, like the students, teachers consider some speakers generally more socially attractive than others, in particular, SW4 (the Michelin-man story) and Cardiff11 (the pool-table story), both of

Table 7.2: Overall means for teachers' evaluations of regional speakers

Speaker	Do you like	Good at school	Like you	Make friends	How Welsh	Good laugh	Interesting story
Cardiff1	2.82	2.61	1.43	3.30	3.02	2.47	2.09
Cardiff11	3.24	2.85	1.85	3.91	3.15	3.91	3.81
NE2	2.95	3.16	1.93	3.59	1.52	3.04	2.66
NE9	3.14	3.14	2.36	3.39	2.16	3.00	3.24
NW7	2.96	2.82	1.69	3.02	4.20	2.81	3.00
NW10	3.31	3.33	2.24	3.24	3.76	2.87	3.09
SW4	3.72	3.11	2.07	3.96	4.54	3.98	3.41
SW13	3.16	3.20	1.80	3.44	4.53	2.72	2.62
Valley5	2.75	2.52	1.70	2.82	4.36	2.32	2.81
Valleys8	2.43	2.22	1.41	3.07	3.70	2.21	2.06
Mid6	3.41	3.48	2.35	3.41	2.30	2.89	2.85
Mid14	2.89	3.11	1.87	3.09	1.98	2.47	2.74
RP3	3.30	3.77	2.68	3.27	1.25	2.38	2.83
RP12	2.95	3.89	2.45	3.34	1.14	2.55	2.70

whom were highly ranked by the students. But the teachers favour SW4 over Cardiff11 (the students' favourite), and rank SW4 highest of all on *you like*, *make friends* and *good laugh*. This finding needs to be considered in relation to the findings in the questionnaire study, where the variety associated with south-west Wales was considered to have the best combination of positive attributes of all the Welsh English varieties – prestige, social attractiveness and authenticity. The least socially attractive speakers for the teachers, however, are not the RP speakers but the two Valleys speakers, and particularly Valleys8 (the sewage and pump story). They concur with the students that the RP speakers are likely to do best at school, but they consider the RP speakers to be most 'like themselves', which the students certainly do not.

As we mentioned above, teachers and students are largely in accord in their rankings of *how Welsh*. In relation to these judgements of *how Welsh*, there is one particularly interesting contrast between the earlier questionnaire study and the narratives studies, and that concerns the position of Cardiff . Along with the north-east, Cardiff was judged the least Welsh of the dialect communities in Wales in the questionnaire study (see table 6.1). In this narratives study, both the students and the teachers give Cardiff a middle ranking amongst the communities in terms of Welshness. This difference is most likely to be due to the different modes of dialect presentation and the different questions the respondents were asked. In the scales section of the questionnaire study, they were asked to evaluate 'the English associated with urban south-east Wales (e.g. Cardiff)'. Dialect presentation through the vocal performances of these Cardiff teenagers may allow the reclaiming of some of the Welshness that is lost in the broader conceptualization given of an anglicized region or city, as provided in the questionnaire study. And perhaps the distinctive English dialect of Cardiff, with its own urban identity and focus, is more clearly perceived, in its audible presentation in the second study, to be less prone to influence from neighbouring dialects from across the border than, say, the north-east. Liverpool would rightly be seen to be strongly impacting on English dialects in north-east Wales, whereas the same cannot be said of, say, neighbouring Bristol on Cardiff (see, for example, Windsor Lewis, 1990).

The teachers also share the students' opinion that the most interesting story is told by Cardiff11. Indeed, Cardiff11 seems to have clearly the most positive profile of all the speakers, even though it is one slanted towards social attractiveness and interest value more than *good at school* or *Welshness*.

As with the students, the teachers' *how Welsh* responses pattern less well with responses to the other items, none reaching significance at the 0.01 level, and three (*make friends, good laugh, interesting story*) not doing so at the 0.05 level. (Given the smaller number of teachers compared to the student sample, it is worth noting these significance levels.) Unlike the students, though, *good at school* seems reasonably in line with the others, with all correlations significant at the 0.01 level. On the other hand, and perhaps understandably, given that these are teachers' evaluations of teenagers, the *like you* scale patterns rather differently, and fails to correlate significantly at the 0.05 level with *good laugh*. But it is interesting to note here too that the highest individual correlation for the teachers is between *you like* and *good at school* (0.70), thus matching judgements of social attractiveness with those of student competence. For the students this correlation is also high, but there are higher ones suggesting that they are more inclined to like those who are a 'good laugh' and with whom they can easily make friends.

Overview of regional dialect effects

The above analysis does not identify the *basis* of the judgements being made. The fourteen speakers are paired in the sense that the describable linguistic characteristics of their speech represent the dialect norms of six different regional communities in Wales, plus (in two cases) RP. But the patterning of the evaluations respects these pairings *only very selectively*. For example, the RP speakers are quite consistently linked in the students' evaluations by being placed at or close to the bottom of the affiliative scales of *you like, good laugh* and *make friends*, and are thus to some extent 'outgrouped' by the Welsh students, and credited only with taking away the prizes at school, which attribution they again share. The north-east speakers are also rated quite closely to each other on several affiliative scales. On the other hand, the Cardiff pair are quite clearly *distinguished* affiliatively, with the teenagers favouring Cardiff11 favoured quite markedly over Cardiff1 (the holiday in Spain story).

The *how Welsh* scale shows that teachers and teenagers *can* respond in very precise ways to the dialectal constitution of the narratives, when this is made salient in a particular question. But *interesting story* pulls the dialectal pairs apart, most strikingly in the case of students' judgements of the Cardiff speakers, and teachers' judgements of the two south-west Wales speakers. Evaluations, then, are apparently conditioned by a range of factors here, which include the connotations of dialect varieties but which are not exhaustively accounted for by these associations. In other words, the social meanings associated with the narrative tellings are multidimensional.

We mentioned earlier that language attitudes studies have repeatedly shown that vocal styles regularly trigger inferences about a speaker's social attractiveness and, as a separate dimension, their prestige and competence. But speakers in the narratives study can receive different ratings on these dimensions, despite sharing dialect characteristics. Being rated a *good laugh* and being easy to *make friends* with may be partly an inference from dialect (and in the case of the RP speakers, low ratings on these scales do seem linked to dialect). Yet these attributions are also very plausibly linked to interactional behaviour, and the discourse of the narratives gives listeners access to relevant evidence by a different indexical/inferential route.

Good at school is potentially another inference from dialect, at least in the case of RP speakers being rated as likely high-achievers. But teachers and students may arrive at their similar rankings for different reasons, the teachers acknowledging the historical correlation of high social-class with educational achievement, but the students perhaps even using *good at school* as a blaming strategy. Teachers' very low rankings on this scale of the Valleys speakers (and to a lesser extent, the Cardiff speakers) again suggest a stereotyped association of low competence or achievement with low-status dialects of Welsh English. But rhetorical style, general animation, narrative framing and creativity might also offer clues to success at school.

This far, then, the analyses have not been able to focus on how the various components of the narrative performances and their dimensions of social meaning might be working *in relation to each other* in listeners' evaluations. Evaluations of speaker performances are likely to be made along competing or complementary dimensions. For example, speakers might be judged a *good laugh* because they can discursively undermine, confirm, or even parody the stereotyped associations of their dialect. It is important to try to tease out these contextual effects, from whatever analytic resources are available.

Multidimensional scaling and cluster analysis

To explore these issues further, multidimensional scaling (MDS) was employed, in conjunction with cluster analysis. Having only two speakers from each community, for reasons given in chapter 4, the conventional (MGT) analysis through analysis of variance would anyway leave too much margin for error. Further motivations come from Giles's (1990) suggestion, in his review of research into the social meanings of Welsh English, for the employment of MDS procedures alongside audio-taped extracts to develop a global set of cognitive maps relating to Welsh English varieties around Wales, as well as from the recent work by Preston and his colleagues (for example, Preston, 1999).

MDS is a set of mathematical techniques that help to uncover the 'hidden structure' of data (for an introduction, see Kruskal and Wish, 1978). By analysing how similar or different objects are perceived to be (in the case of the present study, speakers/narratives), it creates a spatial representation of these as a configuration of points, as on a map. So far, the analysis in this chapter has only looked at the judgements of speakers/narratives along individual scales. But, arguably, more than just regional origin of the dialect is affecting evaluative outcomes, since dialectal pairs are in most cases pulled in different directions. MDS, by looking at the differences and similarities in the quantitative judgements of the range of varieties, locates the variable in relation to more than one dimension. It is then up to the researcher (as with factor analysis) to try to place a meaningful interpretation on those directions in terms of the possible variables at work in the study. One decision to be made when using MDS is how many dimensions should form the basis of the output. The issue is in large part pragmatic, revolving around questions of interpretability and ease of use (Kruskal and Wish, 1978: 48). The results reported below are based on a two-dimensional analysis, following other sociolinguistic studies (for example, Hartley, 1999; Kuiper, 1999; van de Velde, van Hout and Gerritsen, 1997), as well as human communication studies (for example, Baxter and Wilmot, 1984).

Kruskal and Wish (1978: 46) show how MDS is often used in conjunction with cluster analysis (for an introduction, see Aldenderfer and Blashfield, 1984; Everitt, 1993). Baxter and Wilmot (1984), looking at the various sorts of strategies that people secretly employ to gauge how their social relationships are progressing, employed MDS to discover the characteristics influencing the choice of strategies. MDS was employed as a supplement to hierarchical cluster analysis, which determined how these strategies fell into groups (or clusters), located in relation to those dimensions. Cluster analysis, too, requires the researcher to interpret what the most likely bases of the groupings are. It is also necessary to determine the number of clusters to interpret. This is a highly subjective process (Aldenderfer and Blashfield, 1984). Ordinary significance tests and other statistical procedures are of questionable value here, and so studies generally make explicit the criteria they have employed in their decision making (see, for example, human communication research by Baxter, 1992; Baxter and Wilmot, 1984; Marston, Hecht and Robers, 1987). The primary guide in our study was the agglomeration schedule. A relatively large distance between two adjacent agglomeration steps is taken as an indication that further agglomeration into clusters is less revealing, and that the data are best represented by the clusters already identified at that point (see Norušis, 1990). This was supplemented by the criteria, following Baxter and Wilmot (1984), that the number of clusters accepted should have reasonable logical coherence and, following Marston et al. (1987), that the number of such interpretable clusters should be more rather than fewer (where agglomerative gaps were not prohibitively large and where this did not encourage excessive 'clusters' containing only one member). Hence, the seven different scales in our study each had their own solution regarding the number of clusters deemed to be the most appropriate.

THE NARRATIVES STUDY   157

The cluster analysis was hierarchical, using the average linking method. Below are set out the results of these analyses for the various judgement-scales. As dialects and speakers are discussed, the reader may find it helpful at times to refer back to the story transcripts in chapter 4, even though brief references to story content are occasionally provided in the discussion.

Judgements of interesting story

Figures 7.1 and 7.2 show the clusters and MDS displays for the teachers' and students' responses respectively to the *interesting story* question. It should be noted when examining the figures that the axis location of the speakers does *not* match what one might expect from the mean scores discussed earlier in this chapter. This is because MDS and cluster analysis are based on distance data, and are therefore not directly comparable with means.

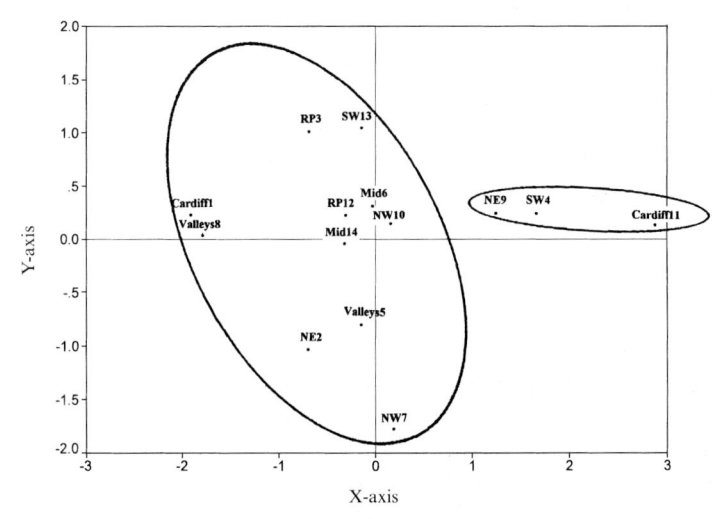

Figure 7.1: MDS and clusters for teachers: 'How interesting does this story sound?'

The teenagers' judgements place the speakers in four clusters, with 50 per cent of them in a single cluster at a very specific point along the X-axis, only slightly spread out along the Y-axis. These are the narratives with the low mean scores, and the clustering suggests a strong tendency

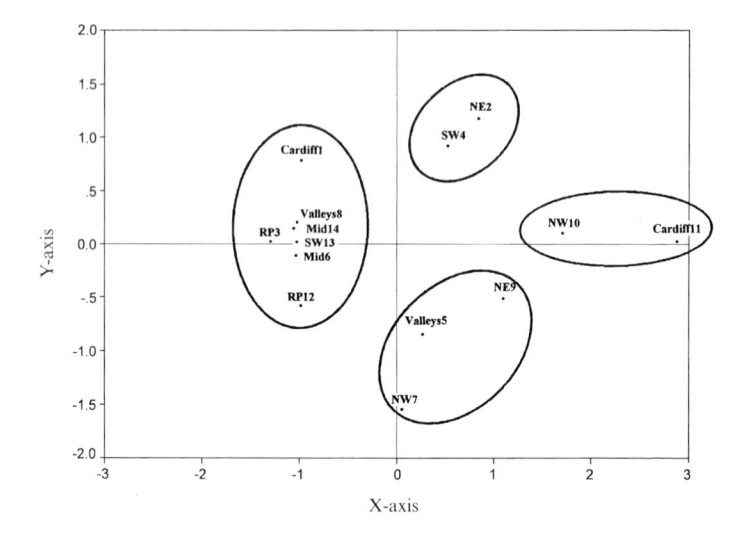

Figure 7.2: MDS and clusters for teenagers: 'How interesting does this story sound?'

to dismiss or relegate disfavoured stories to an undifferentiated 'scrap-pile'.

One interpretive strategy is to look for resemblances in the actual content of the clustered stories. Cardiff1's excerpt tells how he feels sick from too much sun in Spain (though is not actually sick) while staying with his uncle who lives there. RP3 cuts his finger on a belt-sander at school, and the teacher advises him to sit down because it is 'quite nasty'. Mid6's story involves a lot of description of the wheels and weight distribution on a tractor and how the tractor started swaying until his father came to the rescue. Valleys8 is out walking with a friend when they come across an unattended sewage pump. His friend turns it on and sewage sprinkles into the air. RP12 tells of people he saw at a funfair whose carriage fell off a 'big wheel'. He mentions that they were not very high and were not hurt. He reports that he and his friends were 'totally amazed' and 'absolutely flabbergasted', when the person in charge continued as if nothing was amiss. SW13's father tells him and his brother to take a motorbike and trailer to do some work in a field. The trailer comes loose and runs into a hedge. Mid14 thinks he hears a bat when he's in bed, and calls for his father who solves the problem.

It is characteristic of this cluster of 'less interesting' stories that the stories contain mishaps that threatened to occur but did not (Cardiff1), or did occur but were not serious (RP12, Valleys8, SW13), sometimes with adults preventing any real danger (Mid6, Mid14, RP3). In addition, the narratives which are unambiguously rural in character are all to be found in this cluster (Mid6, Valleys8, SW13, Mid14). No one gets into trouble. No one gets hurt. There is relatively little in the way of humorous effect, and we might even say that these narratives are not well performed, according to prevailing norms of interpretation.

The teenagers appear to be more discerning in their ratings of the more interesting stories further along the X-axis. These three other clusters are distributed across both dimensions, and none contains a pair of speakers from the same region, thus indicating that narrative features are more salient in relation to regional dialect in the evaluations of these particular speakers. The cluster containing NW10 and Cardiff11 links stories about what might be regarded as self-inflicted accidents arising from 'unconventional' lifestyles that probably capture the imagination of the teenagers. Cardiff11 gets his hand stuck in a pool-table while attempting to fiddle ('tief' = 'thieve', and is of Caribbean origin) a free game, and has to face the consequences, humorously framed, from a caretaker. NW10 is a story about a third person who steals a metal gate from the fire brigade to build a go-kart, and who later builds a motorbike, on which he injures himself in an accident involving a police car.

The NW7, Valleys5, NE9 cluster groups together three stories that also portray mishaps, but for the teenagers, these probably lack the fun and dynamism of such pursuits as playing pool and riding motorbikes. The final cluster is in marked contrast. Neither NE2 nor SW4 tell stories involving accidents or machines or getting into scrapes with authorities. The evaluations of the speakers in this cluster are instead likely to have been influenced by their vivid description of things happening, people doing things before their very eyes. Both stories are told from a strong affective standpoint ('chuffed', 'a bit sad', 'disgusting'). NE2's story is about himself going out to a nightclub, drinking under-age, meeting rock-bands and getting autographs. SW4 gives a vivid, animated and comic description of a Michelin-man rugby-player trying to squeeze himself into an undersized rugby-shirt.

In various ways, then, the narrative components have a potent effect on the clustering of ratings on this question. Regional dialect features seem to have little impact. Looking at the means earlier, it was noted that the Cardiff pair was pulled apart on *interesting story*. But the two-dimensional spread of the clusters shows that other pairs are separated, too: NE9 and NE2, though close in relation to each other on the X-axis (and in the mean scores set out earlier in table 7.1), are drawn apart along the Y-axis to find themselves in different groupings. The NW, SW and Valleys pairs are also split. Where pairs do occur within a single cluster (RP and Mid), the cluster also contains speakers of other dialects, so that dialectal connotations do not appear uniquely decisive here either.

The teachers' judgements of *interesting story* place the speakers in two clusters, one of which contains eleven of the fourteen. Like the teenagers, the teachers separate Cardiff11 (hand in pool-table), SW4 (massive rugby-player) and NE9 (who finds cockroaches under the table in a restaurant) from the main large cluster. These are also the three stories with the highest mean scores for interest. But unlike the students who placed one of these in each of their three 'best' story clusters pulled apart along the Y-axis, the teachers place all three in a single cluster seemingly unaffected by the Y-axis. It is perhaps most interesting to look at the stories included in the students' 'top three' clusters which are relegated to the teachers' 'less interesting' cluster: NW10 (home-made motor bike), NE2 (nightclub), NW7 (who tells of a local character who tests his crash-helmet by throwing a brick into the air and then puts his hands on his head when the brick comes down), and Valleys5 (who relates how his father had a driving accident in a thunderstorm). Unlike the three narratives in the teachers' 'top cluster', three of these four involve injury: NW7's character breaks all his fingers, Valleys5's father loses his foot, NW10 seriously injures his knee. Perhaps NE2's (unashamed) under-age visit to a nightclub, mixing with 'big fellas' who were 'already drunk' and pop-stars, and regarding the whole thing as an 'ego boost' met with disapproval from the teachers, as much as NW10's stealing from the fire brigade and having accidents involving police cars. In contrast, none of the three narratives (NE9, SW4 and Cardiff11) in the teachers' top cluster shares these qualities. NE9's cockroaches could happen to anyone, and were not going to cause injury. SW4 was simply a well-performed and amusing description of a scene one might see in any TV comedy programme. Cardiff11 was, of course, stealing pool-games, but his story had built-in blame-mitigation in that the caretaker saw and indeed returned the humour in the situation instead of meting out punishment.

The analysis has, then, shown how the respondents' judgements of interest in the stories cannot be wholly explained by the linguistic features of dialect. Narrative performance properties are also at work, and are identified in a structured way through cluster analysis, with these properties affecting the teachers' evaluations differently from those of the teenagers.

Affiliative judgements

Given the correlations among the affiliative scales, discussion can reasonably focus primarily on one of these: *good laugh* (see figures 7.3 and 7.4), but refer to other affiliative scales where appropriate. (The *good laugh* scale shows itself to be the best differentiator of the speakers.)

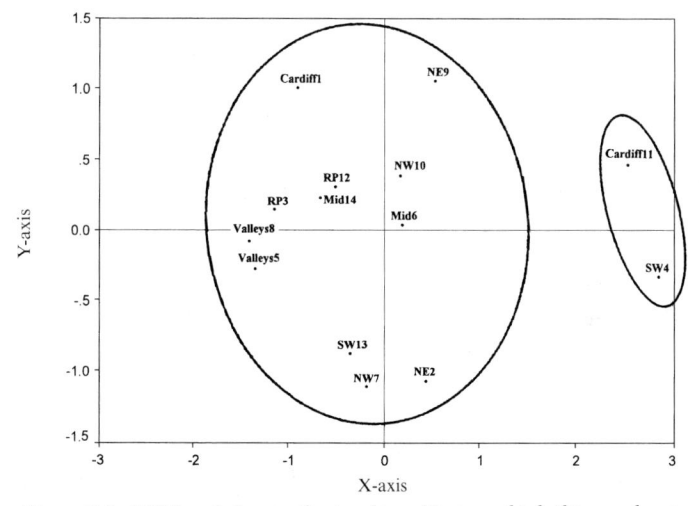

Figure 7.3: MDS and clusters for teachers: 'Do you think this speaker is a good laugh?'

In both figures, the X-axis is an overall reflection of positivity of ratings. For the students, nine of the less favourably rated stories cluster towards one end of this axis and the remaining five stories form two separate clusters towards the other end, with NE2 forming its own 'cluster' drawn away from the others by the Y-axis. For the teachers, there are two clusters, one containing twelve speakers with less-favourable or mid-range ratings, and the other comprising Cardiff11 and SW4 at the favourable end. The large and relatively low-scoring

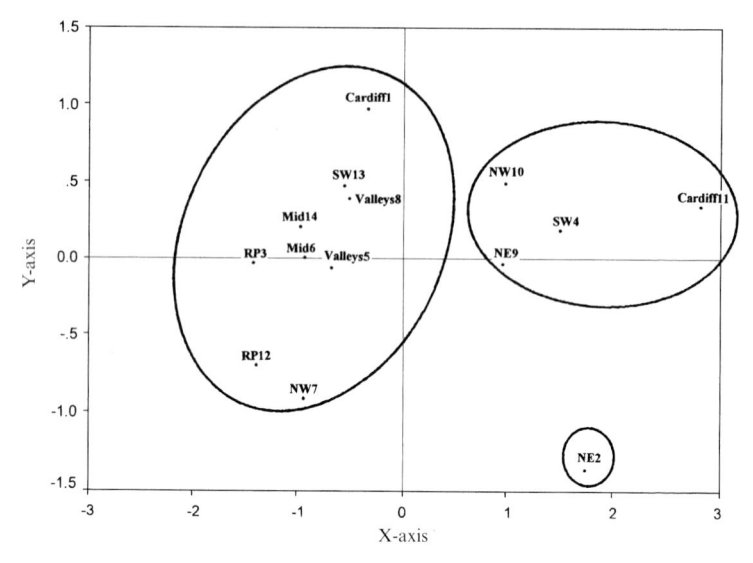

Figure 7.4: MDS and clusters for teenagers: 'Do you think this speaker is a good laugh?'

cluster in the students' display is a common feature for all of their affiliative scales, and it always contains the same narratives. These include a group of stories that can be judged as relatively 'harmless'. Cardiff1 felt sick but wasn't, RP3 cut his finger and had to sit down, RP12's accident victims didn't 'get squashed', Mid6's tractor didn't tip over, Mid14's clicking noise was just a bat, SW13's trailer rolled into a hedge, Valleys8's pump caused no distress. Two more stories are also included: NW7 (brick on crash-helmet), which has the slowest speech-rate of the fourteen stories, and Valleys5 (father's foot), which has the highest degree of hesitation (and, understandably, sadness too) in the delivery.

The number of clusters that forms from the students' data shows regularity across the other affiliative scales: always three, except for *make friends* where there are four (two of these are single-speaker 'clusters'). This regularity is not found in the teachers' data, where the number of clusters ranges from two for *good laugh* to five *you like* (albeit with two singles again). Within the teachers' clusters in the affiliative scales, some patterning is also evident. The two-cluster outcome for *good laugh*, in which the RP speakers fall into the much larger and less well-evaluated of the two clusters in figure 7.3, belies the

THE NARRATIVES STUDY 163

way in which teachers' affiliative judgements of these speakers contrast with those of the teenagers. Whereas the RP speakers are always included in the teenagers' lowest-rated affiliative clusters, they fall into higher-rated teachers' clusters for *make friends*, *like you* and *you like*. And in the latter two, they find themselves separated from each other in different highly rated clusters. There is more consistent patterning in the teachers' affiliative data with regard to the two Valleys speakers, who always appear together in the lowest-rated cluster. NW7 always accompanies the Valleys speakers in this cluster, and these are joined by Mid14, NE2 and Cardiff1 in all but *make friends*. Comparisons with the students' affiliative evaluations are revealing. The position of NE2 as a single 'cluster' in figure 7.4 typifies their view of him. A mid-ranking (mean = 2.97) *good laugh* he may be, but he is distinctive. His excursion into the glitz of nightclubs, alcohol and pop-bands makes his story more remote from their world than the other stories. As with *interesting story*, the teachers do not share this assessment.

There is evidence, especially noticeable when turning to the more favourable clusters, that there is interplay between dialect and non-dialect features influencing evaluative patterns. It is particularly interesting to the concerns of this study that some speakers project strong confirmations of their regional stereotypes through their narratives: SW4's rugby-player is very much in keeping with the sporting image of the rural south-west. NE2's chance encounter with rock-groups reflects the image of youth from the Liverpool-influenced north-east. Cardiff11's story too has urban connotations of streetwise kids holding their own in pool-halls. It may be this well-performed fulfilment of such different regional stereotypes that not only separates them from each other (for example, SW rural versus NE urban), but also separates them from the other members of their respective pairs who do not confirm the stereotypes so well. Cardiff1, for example, is unambiguously not in his urban home, but abroad in Spain in a story that has no Cardiff associations. The division of NW10 from NW7 may reflect a similar process.

In the questionnaire study, the north-west Wales dialect community attracted a clear preponderance of negative over positive stereotyped affective evaluations, vividly exemplified in the comment by one respondent: 'slow, makes speakers seem mentally deficient'. NW7, with his slow delivery about someone who is clearly portrayed as not very bright, does indeed appear to evoke the negative stereotype in his own speech-style. Slow speech-rates can attract negative evaluations on competence and social-attractiveness dimensions, especially for younger speakers (Stewart and Ryan, 1982). NW10 escapes this through a story that is not only faster in its delivery, but is about someone who is skilful and enterprising enough to build machines and do exciting things with them. It is interesting too that SW4's speech-rate is also comparatively slow, but he nevertheless gains favourable ratings. In this case, it may be that his low word-per-minute count results from a performance strategy to enhance the impact of his delivery, as he holds and savours his sibilants in the key words 'massive' and 'disgusting'.

There is no evidence in figures 7.3 and 7.4 of regional provenance alone having an impact on the clustering. It is notable that this is the case for the students' evaluations on all the affiliative scales, but for *you like* and *like you*, there is some evidence of a Welsh–English dimension on the Y-axis, with the 'English' varieties (RP, NE and Mid) falling into one half of the displays, and the 'Welsh' varieties (SW, Valleys, NW, Cardiff) falling into the other half. These trends are not strong enough to cause the speakers to cluster into those groups but are undercurrents in the more salient (that is, clustered) divisions, suggesting an ingroup–outgroup process at work based on Englishness and Welshness as well as (though weaker in their effects than) story features. In the teachers' other affiliative scales, although there are the above-mentioned patterns in the positioning of the RP and Valleys speakers, neither pair ever appears in its own unique RP or Valleys cluster, again indicating that features of the narrative performances are affecting judgements.

Good at school *judgements*

Figure 7.5 shows the teachers' results for *good at school*. Here, there is a conspicuous RP versus Valleys opposition, as they form their own unique clusters. The X-axis moves from 'not good' (to the right) to 'good' (to the left), from the Valleys cluster at the former end to the RP cluster at the other, as if the social background of the RP speakers confers educational advantages that the Valleys cannot achieve. All the other speakers find themselves in a single structure between these two pairs.

How do the students deal with this question? In table 7.1, the RP speakers attracted almost identical mean scores. However, in figure 7.6, they are separated from each other. They are both 'loners', clustering with no one. Mid6 and Mid14 are clustered as a pair. Thereafter, two

THE NARRATIVES STUDY

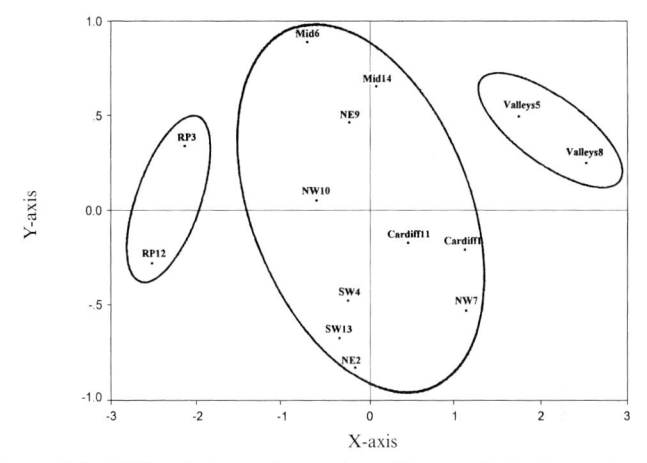

Figure 7.5: MDS and clusters for teachers: 'Do you think this speaker does well at school?'

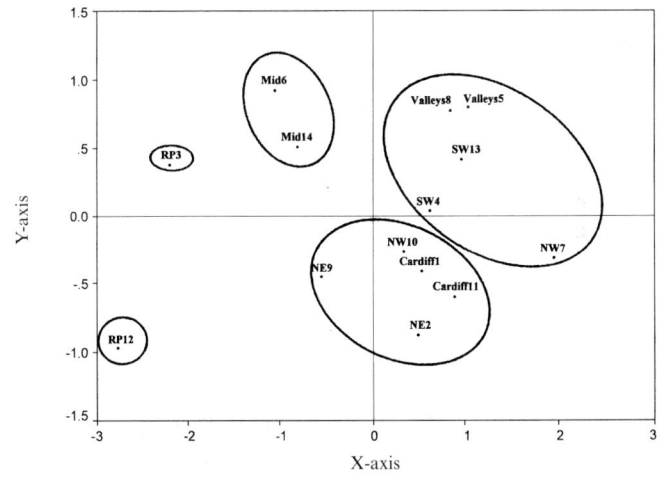

Figure 7.6: MDS and clusters for teenagers: 'Do you think this speaker does well at school?'

large clusters remain. One of these is low on the Y-axis: the two Cardiff speakers, the two NE speakers and NW10. The other group comprises the two SW speakers, the Valleys pair and NW7. The students seem to see this issue of school success partly in terms of an English–Welsh dimension, with the anglicized varieties set in their own cluster, and the Welsh varieties in theirs (NW10 excepted). But there is also a spread along the Y-axis that partly resembles that of the teachers: the content of the narratives and the messages they send out about the speakers are of significance. The bottom half of the model contains narratives about the storytellers indulging in leisure activities: NE2 (nightclubbing), Cardiff11 (pool), Cardiff1 (bars in Spain). NE9 is out at a restaurant (albeit with his family). RP12, a cluster of his own, but far down the Y-axis, is with some friends watching people have narrow escapes at a fairground. None of these speakers is unambiguously projecting a staid home-environment where parents might be ensuring that they do their homework. Despite this, RP12 is singled out from the others; his likely success at school is not doubted by the students.

How Welsh? *judgements*

Figure 7.7 shows the students' *how Welsh* assessments generating four clusters. From left to right, these are interpretable in terms of Welshness on the left, moving towards increased Englishness to the right. Pairs find themselves unseparated, as we noted in our comments on the descriptive statistics, and each pair is held within the same cluster, reinforcing the view that regionality is conspicuously salient for this question. On the other hand, the English cluster is much tighter and less differentiated than the Welsh clusters. This is an important finding,

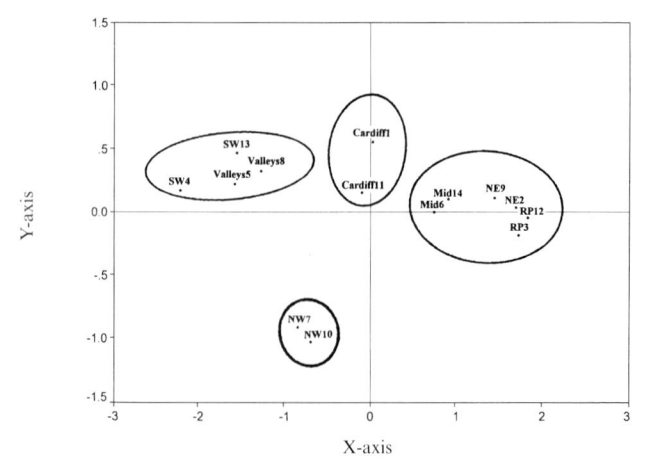

Figure 7.7: MDS and clusters for teenagers: 'How Welsh do you think this speaker sounds?'

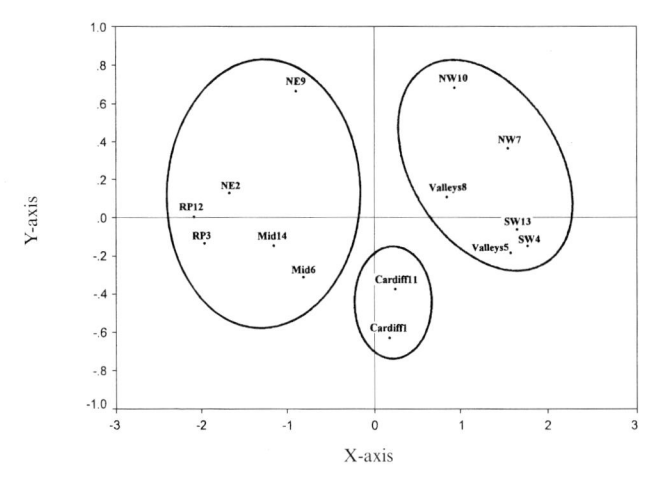

Figure 7.8: MDS and clusters for teachers: 'How Welsh do you think this speaker sounds?'

with NE and Mid speakers perceived to be as English as the RP speakers. SW Wales and the Valleys are represented as conjoined heartlands of Welsh identity. Cardiff finds its space somewhere in the middle, perhaps reflecting its popular image as a relatively anglicized city (but not anglicized enough to be included in the English cluster), and its official status as the Welsh capital (but not Welsh enough to be included in the heartlands cluster).

School students clearly have already well-developed and consistent perceptions of Welshness as indexed in the principal English-language varieties. But the MDS has spread the clusters out across a further dimension that the earlier focus on the overall means could not reveal. Though the other clusters are largely located in the top half of the Y-axis, the NW speakers are far to the bottom, suggesting that Welshness occupies other perceptual spaces. The NW English dialects are far more distinctively influenced by the Welsh language itself, and the NW is geographically more remote from large urban centres are than the SW and the Valleys. Most strikingly, if upper and lower halves are inverted (and since MDS is simply producing a spatial representation of quantitative distance data, this would be perfectly acceptable, as long as the spatial relationships amongst the speakers remain unchanged), it bears a close resemblance to a map of Wales, but with the Valleys shifted into a composite southern heartland. The suggestion here is that the Y-axis is fundamentally a perceptual north–south axis, but with the NE Liverpool-associated speakers coalesced into an 'eastern' 'English' hinterland.

The teachers' clusters in figure 7.8 follow a similar pattern, placing the 'English' speakers together in the left half. Cardiff again finds itself somewhere fairly central on the X-axis, though low on the Y-axis. But although the 'Welsh' speakers find themselves in much the same area of the model, the NW speakers are this time embraced into a single Welsh heartland. We consider this finding in the discussion of the keywords data in the next chapter.

Normative demands: the focus-group discussion data

As a postscript to the more formal analyses of this section, we can look briefly at parts of the focus-group discussion data, to revisit the 'peer performance' aspect of the study. What can we say, with hindsight, about the normative contexts in which the young people's narratives were performed and evaluated? What light do the group-discussion data throw on the cultural norms against which the stories were both performed and evaluated? An informal sampling of comments made in the discussion sessions suggests an interesting pattern of norms, and of 'normative demands', as being the relevant backdrop.

We selected the focus-group discussions held in schools in just two communities, in Cardiff and in south-west Wales (Carmarthen), and transcribed those parts of the discussions where discussants made comments to each other about just five of the fourteen 'targets' – narratives/storytellers. These targets of discussion were Cardiff11, NW10, SW4, Mid6 and RP3. These five were chosen because they spanned the widest extremes of social evaluation, as established by the other forms of analysis we have reported. Table 7.3 lists all the particular comments that were clearly audible in the relevant tape-recordings. Frequent overlapping turns and occasionally quite animated discussion often led to segments being less than fully audible. Italicized syllables mark heavy spoken emphasis. We identify discussants in the transcripts as being male (M) or female (F), but we did not collect any detailed background information on individuals, who would not in any event have been clearly identifiable in the data. Our ambition here is simply to 'test the water' of free-response, group-based, discursive evaluations, to assess the climate of values that was operative.

THE NARRATIVES STUDY

Table 7.3: Transcripts of responses from focus-group discussions with students

Free-discussion responses

Cardiff11 The pool-table

Cardiff kids' views:
1. (M) no he's that's quite *good* actually cos (conspiratorial) he could have *tiev*ed a few *games*
2. (M) 'a massive chainsaw' yeah he ex*agg*erated
3. (M) he's all right I suppose
4. (M) he's a bit stupid (M2) who's gonna stick their *hand* in the *hole*? (M3) *I've* done it
5. (M) he boasts he's a bullsh- sh- (laughs)
6. (M) he's from Cardiff
7. (M) he *saw* the opportunities and *went* for it (.) he didn't do it all the time I don't reckon
8. (M) he'd be all right with *us* cos he's a *bad* boy
9. (F) he acted *tough* (M) he didn't *act* it he *sound*ed it

Carmarthen kids' views:
10. (M) *well* (1.0) not having a good *run* with these now (.) I can't be*lieve* that he'd (.) most probably they just chopped the *edge* of it off not chopped the (.) *whole pool* table ((and all that)) and he wouldn't be concerned about his (.) *food* and *tea* (.) with his *hand stuck* in *there* would he (.) he he he'd be *pan*icking mun
11. (M) he *sound*ed a good *laugh*
12. (M) he sounded like *us* (.) we *we* do *that* every *day*
13. (M) he thought it was a big *joke* (.) after he was *say*ing it (.) and the way he was say he was *say*ing it as well he thought oh- I'm I'm *hard* now I (.) I put my *hand* down a *pool* table and stuff like that
14. (M) he sounds alright
15. (F) he sounds as if he can have a *laugh* without going too *far*
16. (F) I thought he was a bit of an *id*iot to put his hand down *there*
17. (M) like all of *us* (.) when (.) when we got no *less*ons or nothing we just go *out* play a*bout* and all that
18. (M) I got stuck in a horse
19. (M) I don't know if he's got a Welsh accent I don't think he'd be able to speak Welsh (.) I think he speaks English as a first language

NW10 Blaenau Ffestiniog The strange motorcyclist

Cardiff kids' views
20   (M) I think he was *ly*ing (.) lying or ex*agg*erating
21   (M) he's all right
22   (M) he talked like a *girl*
23   (M) he's a *boast*er
24   (M) from *In*dia or Outer Mong*o*lia
25   (F) gets into *trou*ble all the time
26   (F) goes round with all the *gangs* you know
27   (M) he had an accent anyway
28   (M) (stylized) '*mass*ive *whee*lie'
29   (M) just a *dill* innit
30   (M) he sounded daft

Carmarthen kids' views:
31   (M) we all know where *he* came from (.) north Wales
32   (M) bit of a *trou*blemaker
33   (F) Brooksideish (.) Gog
34   (M) go over a car (.) go over a po*lice* car at the same time and br- got his *knee*cap (.) that (would have) been on the *news* mun
35   (M) he sounds a *laugh*
36   (M) sounds like *Swan*sea *gangs* and all of that (.) you go round stealing stuff
37   (M) he knew (.) well he liked I think he liked what *I* liked as well... he knows what he's *talk*ing about like and *I* like bikes as *well*
38   (M) sounded *my* type of person
39   (F) no I think they *could* be a laugh but sometimes they go too *far* (.) *nick*ing a *gate*
40   (F) he sounded quite ad*ven*turous (.) bit of a *trou*blemaker
41   (M) he'll grow *out* of it one day

SW4 Carmarthen The fat rugby-player

Cardiff kids' views:
42   (M) you can't understand half the things he *says*
43   (F1) he's boring (F2) no that's just *Welsh*
44   (M) (stylized) 'belly'
45   (F) I'd think 'get a*way* from me'
46   (M) he sounds like he's *per*fect but
47   (M) oh he's from the Valleys this one Miss (.) he talks too fast
48   (M) (stylized) u:h
49   (M) (stylized) '*mass*ive'

THE NARRATIVES STUDY

Carmarthen kids' views:
(initial laughter)
50 (F) sounds like a guy in our class
51 (M) he's Welsh
52 (M) I was a bit confused what he was saying
53 (F) he's not as good with his language (.) he's probably getting his Welsh and his English mixed up
54 (M) he thinks he's it
55 (M) arsehole
56 (M) overbearing

Mid6 Newtown The tipping tractor

Cardiff kids' views:
57 (M) detailed
58 (M) boring
59 (F) as soon as he said tractor I fell asleep
60 (F) it would *all* have sounded more ex*ci*ting if they were talking about something *diff*erent
61 (M) a *trac*tor isn't a very at*trac*tive thing to talk about
62 (M) (stylized) 'Dorset'
63 (M) farmer
64 (M) (stylized) 'I got the mock like'
65 (M) sounds like a builder like

Carmarthen kids' views:
66 (M) he's all right
67 (F) nice voice not too *loud*
68 (M) if I was a *far*mer I'd turn round and say 'what happened next?' what sort of *dam*age there was on the tractor
69 (F) because we don't live on a farm we think it's a load of rubbish

RP3 Cheltenham The belt-sander accident

Cardiff kids' views:
70 (M) how may people d'you know talk like *that!*
71 (F) he sounds well spoken
72 (F) I feels ready to go to *bed* after that
73 (M) he talks *slow* like
74 (F) he's still a *moan*er (.) he's *E*nglish
75 (F) (stylized) 'oh oh uh my finger wu:h it's just come off uh uh uh'

76 (M) he's a big baby
77 (F) I reckon he's got spots and all that
78 (F) one of those dungareesish people

Carmarthen kids' views:
79 (F) he's got a nicer voice
80 (F) sounds like a *Chris*tian
81 (M) he sounds *swott*y like
82 (M) he was sympa*the*tic about himself
83 (M) I reckon he's a bit posh sounding (.) snob
84 (F) he's got a clearer accent like (.) like the way (to researcher) *you're* talking in English
85 (F) the *tone* of his voice was er bit (.) like (.) he had a better edu*ca*tion or something like private *school* or something
86 (M) I think probably he used his language you know more freely that the other ones (.) they kept to the same sort of words

There is of course the difficulty that individual focus-groups, in the absence of strong direction from a group leader (which we wanted to avoid), will tend to hit on specific themes and in that way develop their own evaluative agenda as a session proceeds. Nevertheless, some discursive themes recur in respect of judgements made about several of the targets. Interestingly, we get a sense that some of the social norms implicit in these evaluative themes are internally quite complex and finely balanced.

This is the case with the perceived dimension that simultaneously involves what we can call 'personal authenticity' and 'interestingly extravagant behaviour'. Note how many of the individual comments in the table attend to aspects of these qualities. Cardiff11 is held to have 'exaggerated' (line 2) and to be a 'boaster' and a 'bullshitter' (the obvious if uncompleted description in 5). There is in fact some extensive debate of Cardiff11's personal authenticity in the Cardiff group discussion. At (10), a male discussant undermines the speaker's claim that the whole pool table was sawn in half, and that he would in real life have been 'panicking'. The Cardiff discussants similarly undermine NW10 for 'lying' (20) and being a 'boaster' (23). Some members of the Carmarthen group agree that 'going over the police car' is implausible, because 'it would have been on the news'. But another member says that 'Swansea gangs' do actually do that sort of thing.

So we have a contested discourse about authenticity and credibility in discussions of Cardiff11 and NW10, which is largely absent from discussions of the other three narratives selected for this analysis. This is no doubt because Cardiff11 and NW10 tell extravagant stories about experientially extreme episodes, for example involving 'a massive chainsaw', and doing 'a massive wheelie' on a motorbike, respectively. We get a sense, however, that the apparently negative comments about how credible these episodes are do not significantly undermine the social attractiveness of the speakers and their stories, and in fact that they might positively motivate it. An interesting story and an attractive teller/protagonist persona in this judgement context might actually require a narrative that skates on the boundary of plausibility, and of course these two speakers are very well liked by their peer-judges overall.

Extrapolating, we might say that we have discursive evidence of two competing narrative demands being made on youthful, male story-tellers and being invoked by the judges in discussion: *be extravagant* but also *be plausible*. The demand to be extravagant predicts that 'good stories' in this context will tend be about life outside the institutions of home and school, and about events that are threatening to those structures, involving a degree of antisocial, rebellious behaviour. They may be more surreal than real, tending towards the bizarre and the exotic. The cultural norms in which these values circulate is of course an aspirational culture as much as an 'actual' culture, and there is therefore a definite appeal in transcendence/extravagance. But 'not boasting' overmuch is a predictable constraint on all this.

A second set of narrative demands seems to exist in relation to tellers/protagonists 'being dynamic' and, at the same time, 'being in control', again with a tension between them. We can refer to them as the 'be intense' demand and the 'be resilient' demand. As suggested by the discussion comments transcribed in the table, to be successful, young male story-tellers have to perform their cultural norms with a definite intensity and certainly with some risk. At turn 1, a male discussant approves of Cardiff11's 'tieving' of a few games while at (7) another discussant commends him for 'seeing an opportunity and going for it'. The Cardiff focus-group reaches the opinion that Cardiff1 was indeed 'going for it' but simultaneously staying in control of the situation. The contributor at (9) is suggesting that Cardiff11 was not only 'acting tough' but that he sounded as if he actually *was* tough. At turns (13–14) some members of the Carmarthen group disagree about how 'hard' Cardiff11 really is, although they agree he treats the event as 'a big joke'. The male's comment at (14) challenges the previous speaker's view that he might not have been as hard as he thinks.

Overall, the groups seem to approve of Cardiff11's survivor narrative – of a kid who (almost literally) goes out on a limb, but copes. If we refer back to the text of Cardiff11's story we see that he actually does, in the narrative account, laugh at his own adversity. A few of the comments made about NW10 seem similarly to express admiration for his persona as 'quite adventurous' and as 'a bit of a troublemaker' (40). There are interesting ingrouping remarks made about each of the two favoured speakers, with claims that their actions and personalities are like those of the discussant group members themselves (see turns 4, 8, 12, 17, 37, 38). Groups who in discussion are relatively accepting and approving of a speaker and his narrativized identity seem to align themselves discursively with him, pointing up the credentials that make him one of them – for example, 'he'd be all right with us cos he's a bad boy' (8).

By contrast, the least-favoured speakers of this subset, Mid6 and RP3, are severely downgraded in the discussions for their lack of dynamism and coping skills. So Mid6 is 'boring' (58) and his tractor topic is not at all 'exciting' (60). RP3 makes one discussant feel 'ready to go to bed after that' (72). He is also held to be a 'moaner' (74) and 'a big baby' (76), an image that is creatively elaborated in following speaking turns. The Carmarthen group refer to RP3 as 'a Christian' (80), 'swotty' (81) and 'sympathetic about himself' (82). In subtly different ways each of these comments characterizes RP3, and to a lesser extent Mid6, as being conventional, dependent and non-resilient. Their reported mishaps are in each case relatively minor, in effect if not in potential – see the tipping tractor and belt-sander incident accounts in the texts of their stories. Dramatically intense possibilities opened up in the narratives (a tractor dangerously tipping over, potentially losing fingers, and being sick) fail to eventuate, and each protagonist seeks help from an authority figure, a father or a teacher, and is helped out of his difficult circumstances.

These themes from the group discussions are necessarily selective, but even the brief, illustrative quotes in table 7.3 merit much closer analysis and development. (Several of the quotations are interesting illustrations of kids' evaluative stances that we discussed earlier in this chapter, and return to later.) At the same time, perhaps the remarks in this section are sufficient to suggest a further useful line of inquiry for language attitudes research, and one that can pick up theoretical threads in linguistic anthropology about discourse, culture and performance. What we see in the group discussions, and in the interface between evaluative discussions and target narrative performances, is what Urban (1993) calls the 'cultural functioning' of discourse at work, or 'discourse in the service of collective social purpose' (p. 241). In fact, in the same source Urban specifically recognizes the potential of narrative in this culturally constitutive process. His claim is that 'narrative ... is capable of playing a normative role in establishing the desirability of certain kinds of contextually situated language use' (p.241). The young people's narratives that we are considering are a form of cultural practice where the norms of adolescence – and in particularly those of young males – are exposed in performance, then tested out, confirmed and challenged. 'Evaluating speech' in this context is partly a matter of assessing the degree of fit between performed identities and a group's partly tacit, partly explicit normative demands.

Conclusions

We pointed out in chapter 4 that young people of about fifteen years of age are at a critical stage in their lives, moving away from family identity towards more individual and peer-group identity. Many are about to move out of relatively stable and rooted sociocultural environments into more fluid and autonomous life-patterns, as they approach employment and new possibilities in their social relationships. Such developments, and their impact on self-concept, as well as, perhaps, the changes in physical appearance (Baker, 1992: 63), are key influences in the rapid sensitization to sociolinguistic norms and re-appraisal of sociolinguistic identities that occur at this age. The data we have reported here have shown how, overall, young Welsh people have in place a complex set of structured perceptions of themselves and their peers. This includes a differentiated set of social meanings, organized as variable value-ratings attaching to Welshness (and strongly divergent intergroup relations to RP-speaking English youngsters), to social attractiveness and to scholastic success. The data also show that only some of these values are carried by dialect. Uncontroversially, Welshness is taken to be marked, to highly variable degrees, through accents of English in Wales, but all other evaluative dimensions in the data relate to a complex interplay between dialect and discourse performance (indexed here through narrative content and style).

Our data reveal a rich stock of resources for young people in Wales to bolster or reconfigure their social identities at this crucial life-stage.

There are resources for maintaining ethnic allegiance to Wales and symbolic Welshness, through distance from RP speakers who are deemed unattractive, alien and to be orientating to mainstream school values. Specific varieties of English in Wales seem to have maintained the full force of their ethnic symbolism for young people, but other varieties (especially in north-east Wales and mid-Wales) are not differentiated in terms of Englishness from RP itself. Wales as a *pluriculture* is again confirmed. 'Anglicization' is not only a matter of Welsh-language shift. The general historic patterning of Welsh-language loss from west to east within Wales is strongly echoed in the perceived Welshness of the varieties of the English language found along the same continuum.

But there is also evidence that the social attractiveness often said to be a recurrent accompaniment of 'non-standard' dialects may be achieved by quite different symbolic routes – and, in these data, just as importantly through innovative and humorous narrative-telling as by dialect alone. The data suggest that the dialect semiotic, while still powerfully active in some dimensions of self- and other- definition, works alongside other factors for young Welsh people, whose verbal performance-styles have at least an equal influence on social evaluations. Future research on Welsh ethnic identity therefore needs to address language attitudes as a far more complex and contextualized phenomenon than has been assumed.

We also noted in chapter 4 how, with their gatekeeping function, teachers are a significant professional group of adults in the lives of these young people. The formal and informal judgements they make about teenagers include the social evaluation of linguistic style, even to the point where this can influence formal school-assessment outcomes. The data show that, on the whole, the teachers were prepared to make rather similar evaluations to those of the teenagers, suggesting some empathy with their perspectives. Despite this, however, there are revealing differences. The teachers gave higher ratings to the more 'innocent' stories, and were less approving of stories involving physical injury or potential scrapes with the law. In so doing, they suggested a cultural gap between themselves and the teenagers in terms of pro-social and anti-social stances. In the affiliative ratings, the same difference occurs again in teachers' and teenagers' judgements of less innocent stories (for example, NE2's nightclub experience), and there is also a comparable pro- and anti-social contrast in the evaluations of the RP speakers.

For both teachers and teenagers, the Valleys speakers find themselves in lower-rated clusters, but in the case of the teenagers, RP speakers are to be found sharing these clusters with the Valleys pair. In contrast, the teachers make a distinction between these pairs in all of their affiliative evaluations except *good laugh*. Considering *good at school* outcomes alongside the affiliative ones, teachers understandably feel more affinity with those speakers who stereotypically strive for and achieve teachers' professional goal of producing successful students (that is, the RP speakers), rather than those who are not stereotypically associated with such success (particularly, in this case, the Valleys speakers). The young adults, on the other hand, do not (and perhaps refuse to) accept a link in their peers between success at school, where they differentiate the likely outcomes for school success, distinguishing the RP speakers from the Valleys speakers, and those for social attractiveness, where these speakers are lumped together.

In this part of our study, the use of uncontrolled-speech data has undoubtedly meant looking closely at a wide range of explanatory factors in the consideration of the data. But this has not led to the hopeless quagmire that is often assumed. Rather, it has proved possible to make use of a variety of statistical techniques that have been relatively little used in language attitudes and other sorts of sociolinguistic research, and these have made it possible to search through the factors to detect some revealing patterns in responses linked to dialects, stereotypes and narrative characteristics. These can be linked to less formal, qualitative, but still revealing commentaries, of the sort that we developed for the focus-group data. Basing our study on reactions to unscripted language in use has allowed interpretations that have gone further than the more controlled research traditions, towards understanding how dialect and communicative performance can work with and against each other in relatively systematic ways along evaluative dimensions.

In the light of findings of the sort presented here, what has often been referred to as 'speech evaluation' or 'accent evaluation' now needs to be reconceptualized as the evaluation of *speech performance*, or of *dialect in discourse*. This simple relabelling seems to us to entail a significant realignment of sociolinguistic studies of dialect. The narratives study so far has suggested that the social meanings of dialect performances lie in the systematic interaction of phonological and other markers with features of rhetorical style (such as speech rate, fluency, key) and probably content (such as local/global, pro/anti-establishment, self/other focus). If this is so, then it will be necessary to transcend the fiction of discrete dialect varieties with apparently bounded meanings. Dialect sociolinguistics will need to address the encoding and reception of dialect forms as part of individuals' and communities' total 'meaning potential', in Halliday's (1978) phrase. Dialect needs to feature as an integrated component of a sociolinguistic theory of language in use, rather than as the focus of an autonomous dialectology.

8

Keyword responses

Our focus in this chapter is on the teenagers' responses to the open-ended item asking them to write down their first impressions of the speakers in what we are calling 'keywords'. It should be remembered that the teenagers were asked to throw these down quickly, so as to elicit their immediate cognitive responses. In order to achieve this, it was necessarily the case that no time was permitted for the careful and thoughtful selection of terms that most accurately and unambiguously summed up their impressions. Moreover, as with any folk comments on language, responses range along a continuum of global to specific character (Preston, 1996). Furthermore, since the teenagers were responding to audio-recordings of fourteen different speakers, each presenting their own narrative, their keywords might refer to some quality of the speaker's narrative (content, performance etc.) or to a quality of the English dialect of the speaker, or to the speaker himself. Inevitably, it was sometimes not clear quite which of these a keyword referred to. For example, the Valleys5 story related events leading to the speaker's father losing his foot in a traffic accident. Hence, in this context, the keyword 'sad' was difficult to interpret. It might have referred to the accident in the story, a quality showing through in the boy's voice, or it could even have been intended as a negative evaluation of the speaker with its contemporary counter-empathetic use (in the UK, at least), as it most certainly was with other speakers. Such variabilities work very much against the convention of attempting to place all the data into rigorous categories for subsequent ease of analysis, a procedure which, as Potter and Wetherell (1987: 41) have rightly pointed out, may also risk obscuring other interesting differences in the data.

On the other hand, it was obviously not feasible or worthwhile to pursue all of the 5,261 keywords individually. Some items grouped together very obviously: for example, 'not interesting' and 'uninteresting', and it would have made little sense to pursue them as separate semantic items. There were, though, some isolated items which did seem to deserve a little checking individually, some of which proved more illuminating (for example, the response 'boring') than others. Hence there is some selectivity in the cases we consider below, discussing some of the most obvious and interesting groupings, but also some single items.

Overall keywords findings

We can certainly make two overall statements at the outset. One is that these young people's evaluations of their peers emphasized *negativity*. The second is that there was a considerable *range* of evaluative content in the keywords. One plausible explanation for these properties is that, if fifteen is an age at which teenagers are *exploring* a range of available identities, this may require an equivalent range of differentiating evaluative descriptors. And positioning themselves in relation to this range of identities is likely to mean rejecting more than they find acceptable, and so lead to more negative than favourable reactions. This developmental phase of experimentation with different roles and behaviours, which seems to prevail during middle adolescence, has been referred to by Marcia (1980) as 'identity moratorium'. Gavin and Furman (1989: 832) also draw attention to the high degree of negative or antagonistic interactions amongst adolescents at fourteen to sixteen years of age, and point to three important functions served by such antagonism at this age. One is that it boosts the teenagers' own self-worth. The other two operate more obviously at the group level. Antagonisms impose similarity among members, with nonconformity being punished. Then, antagonisms lead to greater within-group dominance hierarchies with confirmed leaders and followers, eventually reducing antagonism.

Taboo/pejorative items

Given the fact that the teenagers were encouraged to write down whatever their first impressions were of the speakers and narratives, it perhaps comes as no surprise that a large proportion of the items they wrote were what are here termed 'taboo' items (for example, 'dickhead', 'twat', 'wanker', 'prat', etc.). Also included in this group are items that are not strictly taboo, but pejorative, with similar, albeit milder, force (such as, 'wimp', 'drip'). These items warrant some discussion, since they accounted for a full 10.63 per cent of all keywords, seemingly constituting a considerable proportion of the teenagers' evaluative lexical repertoires, and indeed forming a sizeable repertoire in themselves of some 112 different items. Similarly, de Klerk (1997) found a rich variety of items in a study of expletives, but in that study respondents were specifically asked to produce expletives rather than linguistic evaluations of any nature they chose – expletive or non-expletive. Interestingly, in published language attitudes studies where judges' free responses have been trawled for evaluative terms prior to the main study (see chapter 3), such taboo items are not given even a passing mention. Yet it is hard to imagine that they would not have featured at all. De Klerk (1997: 147) notes that one expects slang and expletives to abound amongst teenagers, since their functions include the reinforcement of group membership and the signalling of shared knowledge and interests. On the other hand, their omission in such research reports might be understandable, if they are seen to be of no real value for the construction of semantic-differential scales, and given, too, the tendency for the messiness of the research process to be hidden from view in most published work (Holmes and Ainsworth, 1997).

Identifying the specific semantic features of taboo words is problematic. As far as possible, items placed in this grouping were those that could be reasonably regarded as not being intended by their users to carry any specific or literal meaning. Some items had some clear reference to another group of items, and so were not included in this general list. For example, it was fairly clear from the juxta-positioning with other keywords that 'sheepshagger' and 'shitshoveller' referred to farming activity, and hence these were included with the other 'farming' words. Hence not all taboo words were included in this taboo/pejorative grouping.

It is striking that some of the regional communities of judges have *used* these items far more than others. Just over a quarter, 25.78 per cent, of all the keywords produced by the Valleys judges fall into this category, and 20.14 per cent of all those provided by the mid-Wales judges. In contrast, the other figures are the north-east (7.16 per cent), south-west (4.72 per cent), Cardiff (4.54 per cent), and north-west (3.72 per cent). However, the data were collected in one single session within each region, so these differences cannot be confidently attributed to significant cultural differences among the regions themselves. The effect of this large proportion produced by the Valleys, however, does mean that they produce fewer other lexical/phrasal items, as is evident below.

Interpretation of the way these items are aimed at the different speakers is, once again, not straightforward. Looking at the mean scores for the narratives scales-ratings data (set out in table 7.1), there is a striking general negativity in the teenagers' quantitative judgements, with scarcely any mean scores rising above the mid-point of the scale. It is tempting, then, to see this large group of taboo items as a reflection of these generally negative evaluations. But this interpretation does not hold, since the most popular and positively (or least negatively) rated speaker overall in the scales results is Cardiff11, who attracts the second-largest proportion of these items (14.56 per cent of all the keywords written about him). Nor is the opposite interpretation tenable that such items are meant favourably – for example, that you have to be a 'prat' to be liked – since the RP speakers are consistently downgraded on all but the *good at school* scale in the quantitative data, yet they too attract high proportions (RP3, 13.24 per cent; RP12, 12.99 per cent). The best interpretation is that many of these items (for example, 'prat') have *variable* force, and others (for example, 'arsehole') might much less variably be meant negatively (but the rich assortment of 112 items was too thinly spread across the judges and speakers to tease out such distinctions). Notwithstanding the low numbers of instances, some support for this view is found by just comparing RP3 and Cardiff11. They are labelled 'prat' seven times and nine times respectively. 'Knob' is used for Cardiff11 fourteen times and four times for RP3. Cardiff11 is seemingly 'enjoyed' because he is seen to be an entertaining and amusing 'prat' or 'knob', alongside other very positive evaluations about his association with pool-halls, for example. RP3 is put down seemingly because he is deemed to sound like an upper-class wimpish 'prat' or 'knob' who cannot manage without teacher's help.

For the most part, this group of labels can be regarded as offensive, at least in traditional terms and taking the 'establishment' view. In addition to this, it is noteworthy that they are overwhelmingly nominal rather than adjectival. Furthermore, they are categorial nominals. Hence, coding a speaker as 'an arsehole' relegates the speaker to a social category of *arseholes*. Many such items then are outgrouping. Thus these evaluative items are not only hanging an attribute on an individual, but also placing an individual in a social space, and indicating where the evaluator stands in relation to that space. This is an important and specific function of evaluation.

Boring

A UK media portrayal of adolescent characters (specifically, 'Kevin' in BBC television's satirical comedy show *Harry Enfield and Chums*) has generated an indelible association between the use of the word 'boring' and (at least young and mid-) teenagers. This characterization is amply supported by the keywords data, with 'boring' being by far the most frequently used single item of all the items, even without taking into account the more specific collocations of 'boring story', 'boring voice', etc. The item 'boring' accounts for 9.77 per cent of all keywords, almost as many as the whole of the above taboo category.

It appears to convey a general sense of lack of engagement by the listener for some or other reason. The use of this item can again be seen as outgrouping, though, we would suggest, by a different route from the taboo items above. This time the speaker is not relegated to a named group or crowd, but is outgrouped through judges signalling that they are not engaged with the speakers or narratives currently. 'Boring' is something of an umbrella response, in that the lack of engagement might be caused by a whole range of factors. This becomes particularly obvious when attempting to look for other items with which it might be grouped – hence it is considered alone here, in its own right. One might try to group it with an item such as 'uninteresting', or, equally, with 'not exciting' or 'not funny', though from the data it would be impossible to justify grouping it with one rather than another of these, and there are at the same time good reasons for wanting to make distinctions among 'uninteresting', 'not exciting' and 'not funny'. At times, the collocation with other keywords by the same judge suggests that a speaker or narrative might be boring because of slow delivery, or frequent pauses, or because he 'goes on'. For the judges, 'boring' can usefully relate to some aspect of the narrative performance (dialect, tempo, monotone) or some component of the narrative content (an uninteresting story, lacking excitement, lacking humour), or both at once, or some more enduring perception of the speaker's personality.

The item would present difficulties to a researcher collecting keywords solely to construct semantic-differential scales. If 'boring' were one end of a scale, what would go at the other end? The choice would be crucial to the interpretation the judge would be most likely to place upon 'boring'. 'Boring' would derive its more specific meaning from the other item and, in doing so, would doubtless lose the sense in which it is used within the evaluative culture of these adolescents. Perhaps the polar opposite is 'acceptable', or 'normal', or 'like us'.

Nevertheless, its general meaning of lack of engagement turns out to be a very useful general measure for the present discussion. In contrast to the use of the taboo items, the negativity of this item can be asserted with more confidence. For example, a brief glance at the data in table 8.1 shows that the rank ordering of the speakers in terms of both *good laugh* and *interesting story* roughly reverses the rank ordering according to the number of mentions of the word 'boring'. It is particularly noticeable that although the most popular of the speakers according to the scales (Cardiff11) attracted the second most taboo items (see above), he attracts almost *no mentions at all* of 'boring' (a mere 1.21 per cent of all his keywords).

Table 8.1: Keyword 'boring' comments about speakers, compared with mean scores for *interesting story* and *good laugh* in the scales data

Speaker	'Boring' as percentage of comments	Interesting story	Good laugh
Mid14	16.76	1.86	1.98
Cardiff1	15.52	1.87	2.34
Mid6	15.01	1.89	1.99
Valleys8	14.13	1.79	2.16
RP3	14.05	1.78	1.70
RP12	13.97	1.99	1.88
SW13	13.60	1.89	2.16
Valleys5	10.79	2.58	2.16
NW7	7.53	2.52	2.27
NE9	5.60	2.71	3.24
NW10	4.13	3.28	2.97
SW4	4.00	2.60	3.17
NE2	2.15	2.87	2.97
Cardiff11	1.21	3.69	3.75

There are differences in the extent to which the different judging communities use 'boring' (and confirm the Harry Enfield stereotype). The north-east (13.08 per cent), Cardiff (12.84 per cent) and the Valleys (12.43 per cent) use the term markedly more than the south-west (8.53 per cent), mid (5.58 per cent) and the north-west (4.92 per cent), suggesting a split between those living in relatively industrial areas and those living in rural communities. Possibly, the more rural communities are operating with higher tolerance or higher 'thresholds of boredom', or at least may be less prone to downgrading speakers of their own age for failing to engage them.

Welshness/Englishness

Of the keywords written by the entire sample of teenagers, 388 (7.37 per cent) referred to the Welshness or Englishness of the speaker/ narrative. This is again a sizeable proportion. Set in the context of the findings in the questionnaire study, and the scaled responses in the narratives study, such data provide further confirmation that this is a particularly meaningful and active component of the evaluation of language in certain (especially post-colonial) contexts, and a particularly salient dimension for these young people in Wales. As we have stated previously, ethnic or cultural provenance is overlooked in much earlier language attitudes work, and hence, presumably for this reason, does not surface among the judgemental dimensions found by Zahn and Hopper (1985). Table 8.2 shows the distribution of these keywords (horizontally) across speakers and also (vertically) across the communities of judges.

Overall, these frequencies are a good reflection of the results from the scaled items on the questionnaire, dividing the speakers into an 'English' grouping of RP and north-east, with the others more frequently attributed 'Welsh' qualities. Mid-Wales finds a somewhat more ambiguous position in the keywords data than in the scales data, though the number of ethnicity comments for both the mid-Wales speakers is low. Cardiff's dual image as, on the one hand, the capital city of Wales and, on the other, a somewhat anglicized urban centre, is reflected once again in the relatively mid position of these two speakers. Interestingly, they are divided here, with Cardiff11 (the most popular of all the speakers/narratives in the scales data) having around the same low proportion of items describing him as 'Welsh' as the 'English'

Table 8.2: Number of keyword references to Welshness and Englishness used by teenage judges in the six communities for the fourteen speakers (figures in brackets are the numbers as percentage totals produced by communities)

Speakers		NE	NW	SW	Cardiff	Mid	Valleys	Totals Eng and Welsh	Totals Eng PLUS Welsh
Cardiff1	Welsh	14 (17.07)	4 (9.30)	7 (8.64)	3 (3.74)	0	0	28 (8.36)	29 (8.66)
	Eng	1 (1.22)	0	0	0	0	0	1 (0.30)	
NE2	Welsh	0	0	0	0	0	0	0	12 (3.23)
	Eng	1 (1.43)	5 (10.20)	6 (6.74)	0	0	0	12 (3.23)	
RP3	Welsh	0	0	0	0	0	0	0	6 (1.62)
	Eng	0	1 (2.00)	5 (5.95)	0	0	0	6 (1.62)	
SW4	Welsh	12 (13.95)	11 (20.75)	4 (4.82)	10 (17.86)	10 (16.95)	5 (7.94)	52 (13.00)	52 (13.00)
	Eng	0	0	0	0	0	0	0	
Valleys5	Welsh	10 (13.70)	13 (20.97)	1 (1.37)	2 (4.00)	2 (3.77)	1 (1.45)	29 (7.63)	29 (7.63)
	Eng	0	0	0	0	0	0	0	
Mid6	Welsh	1 (1.43)	0	2 (2.63)	0	2 (3.28)	0	5 (1.34)	13 (3.49)
	Eng	1 (1.43)	5 (9.62)	2 (2.63)	0	0	0	8 (2.14)	
NW 7	Welsh	0	12 (20.69)	19 (23.75)	2 (2.90)	8 (12.50)	1 (1.45)	42 (9.88)	42 (9.88)
	Eng	0	0	0	0	0	0	0	
Valleys8	Welsh	2 (2.78)	7 (14.29)	18 (24.66)	4 (8.16)	10 (14.93)	3 (4.62)	44 (11.73)	46 (12.27)
	Eng	0	1 (2.04)	0	1 (2.04)	0	0	2 (0.53)	
NE9	Welsh	0	0	0	0	0	0	0	23 (6.44)
	Eng	0	6 (12.50)	16 (21.05)	1 (2.17)	0	0	23 (6.44)	

Speakers		NE	NW	SW	Cardiff	Mid	Valleys	Totals 1	Totals 2
NW10	Welsh	9 (13.85)	6 (9.84)	22 (30.99)	3 (6.12)	9 (21.95)	0	49 (14.45)	50 (14.75)
	Eng	0	1 (1.64)	0	0	0	0	1 (0.29)	
Cardiff11	Welsh	0	4 (7.14)	1 (1.14)	2 (3.23)	1 (1.64)	0	8 (1.94)	10 (2.43)
	Eng	0	1 (1.76)	1 (1.14)	0	0	0	2 (0.49)	
RP12	Welsh	0	0	0	0	1 (1.82)	0	1 (0.25)	23 (5.64)
	Eng	0	6 (9.84)	13 (15.85)	0	1 (1.82)	2 (2.78)	22 (5.39)	
SW13	Welsh	7 (10.45)	15 (26.32)	9 (11.84)	5 (8.06)	4 (7.41)	1 (1.69)	41 (10.93)	42 (11.2)
	Eng	0	0	0	1 (1.61)	0	0	1 (0.27)	
Mid14	Welsh	0	1 (1.89)	5 (7.14)	0	0	0	6 (1.76)	11 (3.42)
	Eng	0	3 (5.66)	1 (1.43)	1 (1.79)	0	0	5 (1.47)	
Totals for Welsh		55 (5.29)	73 (9.71)	88 (7.99)	31 (4.03)	47 (6.39)	11 (1.28)		
Totals for English		3 (0.29)	29 (3.86)	44 (3.99)	4 (0.52)	1 (0.14)	2 (0.23)		
Totals for Eng PLUS Welsh		58 (5.58)	102 (13.56)	132 (11.98)	35 (4.55)	48 (6.53)	13 (1.51)		388 (7.37)

group has. However, in terms of comments about Englishness, Cardiff11 is here aligned with the 'Welsh' group. So the most likely explanation for Cardiff11's lack of comments about Welshness is that, given the comparative success of this speaker, respondents may have found themselves with a far richer stock of other first impressions to jot down in the three keyword slots available, so much so that Welshness, while important, may have been washed aside.

In terms of the numbers of comments about Welshness, the speakers from each dialect community tend to pair off, concurring with the earlier (MDS) findings from the narratives study. Despite the larger gaps in the numbers of Welshness comments between Cardiff1 and 11 (mentioned above), and between Valleys5 and 8 (twenty-nine and forty-six comments respectively), the overall pattern does again appear to suggest that these judgements are based primarily on dialect features rather than on any of the other variables in the speakers and narratives.

If the proportion of comments about Welshness is compared with those about Englishness, the proportion is comparatively low for Englishness. If all the Welshness and Englishness comments are collapsed into one 'ethnicity' category, then the five speakers that attract most of these comments are NW10 (14.75 per cent); SW4 (13 per cent); Valleys8 (12.27 per cent); SW13 (11.20 per cent), and NW7 (9.88 per cent). In all these cases, the comments are solely or almost solely about Welshness. And, taking all of the ethnicity words from the judges in all the communities about all of the speakers (388 words), it is striking that 78.6 per cent of them are references to Welshness. So, as a generalization for the whole pan-Wales set of judges, then, it might be argued from these keywords data that Welshness is a more salient characteristic in English than Englishness is for these teenagers.

This overall claim finds some support in the fact that those speakers attracting fewest comments about ethnicity (Cardiff11 aside) are RP3 (1.62 per cent); NE2 (3.23 per cent); Mid14 (3.42 per cent); Mid6 (3.49 per cent); RP12 (5.64 per cent); and NE9 (6.44 per cent), who are seen as mainly 'English' or fairly balanced (the mid-speakers). Englishness does have some salience, of course, and it is noticeable that it appears to hold more salience for certain communities. Table 8.2 shows that almost all of the eighty-three comments about Englishness (mainly directed at the north-east, RP, and mid speakers) come from the judges in the north-west (twenty-nine comments, or 3.86 per cent of all their keywords) and the south-west (forty-four comments, or 3.99 per cent). However, these are still far fewer than the comments they make about Welshness, even allowing for the fact that there was a greater number of speakers remaining for whom Welsh labels might be used (the north-west, south-west, Valleys, and Cardiff speakers). The south-west judges make eighty-eight comments about Welshness (7.99 per cent of all their keywords), and the north-west judges make seventy-three (9.71 per cent).

The above 'pan-Wales' observation needs some additional qualification. Most of the comments rained upon RP3 and RP12 about Englishness come from the south-west. These are sometimes expressed simply as 'English', with the same judge using other keywords such as 'posh' and 'snob', as if the term 'English' itself carries a pejorative intensity rather than a mere factual reference. Elsewhere, Englishness is expressed with more conspicuous hostility: for example, 'English, enough said!', and the word 'English' accompanied by a swastika and skull-and-crossbones! This is an illuminating supplement to the scales data. Here the teenagers are turning their attention to the outgroup, vividly elaborating on how they view Englishness. The inclusion of a *How English do you think this person sounds?* scale would not have made so clear the character of such hostility and intensity, nor the pragmatic force of 'Englishness' for the south-west judges.

The south-west and the north-west are the communities that have most to say about ethnicity (11.98 per cent and 13.56 per cent of their comments respectively). These are the two heartlands of Welsh identity and areas where the Welsh language is still relatively strong (Aitchison and Carter, 1994), and connotations of Welshness are high, as findings we considered earlier have shown. Those with by far the least to say about ethnicity are the Valleys judges (1.51 per cent). However, even if one cannot describe the Valleys as a stronghold for the Welsh language, the region undoubtedly holds clear connotations of Welshness, just as the south-west and north-west do, so one might expect to see more comments about ethnicity on the same sort of scale as from the SW and NW judges. It is possible that the reason for this lack of comment on ethnicity is caused by the exceptionally high proportion of their keywords that were 'used up' in the taboo category.

The 'how Welsh' scale results also have further light cast on them from an examination of the comments made by the south-west and north-west judges about each other's speakers. Table 8.2 shows that this is in fact where the greatest exchange about Welshness takes place. The south-west judges' comments about the north-west speakers are arguably exclusionary. They make nineteen Welshness comments aimed at NW7, of which sixteen are accounted for by the items 'gog', from the Welsh 'gogledd' 'north', (twelve occurrences), 'North Wales' (two), and 'North Walian' (two), indicating that the south-west see Welshness as having regional differentiation. Their twenty-two similar comments about NW10 include six 'gog', four 'North Walian', four 'from North Wales', and three 'North Wales accent'. In contrast, of the north-west informants' eleven Welshness items about SW4, nine are simply 'Welsh', as are thirteen of their fifteen comments about SW13, as if ingrouping their SW neighbours. Although we have mentioned earlier the idea of the north-west being perceived as 'differently' Welsh, the keywords suggest that this view may not be shared by the north-west (for example, in a claim to be exclusive), and that the south-west plays a strong role in this dynamic.

Farming and other activities

Table 8.3 shows the results for a group of items exemplified by 'farmer', 'country type', 'sheepshagger', etc. These comments are made mainly about Valleys5 (10.26 per cent), Mid6 (14.26 per cent) and SW13 (9.87). The stories themselves are rural in content, each of them relating an event which happened to the speaker himself. There is one other unambiguously rural story involving the speaker (Valleys8) that does not attract so many comments of this type (1.6 per cent), possibly because this one differs from the others in that it does not involve an accident and is more about having fun, and there is no suggestion that the speaker himself actually lives on a farm.

It is also worth noting that most of these comments about 'farmers', 'farmer's boys', etc., are made by just three communities of judges: mid (5.71 per cent); south-west (4.17 per cent) and north-west (4.12 per cent), the others making far fewer (north-east, 1.44 per cent; Cardiff, 0.91 per cent; Valleys, 0.46 per cent). These connotations of farming and rural life are most powerful, then, for the judges from the first three communities, and this can be attributed to the rurality of the judges *themselves*. The salience is undoubtedly generated by the contact (for example, in rural market-towns), throwing agricultural life into sharp contrast with the lure (perhaps especially for adolescents) of global culture and urban lifestyles. These rural stories were rated negatively on most of the scales in the data, so these comments can be reasonably interpreted as a rejection of farming and country life.

With large areas of Wales still very much dependent on agriculture, currently in crisis economically, the prospect of few obvious alternative local opportunities for their future may be making this evaluative factor a very sensitive one, in some regions in particular. For the teenagers in relatively urbanised industrialized regions, the lifestyles and social attributes of farmers are not an issue, of course. They do not come across them to the same extent (if at all).

In some ways, it might seem unremarkable that stories about farms should attract these sorts of comments. But the results take on more importance if considered alongside other keyword findings. It is notable that Cardiff11, though a city kid engaged in playing pool, does not attract a lot of comment about the activity of playing pool. It is also worth noting that RP12 does not attract comment about going to funfairs. One might argue that the cases of Cardiff11 and RP12 are quite different in that they do not concern economic activities but recreational

Table 8.3: Number of references to 'farmer', 'country-type', 'sheepshagger' etc., in the six judging communities for the fourteen speakers (figures in brackets are the numbers expressed as percentages of total keywords produced by communities)

Communities

Speaker	NE	NW	SW	Cardiff	Mid	Valleys	Speaker total
Cardiff1	0	0	0	0	0	0	0
NE2	0	0	0	0	0	0	0
RP3	0	0	0	0	0	0	0
SW4	0	0	0	0	1	0	1 (0.25)
Valleys5	2	7	12	1	15	2	39 (10.26)
Mid6	6	10	18	2	17	1	54 (14.48)
NW7	2	1	0	0	0	0	3 (0.71)
Valleys8	0	0	1	1	4	0	6 (1.60)
NE9	0	0	0	0	0	0	0
NW10	2	0	0	0	0	0	2 (0.59)
Cardiff11	2	0	0	0	0	0	2 (0.49)
RP12	0	0	0	0	0	0	0
SW13	1	12	15	3	5	1	37 (9.87)
Mid14	0	1	0	0	0	0	1 (0.29)
Community totals	15 (1.44)	31 (4.12)	46 (4.17)	7 (0.91)	42 (5.71)	4 (0.46)	145 (2.76)

ones, and that one would not expect recreational activities to attract the same level of comment. But SW4 attracts a great deal of comment about rugby, and, though a recreational activity, this again is an activity that goes right to the heart of Welsh cultural traditions and stereotypes: 11.25 per cent of the comments about SW4 are connected with rugby and sport. (There are almost no other comments about sport for the other speakers, even for Cardiff11.) The evaluative profile of SW4 in the scales data is generally very favourable, so it is reasonable to see these comments about rugby and sport in positive terms. This time, it is the Cardiff judges who loom largest with such comments: 21.43 per cent of their comments have this rugby and sport focus. Though perceived as relatively anglicized with relatively few Welsh-language speakers, Cardiff has at least one jewel of Welsh culture embodied in its rugby-playing and its national rugby-stadium – the Millennium Stadium. Mid-Wales, too, attributes importance to this property (13.56 per cent), along with the south-west itself (13.25 per cent) and, to a lesser extent, the north-east (9.30 per cent). By comparison, the north-west (5.66 per cent), along with the Valleys (4.76 per cent) gives little attention to this aspect of SW4. These data offer a clear illustration of how evaluations are made in terms of categories and qualities available in the culture, either locally (for example, farming), or more widely (for example, rugby), and that the loadings of such evaluations will vary accordingly.

Sexuality

The judges had much to say about sexuality, with comments referring to a range of features, from someone having a 'sexy voice', to another being a 'ladies' man' to references to homosexuality, and account for 2.24 per cent of total keywords. Of these, 1.69 per cent of the total 5,261 keywords referred to homosexuality ('gay', 'poof', 'bent', etc.). It is not clear whether they are used with any serious suggestions of homosexuality, and they may simply belong to the taboo/pejorative category above, relative to punitive group norms and values. Nevertheless, the significant proportion of items concerning sexuality would appear to reflect teenage developments. The awareness and preoccupations that accompany the onset of puberty are well-documented, of course (for example, see Heaven, 1994), but this sexual dimension of evaluations does not appear to feature in published work on adolescents' language attitudes.

'Rich'/'posh'

Socio-economic factors were referred to in 3.93 per cent of all keywords: 'posh', 'rich'. Predictably perhaps, the RP speakers attract most of these: 24.51 per cent of the comments about RP12 fall into this group. The figure for RP3, though much lower at 10.54 per cent, is nevertheless way ahead of the others. The only others attracting numbers of such comments worthy of mention are Mid6 (6.97 per cent), who probably projects an image of himself not as the son of a poor farmer, but as the offspring of a more affluent one, who is allowed to drive his father's tractor and carry out farming tasks with it, and Cardiff1 (4.78 per cent), who talks about events on his holiday in Spain. This dimension effectively separates out these four speakers from the rest. 'Posh' is frequently found collocated with 'snob', pointing to outgrouping processes once again.

There are also differences in the degree to which the different judge communities focus on richness, poshness, etc. The dimension seems most salient for the mid-Wales judges (5.31 per cent), the north-west (5.19 per cent), Cardiff (4.80 per cent) and the south-west (4.72 per cent), and less so for the north-east (2.21 per cent) and the Valleys (2.02 per cent). A group of words relating to intelligence, braininess, also separated out the RP speakers (this time, along with NE9) from the others, with the Valleys judges again hardly mentioning such attributes at all.

Drugs

This grouping of items (1.60 per cent of the keywords total) included items such as 'likes the odd one' and 'on booze' as well as 'drug user', 'junkie, in touch with the drug world', etc. Unsurprisingly, NE2, with his story of his visit to a nightclub, was the speaker who attracted considerably more such keywords than the other speakers: 8.06 per cent of the keywords about him fell into this grouping (35.71 per cent of these drugs keywords were about him). Beyond that, there is general noteworthiness in the proportion of such items in the keywords, and also in the fact that a good number of the narratives themselves make reference to drugs and alcohol, pointing to some overall salience of these to fifteen-year-olds.

'Boasters' and 'bullshitters'

These two groupings are considered together here, since they both concern perceivedly unacceptable excesses in speakers: the first in terms of overstepping a norm concerning modesty, and the second a norm concerning truthfulness. These judgements thus suggest another process of exclusion or outgrouping by the teenagers. Together these items account for 3.52 per cent of total keywords, and there is a reasonable spread of them across speakers and judge communities. But as with the taboo items, the Valleys judges make the most comments for both of these groupings, especially in the case of 'bullshitters', where they account for 51.5 per cent of the comments. The north-west makes the least in both groupings combined (4.86 per cent of all the items in the groupings) and, interestingly, the south-west judges make no allegations of bullshitting at all. Of the speakers, the big 'boaster' (39.53 per cent of the 'boaster' comments) is NE2 with his story about under-age entry to a nightclub, rock-stars and TV filming, and he also scores highly on the 'bullshitter' ratings (13.13 per cent of them). Regrettably, since his story is true, Valleys5, telling about his father losing his foot in an accident, is seen as by far the biggest liar (22.22 per cent of all the comments). It is certainly unique amongst the stories with its personal tragedy, and perhaps a story the teenagers would not want to believe was true.

'Troublemaker' and 'funny'

'Funny' was quite a large grouping of 6.23 per cent of total keywords – 'sense of humour', 'hilarious', 'amusing', etc. 'Troublemaker' was a somewhat small grouping of 1.12 per cent (coming largely from the south-west and Cardiff judges). The communities with the most to say about 'funny' were the north-east (7.7 per cent of their keywords) and Cardiff (7.39 per cent). Given the comments above, it is perhaps no surprise that the Valleys used these terms the least. By far the funniest of the speakers was Cardiff11 (21.84 per cent of his keywords), followed by SW4 (15.25 per cent). The speakers are almost divided neatly into one high-scoring and one low-scoring group, with NW10, NE2 and NE9 joining Cardiff11 and SW4 in the top group, much in line with the scale-findings for *good laugh*. The two speakers attracting fewest comments of this type were RP3 and Mid6 (both 0.54 per cent of their totals), again largely in step with the scale-findings. RP12, though not amongst the very lowest scorers here, was still low, again reflecting the poor showing of the RP speakers as *good laughs* in the scales data.

Two of these high scorers also attracted the many comments about being 'trouble' ('criminal', 'mischievous', 'mucks about a lot', etc.): Cardiff11 especially (4.13 per cent of his comments), and NW10 (3.54 per cent), suggesting that causing trouble might be an important component of their 'funny' stories. Both of these speakers break adult rules, with Cardiff11 fiddling pool-games and NW11 building go-karts and almost crashing into police cars. But troublemaking as a factor in 'funny' is qualified when one looks at the other highest scorer for 'troublemaker' (Valleys8, 4.53 per cent) who is simply up to mischief with less glamorous farm-machinery, and anyway does not appear to get into any trouble for it, and is one of the lowest scorers for 'funny' (1.07 per cent). Nor does a story have to involve mischief to be 'funny'. The teenagers are apparently amused by SW4's clearly 'unmischievous' (0 per cent) vivid description of a rugby-player trying to squeeze himself into an undersized shirt.

Keywords conclusions

Our motivation to include the collection of keywords in the main part of the narratives study (rather than just the pilot) was to argue that keywords can be of wider value than as merely a preliminary stage in designing language attitude measurement scales. They are informative both alongside such scales and also in their own right as evaluative data for investigating attitudes. Our intention with these data has been to demonstrate that keywords can give deeper insights into data elicited from one-dimensional scales, allowing better access to the multi-dimensional character of attitudes. This multidimensional nature of language attitudes and of the semantic items that express them makes simple comparison more difficult, and indeed ease of comparison has always been one of the advantages claimed for such scales. But attitude-rating scales alone may at times not delve deep enough.

Keywords, then, can allow a clearer view of the wider picture. Furthermore, even if examined without reference to accompanying scales, they do not necessarily altogether sacrifice qualities of intensity, direction, or comparability. Many items do suggest directionality and at least some rough idea of intensity. For example, 'English, enough said!' suggests negative directionality and strong intensity. But it also carries an emotional reaction that would be missed by a circle around 'very English' on a seven-point scale. 'Sheepshagger', too, suggests these qualities, and also projects quite precise stereotypical imagery. Such items may form the basis of some useful qualitative comparison – for example, of 'sheepshagger' as an image of one community and 'townie' for another, or of how drugs connotations may be far more salient in people's evaluations in one region than they are elsewhere.

Needless to say, caution needs to be exercised with this kind of data when making numerical and percentage comparisons, and it is possible that in some cases, above, these have been stretched a little further than the data comfortably allow (especially perhaps by region). For example, a dearth of comments from one judging source might be attributable to their having 'used up' their three keywords on other dimensions, thus making it less secure to compare percentages than it would be with forced-choice items. However, there is considerable value in being able to draw out some intriguing socio-semantic dimensions, which later studies can subject to more detailed analysis. Discussion should not be restricted to the use of keywords against the background of using semantic-differential scales in language attitudes research. Their value undoubtedly extends to other sociolinguistic traditions too. Keywords could usefully supplement the tradition in which correlations are explored between sociolinguistic variables and social groups to investigate in more depth the various motivations and social connotations with which language users are operating (see Kristiansen, forthcoming).

Keywords, then, offer an intriguing shorthand for evaluative discourses, and how they are structured within particular groups. They can show how evaluative language does more than hang qualities or attributes on targets. For example, to return to the earlier mention of evaluation as a set of functional processes for group formation, keywords can actively 'promote' or 'relegate' individuals to membership of ingroups and (especially here) outgroups. Keywords often impute group membership directly, as nominals, rather than simply describing personal attributes, as adjectives. They also allow access to a complex set of theoretical issues to do with salience (which are far from resolved in our work here). The data show how unlikely it is that speaker/language evaluations can ultimately be captured via a universal set of dimensions. Specific groups (here, adolescents in Wales) have their own sociolinguistic repertoires for doing evaluation, just as specific targets are evaluated via attributes considered meaningful to assess them. The data have also suggested that salience is linked to the cultural constitution of judges' own communities: for example, where farming is an experiential reality. But how a dimension is salient again depends on a local cultural process: being a farmer is mainly attributable as undesirable by teenagers in rural communities, who can conceive feasible and more attractive alternatives to farmers' lives.

Keywords, then, provide a valuable window to the aspirations of teenagers, to their cultural and spatial outlooks, and to their aspirations as to the range and nature of the opportunities, relationships and identities that might be available to them. The general negativity in the evaluations collected here is striking, and it is clear that they have multiple means of rejecting many of their Welsh peers. They may do this on personal criteria such as 'boring', 'bullshitter', etc. and also on sociocultural criteria, being 'farmers' or indeed 'Welsh'. And while Welshness itself is seen from an English-language vantage point, Englishness, too, is strongly outgrouped and even pilloried in our data by informants from the south-west. The processes operating to generate such negativity at this age have been mentioned earlier: for example, the moratorium period in which there is a searching through the proliferation of potential identities at this age, and a concomitant need for teenagers to distance themselves from such a large number, compared to those with whom they wish to identify themselves more closely. But although a moratorium is seen as essential for identity achievement (Marcia, 1980), there is no guarantee that all teenagers move into early adulthood having achieved fully-formed identities (Heaven, 1994: 33), and, at worst, these data arguably breed some concern that the evaluative patterns might not leave much space for positive and satisfying personal or sociocultural identities. That said, the study of teenagers' evaluative repertoires shows itself to be of great value in reaching a better understanding of the comparisons they are making and the stereotypical images and dimensions they are working with, and gives more insight into their life-views and how they are negotiating their identities.

9

Recognition of dialects

We mentioned in chapter 4 that research in dialectology and variationist sociolinguistics has tended to work with the assumption that people recognize dialects with reasonable accuracy. We noted that Preston (1989: 3) had called for the inclusion of a recognition item for respondents in language attitudes studies to complete when varieties were aurally presented to them. We also suggested that recognition might be regarded as a relatively complex process, closely bound up with affective and evaluative processes. How then did the teachers and students respond to the recognition item in the narratives study? Their most frequent answers are set out in table 9.1.

Recognition rates

It is evident from this table that, overall, the teachers have been more successful on this recognition item than the adolescents were, in terms of accurate identification of where the speakers were from. The teenagers responded with 'don't know' more often than the teachers did. And where the most frequent response by the teenagers was accurate, the teachers always identified the speaker accurately and with higher frequency.

We discuss the recognition findings relating only to the teenagers, since these data are more extensive and more differentiated. Our discussion is motivated by two questions. One, which is dealt with more extensively, is whether these results provide any insights into the processes involved in so-called 'recognition'. The other is whether the low degree of accurate identification discredits the findings in the scales

Table 9.1: Most frequent responses from young adults and schoolteachers to question concerning where the speaker was from

Voice	Teachers' answers		Young adults' answers	
Cardiff1	Cardiff	68%	?	21%
Cardiff11	Cardiff	53%	Cardiff	42%
NE2	England	47%	?	28%
NE9	England	30%	England	27%
SW4	South-west	45%	Valleys	39%
SW13	South-west	47%	Valleys	26%
Valleys5	Valleys	53%	Valleys	22%
Valleys8	Valleys	68%	Valleys	33%
Mid6	MidWales	34%	MidWales	28%
Mid14	?	28%	?	27%
NW7	North-west	49%	North-west	29%
NW10	North-west	47%	North-west	26%
RP3	England	77%	?	34%
RP12	England	85%	England	44%

Key: ? = don't know.

and keywords parts of the study. To some extent, discussion of the first question itself leads to the conclusion that the findings considered above are not at all devalued. Edwards and Jacobsen (1987: 377), who included a recognition item in their study of Canadian and US accents, and who also found that recognition rates differed considerably, concluded that, where there are consistencies elsewhere in the data, 'errors in placing speakers do not invalidate judges' assessments'. And they refer to an earlier discussion by Milroy and McClenaghan (1977: 8ff.) making the same point. As will be shown below, there are striking consistencies in the Welshness findings suggesting that recognition is occurring at some level, and that the students' other evaluations are therefore not automatically invalidated.

For the teenagers, then, the recognition rates were generally low. Table 9.1 shows that, overall, the fourteen speakers were correctly identified by between 20 per cent and 44 per cent of all the young adult listeners. Two speakers were correctly identified by more than 40 per cent of the adolescents: Cardiff11 and RP12. Given the considerable exposure to RP (most notably in the broadcast media), a high recognition performance for this variety was anticipated, although we should bear in mind that correctly identifying one speaker's provenance as 'Cardiff' and another's as 'RP' are qualitatively different judgements. RP represents a far more widespread and culturally-prominent speaking cohort than do the other dialects in the study. Indeed, it is more striking that RP12 was *not* recognized by more than 26.6 per cent of all judges (see table 9.2).

Table 9.2: Percentage of young adults who achieved correct recognition of where speaker was from

	Young adults' communities (judges)						
	Cardiff n = 23	NE 30	SW 33	Valleys 29	Mid 25	NW 29	All 169
Speakers							
Cardiff1	**43.5**	13.3	21.2	17.2	20.0	10.3	20.1
Cardiff11	**100.0**	30.0	36.4	34.5	36.0	27.6	42.0
NE2	8.7	**73.3**	3.0	6.9	4.0	20.7	20.1
NE9	21.7	**23.3**	18.2	6.9	40.0	13.8	20.1
SW4	8.7	10.3	**72.7**	3.4	24.0	31.0	26.6
SW13	21.7	14.3	**54.5**	13.8	28.0	13.8	24.9
Valleys5	34.8	23.3	39.4	**13.8**	4.0	13.8	21.9
Valleys8	26.1	3.4	45.5	**41.4**	64.0	17.2	32.5
Mid6	17.4	30.0	36.4	10.3	**44.0**	27.6	27.8
Mid14	21.7	3.3	9.1	0.0	**28.0**	31.0	14.8
NW7	17.4	23.3	54.5	10.3	24.0	**37.9**	29.0
NW10	8.7	16.7	60.6	3.4	36.0	**24.1**	26.0
RP3	43.5	20.0	39.4	17.2	32.0	10.3	**26.6**
RP12	82.6	40.0	54.5	27.6	44.0	20.7	**43.8**

(Figures in bold indicate judges' identification rates with speakers from their own communities.)

It is initially hard to explain why Cardiff11 was so well recognized compared to Cardiff1. Given that the pairs of voices representing each dialect type were selected on phonetic/phonological criteria, it is difficult to establish why there should be divergent rates of recognition between members of these pairs. In table 9.2, which gives a breakdown of how each community of judges fared on this task, it is even more puzzling why teenagers' recognition of voices from *their own* dialect communities (see bold figures) should in some cases differ so much between the pairs of speakers. McNemar's tests showed that the differences in recognition between speaker pairs by judges in their own communities were significant in the cases of Cardiff (chi square = 13.00; $p < 0.01$), Valleys (chi square = 5.33; $p < 0.04$) and the NE (chi square = 13.20; $p < 0.01$).

It is tempting to explain these results by attributing them to 'simple misrecognition'. If recognition is merely a matter of the individual mapping the speech features they hear on to their perceptual records of speech community norms, then 'wrong' answers to the recognition question could be caused by the individual not having reliable perceptual records of the outgroup norms. In other words, perhaps these adolescents do not have sufficient experience and awareness of these varieties. It was noted when reviewing the developmental studies in chapter 4 that those studies did not involve the elicitation of attitudes to a whole range of non-standard varieties, as the present study does. It seems reasonable to assume that this does indeed account for *some* of the instances of wrong responses in the data. In the case of their own dialects, misrecognition might imply adequate experience but inadequate cognitive representation (or awareness) of ingroup speech-norms. The variable levels of ingroup recognition are indeed striking, varying from 100 per cent to 13.8 per cent, with a mean for ingroup recognition of just below 45 per cent.

The picture becomes more intriguing when we examine more closely some of the 'misrecognitions'. One might expect misrecognitions to lead to fairly random responses, but in fact there are some very consistent patterns in the data, not represented in table 9.2 (which records only levels of correct recognition).

Of the Cardiff listeners, 44 per cent thought that Cardiff1 was from south-west Wales, 39 per cent thought Valleys8 was from south-west Wales, and 20 per cent thought Valleys5 was from south-west Wales, and these are not untypical values for *correctly* recognized varieties. Such a regular pattern leads one to wonder what there might be about these speakers, or about the listeners, that leads Cardiff judges to attribute them to the south-west of Wales. In the opposite direction, 52 per cent of the Cardiff judges thought NW10 was from *their own* dialect community. But these are in fact two very distinct varieties of English in linguistic terms. Whereas north-west Wales English is very dependent upon the Welsh language for its distinctive features, Cardiff English is only marginally influenced by Welsh. Amongst the Valleys listeners, it is fair to say that there was an overall failure to recognize Valleys5. Conversely again, 51 per cent of the Valleys judges thought SW4 was from the Valleys, and 10 per cent of them thought Cardiff11 was from the Valleys.

These regularities could be taken as evidence that this is not 'simple misrecognition' here, but that other processes are at work, and these might be social-evaluative processes. These processes could be either competing with and overwhelming what are in fact quite reliable perceptual records in the adolescents, or they could be taking compensatory effect where the adolescents' perceptual records are not yet fully developed. We come to these shortly.

But to return first to the notion that recognition is a question of mapping the speech features heard on to a cognitive template; a further possibility that needs to be considered for 'misrecognition' is that the speech features themselves are misleading the teenagers (but the teachers far less so). Perhaps some of the individual dialect-samples contained more, or more salient, phonological cues than others did, linking them to community norms. Or perhaps, since these were all authentic recordings, rather than controlled matched guises, they contained different content cues, narrative characteristics, etc., that might lead to faulty identification. In one case, there is a simple explanation. In table 9.1 we see the tendency for both teachers and pupils to identify north-east Wales speakers as 'English'. This is clearly due to the strong influences of the nearby Liverpool conurbation on north-east Wales speech, as pointed out earlier. To a considerable extent, the English of north-east Wales is, indexically, 'English' (in the same sense that it indexes the variety spoken in an urban enclave centred in England, not in Wales). There may be a phonological explanation for the above-mentioned identification of NW10 as 'Cardiff' by Cardiff listeners, since both speech communities share the fronted and somewhat raised long /a:/ feature (Coupland, 1988), and indeed the word 'car' is repeated five times in the thirty second recording of NW10's story, along with single instances of 'bar' and 'go-kart'. On the other hand, given the distinct differences in the varieties in other respects, one might expect the Cardiff listeners to be the least likely of all to confuse them. And this has also to be seen against relatively good rates of accurate recognition of NW10 by south-west Wales (60.6 per cent), and Mid-Wales (36 per cent) listeners.

Although such phonological and content factors might account for some proportion of the lack of accurate identification, results relating to another item on the questionnaire given to respondents make it questionable that these factors can explain all of it. For the same reason, there is reason to doubt that the results can be fully explained by the earlier suggestion that the perceptual records of these adolescents might not be adequate for this task. Let us return to the item on the questionnaire that asked respondents to rate the voices according to how Welsh they sounded to them.

Welshness

It is useful at this point to extract, from tables 7.1 and 7.2, the students' and teachers' scores for the Welshness scale, and set them out side by

Table 9.3: Mean scores of young adult and teacher judges on the item: *How Welsh do you think this speaker sounds?*

Students		Teachers	
SW4	4.47	SW4	4.54
Valleys5	4.01	SW13	4.53
SW13	3.91	Valleys5	4.36
Valleys8	3.76	NW7	4.20
NW7	3.44	NW10	3.76
NW10	3.41	Valleys8	3.70
Cardiff11	2.88	Cardiff11	3.15
Cardiff1	2.83	Cardiff1	3.02
Mid6	2.29	Mid6	2.30
Mid14	2.14	NE9	2.16
NE2	1.88	Mid14	1.98
NE9	1.60	NE2	1.52
RP3	1.56	RP3	1.25
RP12	1.51	RP12	1.14

side, as in table 9.3. There is evidence of pairing of the samples for each dialect in these mean scores, as previously discussed. What is also evident here is that the pairing occurs for both the adolescents and the teachers, who achieved higher rates of recognition. It would seem from this that the adolescents do in fact recognize (at some level of awareness) that there are pairs of speakers from the same dialect community.

The possibility that these pairings can be due to chance can be safely dismissed for two reasons. One is the similar hierarchical structure for judgements of Welshness in the questionnaire study, where no story content or phonological features were present. The other is the similarity between the students' and the teachers' results in the narratives study, both in terms of the pairing and the rank ordering of the dialects. To illustrate this more clearly, in table 9.4, the mean scores for the two members of each regional pair of speakers are averaged to show a single score for each community. The resulting rank orderings of the communities by the teachers and the teenagers are identical, and the similarity with the rank ordering for Welshness in the questionnaire study (taken from table 6.1) is also striking. Only the position of Cardiff differs between the studies (a point we addressed in chapter 7).

The notion that the adolescents are operating with an awareness *at some level* of what these varieties are is not as problematic as it might first appear. Preston (1996) sets out a taxonomy of folklinguistic awareness in which he identifies four independent continua along which

Table 9.4: Rank orders from averaged scores for speaker pairs on the Welshness scale in the narratives study (students and teachers) and from the Welshness mean scores from the questionnaire study (teachers)

Narratives study (students)	*Narratives study (teachers)*	*Qu'aire study (teachers)*
SW 4.19	SW 4.54	SW 2.10
Valleys 3.89	Valleys 4.28	Valleys 2.43
NW 3.43	NW 3.98	NW 2.52
Cardiff 2.86	Cardiff 3.09	Mid 4.41
Mid 2.22	Mid 2.14	NE 4.86
NE 1.74	NE 1.83	Cardiff 4.87
RP 1.54	RP 1.20	RP 6.66

Note: The higher the scores in the narratives study, the more Welsh-sounding the speaker. The scale in the questionnaire study was in the opposite direction.

awareness might be identified at different *levels*. These independent dimensions are *availability, detail, accuracy* and *control*. Figure 9.1 shows these dimensions, with hypothetical settings marked on them to illustrate their independence from each other. Preston also lists a number of factors that might contribute to these levels of awareness. These include such features as formal training and/or knowledge, publicity (such as popular culture, media exposure), correctness (transmitted formally or informally) and folk culture artefacts.

AVAILABLE ___X_____UNAVAILABLE

DETAILED_____X_____ ___GLOBAL

ACCURATE_____X_____INACCURATE

FULL CONTROL_____X____NO CONTROL

Figure 9.1: Variable independent continua of the modes of non-linguists' language awareness, with hypothetical settings (after Preston, 1996)

Facets of language differ in their degree of *availability* to non-linguists. Some are common topics of discussion, whereas others are never discussed, or are commented on only with some prompting (= availability), some are not at all salient to them. Secondly, their comments about language may differ in their degree of *detail*. Compared to linguists, non-linguists might operate with a much less differentiated understanding of a phonological or other feature. Thirdly, non-linguists' descriptions of language may differ in their degree of scientific *accuracy*. That is, even if a non-linguist's 'analysis' of a feature was detailed, it could technically be 'wrong'. Fourthly, people may or may not be able to *control* a feature, for example, to perform a language variety (= control). Most relevant to our present concerns are the first three continua, since the recognition task precludes 'performance'. Recognition can be interpreted as one form of 'availability', in this case prompted by audio-recordings. Correct recognition of the dialect would reflect 'accuracy'. The 'detail' continuum is of interest here, because the questionnaire predetermined the level of detail at which the adolescents were being asked to comment when they made their judgements of recognition. It is possible that some of the 'wrong answers' can be explained by this. For example, a number of instances were pointed to earlier where speakers from the Valleys were identified as coming from south-west Wales, and vice versa. The questionnaire gave multiple-choice options for respondents to select from, which included three regions from south Wales: the urban south-east (that is, Cardiff), south-west Wales and the Valleys. Conceivably, some respondents were only able to operate at a lower level of detail than was asked of them, and so might have felt confident that the voice they heard was from a non-urban (or non-Cardiff) area of south Wales, but not been able to select confidently from the two alternatives of south-west Wales or the Valleys. Their recognition would be 'available' and 'accurate', but not sufficiently 'detailed'.

Table 9.3 provides some evidence that such a process might be at work. There appears to be more pairing of voices by dialect community for all the regions except south-west Wales and the Valleys. For the young adults in the study, these latter two intermesh. (However, these are only descriptive statistics.) On the other hand, it is still striking that percentages choosing south-west Wales rather than the Valleys (or vice versa) in response to the recognition item tend to point markedly more in one direction than the other, in each instance. One would expect that if these responses were simply due to a lack of detail in their awareness, results would not tend to pull in one direction much more than in the other. Hence, again, it is likely that there are some additional factors operating.

Why is it then that, although there seems to be some degree of accurate recognition detectable in the responses to the *how Welsh* item, this degree of recognition is not so evident in the responses to the recognition item itself? What factors might account for this? On the *how Welsh* item, one might, for example, expect influence from several of the factors that Preston lists as affecting the settings on the continua: publicity, folk culture artefacts, correctness, etc., all contributing to a cognitive-mapping process. On this issue of recognition, however, a further factor needed to be explored. Possibly, recognition amongst these teenagers did not simply require a mapping of speech features on to a cognitive template. It is important to pursue the possibility that there are *affective, group-level* factors at work: recognition might be influenced by an *active ingrouping* process (Tajfel, 1974). In Preston's taxonomy, affective factors are not included in the list of factors influencing settings on the dimensions, but if there were evidence of them in these data, they would make a useful addition to this theoretical model of dialect awareness.

Likeability

Accordingly, we conducted further analysis on the speaker pairs in which one was significantly more recognized than the other to test the hypothesis that the more-recognized speaker would be rated higher on affiliation by their ingroup community. The hypothesis was tested by calculating t-tests, comparing speaker-pair means for the three communities in question on two other items on the questionnaire, which measured how much the listener *liked* the speaker, and to what extent they thought the speaker was a *good laugh*. For Cardiff, this hypothesis was supported for both *liking* and *good laugh* at the p<0.01 level. The hypothesis was also supported in the case of north-east Wales for both *liking* and *good laugh* at the p<0.01 level. The hypothesis was not supported in the case of the Valleys speakers, however, for *liking* or *good laugh*, as neither of these speakers was rated as particularly *likeable* or a *good laugh* by the Valleys judges.

There is further support for the hypothesis elsewhere in the data. For example, the results for the Valleys listeners show that, while 24.1 per cent recorded a *don't know* for Valleys5, who did not score high on *likeability*, 51 per cent thought SW4 was from the Valleys, and 10 per cent thought Cardiff11 was from the Valleys. Both SW4 and Cardiff11 scored high on *likeability*. Similarly, 52.2 per cent of Cardiff listeners thought that NW10 was from Cardiff, whereas there was a weaker misattribution for NW7, a difference which is echoed in their *likeability* ratings.

There is evidence, then, of what we can call an ingroup process of *claiming* (and indeed, in the case of misrecognition, *outgrouping*) processes at work in the recognition data. Most striking of all in this respect are the results for the Cardiff11 speaker, who scored highest of all on the *likeability* ratings. Although he was correctly identified as a Cardiff speaker by the majority in all the judging groups, he was also the most *claimed*: 26.7 per cent of the north-east listeners claimed that he was from north-east Wales, 18.2 per cent of the south-west Wales judges said he was from south-west Wales, 16 per cent of mid-Wales listeners thought he was from mid-Wales, and 10.3 per cent of Valleys listeners claimed he was from their dialect community. Also, in contrast to the other results, he was 'correctly identified' as a Cardiffian by 100 per cent of the listeners from the Cardiff community.

The processes of claiming and denial illustrated above find a theoretical foundation in theories of social identity and self-categorization (Hogg, 1992), and are essentially concerned with social attraction. The focus of social (as opposed to personal) attraction is the set of prototypical properties of the group (though social and personal attraction may coexist). Intergroup relations define groups, and the groups to which one belongs are a resource for defining one's personal identity. So there is a continual process of competition and innovation to establish and maintain a relatively positive evaluation of one's own group. A consequence is that ingroup prototypes are generally evaluated positively. In the recognition task given to the teenagers, they were arguably able to decide themselves whether the speakers they heard were ingroup or outgroup members. Hence, from the speech performances they heard, listeners were able to focus on the salient dimensions of group identity, and decide whether speakers approximated to the prototype they valued most or not, or even whether they more closely approximated to some outgroup prototype that the listeners knew well and valued negatively. The apparently simple task of giving a community label to a particular speaker may well have tapped into these group-level cognitions, and influenced the frequencies with which particular speakers were 'recognized' as members of ingroup and outgroup communities.

Summing-up of recognition issue

Including the recognition item on the questionnaire, then, has led to consideration of various possible ways of defining 'recognition' itself. Recognition *can* be construed as the cognitive mapping of audible speech-features (or stylistic configurations of features in combination) on to individuals' records of the usage norms of particular communities. By this account, 'recognizing a dialect' involves identifying values of variable features and then succeeding or failing to make the appropriate mapping. In Preston's terms (figure 9.1), 'failing to recognize a dialect' is one form of non-availability at specifiable levels of (in)accuracy and detail.

The important general finding that the teenagers in the narratives study produce lower levels of recognition than the teachers can in this sense be accounted for by their predictably lower levels of dialect experience. They have probably experienced lower geographical mobility, and less access to dialect speakers, face-to-face or in the broadcast media. The young adults show lower levels of availability (in this particular, receptive sense of availability), which might be the result of less accurate or less detailed cognitive templates of English language sociolinguistic variation in Wales. Even if levels of exposure were similar between younger and older people, secondary school-age youth might still have less inferential experience than their teachers – less experience of assessing the social significance of the sociolinguistic differences they encounter.

Dialect recognition, to the extent that this label is an adequate one for the sociolinguistic processes activated in asking the question 'where is the speaker from?', is of course a cognitive process. But the analysis of the teenagers' responses above suggests that it is also part of *social* cognition, people's cognitions about social-group memberships, group identities and group boundaries. They did not merely recognize or fail to recognize speakers as belonging to specific communities. In some respects, their identifications responded to and manipulated the group designations that were offered to them to select from. Most notably, there was a tendency for a very likeable speaker to be actively appropriated into the ingroup.

The group-level, affective dimension of dialect recognition, and of language awareness, deserves more attention. Affective factors could usefully be added to Preston's summary list of factors that influence an individual's set of locations along his independent modes of language awareness. It could be argued that such factors are likely to dominate in recognition tasks where accurate cognitive mapping cannot be achieved: for example, when listeners are inexperienced. But social cognition about dialect can equally well be seen as a relatively sophisticated sociolinguistic activity, responding to preferences and ideologies that dominate in listeners' own communities, and which also influence other evaluative judgements they make. Processes such as claiming and denying or disavowing may be an intrinsic part of dialect-recognition processes, even where listeners' records are well developed and speech cues are unambiguous. Sociolinguistic studies need to ask not only what speech community members know about varieties, but how they construct this knowledge, and how they use it creatively to reflect and refine their group priorities and memberships. The study of dialect recognition, linked to studies of dialect variation and other aspects of dialect awareness, seems to be a profitable new direction.

Closing comments

In these last three chapters, four sets of data have been analysed. The first of these three sets of data to be analysed was that from the attitude-rating scales, where, to begin with, mean scores were looked at for the teachers and teenagers in turn, and then the output from multidimensional scaling in conjunction with cluster analysis was considered, giving insights into how and on what basis teachers and judges evaluatively differentiated and grouped the dialect performances. The second set of data was the focus-group data, where teenagers were engaged in free discussion of the speakers and narratives. The third set was the qualitative-keywords data from the teenagers, showing salient dimensions of intergroup comparisons for this age-group. And the fourth set of data came from the recognition item, which proved to be not the simple outcome of cognitive-mapping processes that one might anticipate, but which once again, in the case of the teenagers above all, showed signs of intergroup processes at work. From these various approaches and manifestations, different facets of attitudes have emerged and been considered. In the concluding chapter, we consider the data and findings from both the questionnaire study and the narratives study in relation to the research questions that we set out in chapter 1.

10

Conclusions

In chapters 5 to 9, there has already been a great deal of discussion of the findings of the composite strands of data in this research. In our concluding chapter, we now draw together and sum up three themes. These are inevitably interwoven, as our methodological focus has been demonstrated through a series of studies that have thrown up original findings of their own. One of the three themes is *Wales itself*, and what these language attitudes studies have contributed to knowledge about social identification in Wales. This theme connects with research questions *5* and *6* set out at the end of chapter 1. A second theme concerns the respondents, in terms of their contrasting *social and cultural positions as teenagers and their teachers*, and in part, in terms of their orientation to language use in Wales. This second theme addresses research questions *7* and *8*. The third theme is about developments in *research methods*, and the methodological contribution of these studies in Wales to language attitudes research in general. In terms of our research questions, the third theme addresses numbers *1*, *2*, *3*, and *4*. We discuss these three themes in the order in which we have introduced them here, though inevitably with overlap at all stages.

An attitudinal map of Wales

As regards language attitudes in Wales, our starting point in this book was the ambiguity of earlier research findings, with Price et al. (1983) arguing that area-wide surveys should be conducted. It is possible to claim that there now is, at least in outline, an attitudinal map. It is inevitably limited in what it can reveal (as with all cartography) in that it is restricted to attitudinal data from teachers and young adolescents, and it is also important (again as in all cartography) to keep in mind the scale of this map. It captures relatively macro-regions across Wales as a whole, rather than providing something equivalent to the highly detailed topography of a hiker's map, or to the minutiae of urban layout in an A-to-Z. This is of course the scale it sought to capture, and the scale that Price and colleagues argued needed to be captured. Indeed, it is an issue of methodological choice. And, to repeat the analogy with cartography in general, maps of other scales will also be of value in language attitudinal work, focusing on particular regions or communities in Wales, as we argue below. With this in mind, what do the map that has evolved in these last chapters, and the research which underlies it, nevertheless tell us about social identification in Wales, mediated through English language use?

Clarification of some earlier inconsistencies

To begin with, it is now clear that the ambiguities or inconsistencies in the earlier matched-guise studies were not random, but were in part due to some degree of underlying systematic variation that small-scale 'one-off' localized studies were much less likely to capture. The six broad dialect communities upon which much of our research was based have been found to vary along a number of independent evaluative dimensions, with each community holding its own sociolinguistic stereotypes, its own differentiated attitudinal profile. Nor are these profiles restricted to those dimensions traditionally found in language attitudes work: prestige, social attractiveness and dynamism. Rather, a further key discriminating dimension of perceived 'Welshness', or 'authentic Welshness' in English has surfaced, not tapped into in any depth in earlier studies. And this has been found, like the other dimensions, to be a gradeable rather than categorical property, with some dialect communities being deemed 'more Welsh' than others, both linguistically and culturally. While the use of a semantic-differential scale has facilitated the simple measuring of different levels of Welshness, open-ended data have added depth and texture to this dimension, suggesting not just different levels of Welshness (or Englishness) but a whole array of different kinds of Welshness, too, as well as orientations towards those different types. Some projected city-focused images, such as 'Swansea Jack', while others projected a rural association that certain community members seemingly reject and seek to distance themselves from, such as 'farmer's boy'. Furthermore, the Welshness that the south-westerners exhibited in their labelling of north-west Wales appeared more exclusionary – 'north Walian' – compared to the Welshness identified in different parts of Wales by the north-westerners, which seemed more embracing – 'Welsh'. Whether speakers of English are perceived also to be Welsh speakers was another salient basis of stereotyped judgement, for example, in the focus-group discussion data. More investigation of such dimensions of Welshness are needed, perhaps, as Coupland (2000) suggests, also in terms of Celticity, rurality and social class. Such indications of internal competition and opposition amongst these views of Welshness have afforded glimpses of unfolding and complex dialectics of Welsh identities, particularly amongst those who, as teenagers, are experiencing and negotiating their own tensions and dialectics of identity development.

It has also been found that the lack of clarity in earlier findings can in part be attributed to a degree of systematic variation relating to the social and cultural characteristics of the respondents or 'judges' themselves. Hence, Welsh and non-Welsh speakers, those in northern areas compared to those in southern areas, differed to a significant degree on some evaluative dimensions with regard to a few of the dialect communities (for example, non-Welsh speakers downgrading south-east Wales on prestige compared to Welsh speakers). The teachers and students in the narratives study were also found to differ in some of their evaluations: for example, in their evaluations of the social attractiveness of the RP speakers. Our Wales-wide survey of language attitudes has allowed such systematic differences amongst the respondents to emerge in a way that affords some clarification rather than leading to the confusion of results from the earlier, small-scale, mainly matched-guise studies. A clearer picture has at least begun to emerge of the cultural and social viewpoints of some of the broader groups (in terms of location, age, language background) in Wales. But there is a great deal more to do. There are other groups of gatekeepers and advisers to compare with the teachers; such as health professionals, law enforcers, personnel managers, youth workers, social-services managers, career officers, etc. And, although the design of the present study has facilitated the comparison of attitudes between two broad age-groups, there may well be other important age-effects. Older people, for instance, barely feature in language attitudes studies.

Current demographic changes, leading to an ageing population profile in so many western countries, and a growing interest, academic and governmental, in intergenerational communication, suggest that more attention to comparing language attitudes across the lifespan is timely (for example, Williams and Garrett, 2002). Indeed, in terms of the mid-teenage school-students in the narratives study, considering their language attitudes within the context of the recent human communication research into identity building at that age has been a distinctive feature of the work we have been discussing, and has, we hope, provided a useful initial framework for understanding the contemporary tensions in Welsh identities at that age.

There is also the issue of comparing attitudes towards Welsh English within Wales to attitudes towards Welsh English by those outside Wales. What, for example, are the attitudes of those who have moved out of Wales? Such work can be extended to investigating Welsh identity and attitudes under globalization (see Wray, Evans, Coupland and Bishop, 2003; Coupland, Bishop and Garrett, forthcoming). Increased mobility and new communication technologies can foster global networks which unite people in new kinds of communities, and so help to create new common identities that are not necessarily linked to a common territory or political locality. Cymdeithas Madog (the Welsh Institute of North America), for example, organizes support for Welsh learners through online and written networking, as well as through residential courses. Similar groups operate in Australia and New Zealand. What beliefs, attitudes and priorities do members of such communities have to Welsh, to Welsh English, to bilingualism and to Welshness? And how (if at all) do such diasporic factors impinge on beliefs, ideologies and policies within Wales?

Further insights into Welshness

The findings from our studies have also cast more light on previously published accounts of linguistic and cultural divisions within Wales, and of English and Welsh identity. Some aspects of the language and identity contours and labels on maps produced by Balsom (1985) and Williams (1985) – figures 3.1 and 2.2 respectively – have been supported. For example, in these attitudinal data based around *English* language use in Wales, the notion of the Welsh heartland, *Y Fro Gymraeg*, is confirmed as a perceived reality, with the teachers' labels keeping separate south-west and north Wales, and perceptually 'Welsh' zones. Also, its division indicated by Williams into northern and southern parts is supported by the attitudinal divisions, if not oppositions, that are evident in both studies, and with the northern region's profile less favourable than that of the south-west. But Balsom's 'Welsh Wales' and, in particular, his 'British Wales' are to some extent problematized by the data from these studies. Balsom's 'British Wales', for example, contains regions that differ significantly in their degree of non-Welshness – a high degree in the north-east and Pembrokeshire, but a lower degree in the mid-Wales region, close to the border with England. We would again want to emphasize that a purely regional basis for ethnolinguistic distinctiveness, objective or subjective, is inadequate. We need to factor in crucial contextual components.

This notion of an incremental and contextualized rather than dichotomous and absolute Welshness is an important finding in these studies, facilitating the sorts of distinction just referred to, and allowing a far more variegated picture of identity in Wales to emerge. It has also allowed insights into how issues of identity link with political ambitions and affiliations in contemporary Wales (figure 6.1). It is important throughout this discussion to realize that this is a time of considerable change in Wales, not least through the establishment of the National Assembly for Wales and, many hope, increasing political autonomy, but also in the virtual disappearance of some of the industries that have until recently contributed to some strong components of Welsh identity in some regions: for example, coal, steel and slate industries. Farming, too, at the present time, is in economic crisis, so in this way, too, the traditional and 'modern' structuring institutions of Welsh social life have already crumbled. On the other hand, Wales is now seeking to discover and define its orientation towards the European Union, and is searching for new social, economic and political identities.

The Welsh language maintains its salience as a cultural icon in several domains. It is now firmly established as a compulsory part of the national curriculum in Welsh schools. There is now a renewed interest in the Welsh language amongst young people in the anglicized south-east, which is where the greatest growth in the number of self-reporting users of Welsh was evidenced in the 1991 census. At the same time, efforts to boost ethnolinguistic vitality (see, for example, Giles et al., 1977) through institutional support for the Welsh language in key areas such as the media are regarded differently by different groups. Some non-Welsh speakers whose families have lived in Wales for generations feel their Welsh (or, as the traditional label has it, 'Anglo-Welsh') identity is being stripped away from them, and claim they are denied access to key jobs in Wales, where to be Welsh-speaking has become a requirement. Others, including the Welsh Assembly government, argue the case for new packages of policy measures and funds to shore up communities in 'heartland' areas where Welsh continues to be under threat. It is evident how people in Wales are struggling, with each other and no doubt within themselves, dynamically to express, project, and promote identities of Wales and of themselves to which they aspire for the future, and which they hope to establish in their lives. In order to capture some of these dynamics in language attitudes research, the lens that was used in the studies discussed in chapters 5 to 9 may benefit from being re-set to take an in-depth look at certain specific communities, where such changes are particularly evident. There needs ideally to be research at more than one level, and this is one principle that the work we have been discussing has surely established. Smaller-scale work needs to be located in the context of larger-scale and more comprehensive frameworks.

Standardness in Welsh English

Intrinsically bound up in issues of political goals, cooperation, conflict, power and ideology is not only the broader notion of prestige, but also the more specific one of 'standardness' in language. This notion was to all intents and purposes entirely bypassed by the earlier spate of matched-guise studies in Wales, in which Welsh English was implicitly viewed as 'non-standard', relative to RP, especially in its 'broad' versions. Our concerted data-sets from throughout Wales have facilitated a comparison of profiles that has revealed a good candidate for a regional standard of English in Wales, with relatively favourable evaluations across all dimensions, echoing the typical pattern of differentiation between regional standard and 'national' standard varieties that has been previously identified by Edwards and Jacobsen, in their research into Canadian and US varieties of English (1987). At this time of increased political independence and change in Wales, with the advent of the Welsh Assembly, it remains to be seen how this evaluative relationship between RP and the south-west regional accent/dialect of Welsh English in particular evolves, and whether the latter will extend its pre-eminence into further contexts. It is conventionally held that RP is a 'regionless' variety in England and Wales, defined socially in terms of status and prestige rather than by region. Our data, however, suggest various ways in which RP speakers are outgrouped by Welsh teenagers, and to some extent, even by teachers. RP may retain its perceived value as the 'voice of success' in Wales, but it is also very much 'not *our* voice'.

Attitudinal effects in classrooms

As members of the sociolinguistic community, teachers are likely to share many of the same evaluations of language use as other members. One of the most sensitive controversies about language attitudes and teachers has always been whether, given professional norms and gatekeeping responsibilities, these evaluations permeate their activities to the point of having detrimental effects on the life-opportunities of any of their students. The data in our studies do not answer that question, and indeed did not ask it directly, although the findings certainly raise the issues again. On the one hand, the fact that teachers' stereotyped judgements in the open-ended data did not raise prestige as a salient discriminator of dialect communities can be seen as reassurance to educationists concerned about the deterministic circularity of self-fulfilling prophecies in the classroom. On the other hand, given the degree to which (in the questionnaire-study scales data) teachers did differentiate the communities on the prestige dimension, there is still an open verdict upon whether the absence of mention of prestige in the open-ended data was a result of a professional taboo rather than a genuine principle that the issue is of low significance to them. One can argue that 'professional blindness' to social difference and to social prejudice is in fact less desireable than 'professional critical awareness'. Teachers in our sample showed awareness of the linguistic basis of social classification, and it is quite likely that they use this awareness critically in their professional dealings with young people. Further research could be designed to address this issue in Wales and beyond.

Teacher–student comparisons

In general, though, the teachers' judgements were similar to those of the teenagers, especially in the narratives study, where a direct comparison was more readily discernible through the design of the study. In particular, of course, they had very similar perceptions of Welshness, which do seem to be deeply entrenched in the fabric of the community. But there were interesting differences, too, such as the teachers giving higher ratings to the apparently more innocent stories. This suggests a cultural gap between the teenagers and teachers in terms of pro/anti-establishment stances, perhaps reflecting other teacher/student divisions found in secondary schools (for example, Hargreaves, 1967). Teachers and teenagers showed that they hold clear evaluative profiles not only of Welsh English speakers, but also of RP speakers. Also, the way in which the teachers seemed to see a link between the social attractiveness of speakers and success at school, where the teenagers did not equate these two attributes, was a telling finding, pointing to contrasting views about those who are thought likely to achieve scholarly success.

It is inevitable that teachers and students approach the scholastic enterprise from their different institutional positions. A notion like 'success at school' must mean different things to those with an institutional responsibility to instil or elicit success, and to those who are still coming to terms with the school's ideological values. On the other hand, the students *are* discriminating about who among their peer-groups is and is not likely to succeed, and the studies show that this judgement is, even for school students, sociolinguistically mediated. In addition, though, the data give a sense of social evaluation being carried out in different experiential domains. The students can and do evaluate their peers in terms of the school's values and norms, but they also have a rich repertoire for evaluating them in terms of their social attributes. Indeed, one can argue that the dimension of social attractiveness, as it is traditionally seen and discussed in the language attitudes literature, seems extremely thin, compared to the semantics of the teenagers' spontaneous evaluative repertoires in the narratives study.

Identity dynamics in the teenagers

In the teenagers' subjectivities, the data showed a complex but nevertheless structured set of perceptions of their peers and themselves. Apart from their perceptions of Welshness in the speakers they heard being clearly attributable to dialect differences, the other values they displayed emanated from the complexities of the interplay between dialect on the one hand and narrative performance on the other. And the open-ended keywords and group discussions in particular provided bold and vivid insights into the identity negotiation that is going on in their lives at this time, and the rich resources they are able to draw upon in constructing and restructuring their social identities. Welsh identity is clearly important in these young people's lives, whatever happens at that age with their attitudes to the Welsh language itself (if this is relevant to them). In some parts of Wales there are seemingly powerful, if not vitriolic, intergroup processes at work against English identity. But, as has been noted earlier in this chapter, there are also competing definitions of Welshness for the teenagers – for example, the separate 'northern' Welshness of north-west Wales in the eyes of the south-westerners, and the urban ('townie') and rural ('sheepshagger') divide in the market-towns areas, usually suggesting a rejection of a future based on traditional Welsh rural occupations. On the other hand, the very nature of the task that these young people were asked to complete – listening to audio-recordings of speakers of different dialects, with the objective of investigating how these dialectal differences are reflected in evaluative differences – probably militates against the emergence of potential, more widely shared Welsh identities: for example, the youth-oriented, rock-music focused identity of 'cool Cymru' projected across all of Wales through the (in particular, Welsh) media.

Research methodology

Critical accounts of the main approaches to language attitudes research were set out at some length in chapters 1, 2 and 3, with a particular emphasis on the various methods subsumed under direct approaches, including perceptual dialectological techniques, and those under indirect approaches, especially the MGT. It was emphasized there that what in particular makes the study of language attitudes a methodological challenge is their latent qualities as constructs. Hence, although one might get apparently 'straight answers' to 'straight questions' about attitudes in direct methods, there is often some uncertainty about whether these answers really do express the attitudes the researcher aims at accessing, or whether they have been influenced by other processes, such as social acceptability, acquiescence and so on.

Indirect methods designed to reduce the risk of such processes 'contaminating' the data (most notably, in language attitudes work, the MGT) were shown to have their own problems of validity. This has led to the studies we have been discussing, comprising several techniques directed at overlapping research issues, to see how they might complement each other to provide more certainty to the findings, as well as a greater range of insights and more contextual specification into the language attitudes they investigate. What advantages have accrued from the methodological explorations of this book?

Perceptual maps and labelling

Asking respondents to draw their perceived dialect-boundaries on (more or less) blank maps of Wales in the questionnaire study accessed some relatively consistent perceptual patterns of differentiation and distribution, showing where informants believe English language differences exist geographically in Wales. It has been valuable to see where their maps overlap with and differ from maps, whether intuited or empirically grounded, based on descriptive dialectological work and other sorts of sociocultural analysis in Wales. However, in this study, perceptual maps were used mainly to form the basis of open-ended tasks to see not only where informants perceive dialect differences, but also how they characterize this variation descriptively and evaluatively. These characterizations have congealed into evaluative and representational dimensions, mainly displaying the salience of affective factors, linguistic forms and qualities of Welshness. At the same time, they have not shown much evidence of a discriminating dimension that is otherwise long-established in language attitudinal research – prestige. In much previous language attitudes research, it has been shown how evaluative dimensions operate independently of each other; indeed, this is very much how attitudinal 'dimensions' are defined. And in these labels and characterizations, evaluative dimensions do also appear to operate independently of one another, generating different profiles for different perceived dialect-zones. Hence, for example, Welshness is not necessarily associated with co-varying positive affective qualities. On the other hand, there seems to be less independence between the linguistic-forms dimension (arguably not an evaluative 'dimension' of the sort typically identified in language attitudes research) and the affective dimension. Linguistic characterizations, which are often non-technical or semi-technical, seem to be more likely to be mentioned in cases where a dialect zone is perceived in terms of negative affect than positive affect, as if serving the function of external and fixed causal attributions (Hewstone, 1989) for such reactions. This suggestion that linguistic forms are more likely to achieve salience where they link with negative rather than positive affective connotations also deserves to be pursued further. Indeed, there is a broader related issue here of delving deeper to try to gain a clearer picture and understanding of the processes that make a dialect prone to imitation or parody.

Attitude scales

The scales section of the questionnaire study demonstrated the importance of not simply basing the selection of evaluative scales and dimensions on what has been found previously in other studies. In chapter 3 we pointed to the risk of circularity in such an approach, and to the risks of missing important parts of the specific picture in Heise's (1970) claim that the basic goal of using semantic-differential scales is to load measurements on to the three previously (and long-) established major dimensions. The inclusion of the Welshness scale in the first study, and its impact, stand in clear opposition to Heise's view.

Indeed these scales findings, based on inferential statistical analysis, have also given a firm, if somewhat traditional, reference point for the other, open-ended, data in the questionnaire study, as well as contributing to the cumulative picture that is further developed in the set of narratives studies. These statistical comparisons of community profiles have required the initial search for associations amongst the individual scales to see whether or not they merge into dimensions. Thus, it has been possible to posit the separateness of the Welshness dimension with statistical probability. Furthermore, the use of scales has meant that statistical procedures have also found differences on various social-contextual variables: north versus south Wales, Welsh speakers versus non-Welsh speakers and, indeed, the evaluative profiles of the specific communities.

All of these have provided a secure backdrop for the open-ended data, setting out the perceptual reality or salience of the main social categories, bringing more confidence to interpretations when similar patterns have emerged in the open-ended data, too. In a sense, the scales data in both studies have sketched out a fairly clear and confident outline for the open-ended data to elaborate on, often with vivid stereotypic sociolinguistic profiling. In this way, too, the open-ended data have highlighted the limitations of relying upon scales alone, and we would not want to argue that there is a clear priority in using closed-ended over open-ended (or quantitative over qualitative) data. As we have already commented, perhaps one of the most interesting instances of the need for multiple methods in the questionnaire study was the relative absence of the prestige dimension in the open-ended data, possibly illustrating a shortcoming in some of the previous language attitudes research that has employed semantic- differential scales. This is that, even where respondents differentiate between languages or language varieties on certain scales or dimensions, we cannot simply assume that these scales or dimensions are therefore more important to them than – or even as important as – other scales or dimensions, even those where no differentiations are made at all. This shows the value of experimenting with dimensions, and of not foreclosing on methods too early.

Future work

This range of techniques combined in a single questionnaire instrument, and relying in part on the abilities of respondents to conceptualize a number of dialect communities across Wales, has given a fairly consistent record of perceptions and attitudes across Wales, with each technique (maps, labels, characterizations, scales, the social acceptability item, asking how these dialect communities are viewed outside Wales) providing further manifestations of attitudes, and illuminating some additional facets of attitudes and stereotypes.

There is undoubtedly more analysis that could be usefully conducted on the perceptual maps drawn by respondents. Some studies have produced composite maps of various kinds with small numbers or sub-samples of informants, or by selecting in advance a specific dialect area of which to examine perceptions (for example, Long, 1999a, 1999b), or by using pre-established (such as political or administrative) divisions or boundaries (for example, Preston, 1989; Dailey-O'Cain, 1999; Hartley, 1999). Other perceptual studies, however, have sought to produce more comprehensive composite maps, based upon the frequencies with which boundaries are drawn around particular areas, and these approaches seem to us particularly worthwhile directions to take with Welsh data in future. These involve finding software solutions, perhaps via software that digitizes maps, in order to construct and compare composite maps for subgroups: for example, from within the various dialect communities, and different age-groups. Such maps might then also serve as a basis for further scaled evaluative reactions, rather than, as in our questionnaire study, asking respondents to give scaled evaluations to communities determined largely by intuited descriptive dialectological research. We mentioned in chapter 5 that language use and language change may well respond to or correspond with such mental maps and evaluations of the zones and varieties within them. The geolinguistic trend of language attitudes research is therefore one that needs to continue.

Dialect performance

One of the arguments raised by exponents of the MGT against presenting each speech variety in the voice of an individual community member, and hence including several different speakers in order to include a range of varieties, was that it would introduce too many interfering variables. Not only would judges be evaluating, say, different *accents*, but also other, idiosyncratic voice and performance qualities (pitch, rate, etc.), even if content was kept constant. Having a large number of people producing each accent instead of one representative speaker per language variety, but still at least keeping content constant, it was sometimes argued, might help to reduce or cancel out effects from these intervening variables. Scores for each variety might then be arrived at by averaging across all the speakers representing that variety. But, in turn, the large number of speakers involved could make the listening task so long that fatigue effects would lead to such a study becoming unmanageable.

The design implemented in our narratives study, then, with just two speakers selected from a much larger set of audio-recordings made in each of the communities, challenges the weight of these arguments. This in itself was not the first time a language attitudes study had been based around two 'real' speakers for each community. For example, Edwards and Jacobsen (1987) also did this, but they were motivated to do so in large part because of the difficulty or impossibility of finding a single person to perform the matched guises they required. In contrast, the decision in our study was also motivated by the important theoretical arguments concerning authenticity issues in the MGT. It was motivated, too, by issues regarding the integrity and cultural constitution of dialect varieties, even at the expense of the methodological 'elegance' of the MGT approach. These are arguments that led us to the analysis of dialect performances by community members, performances not controlled for content, but guided towards a degree of uniformity in their communicative design (telling narratives about frightening, embarrassing or funny things that have happened to them, or to people they know).

'Presentations of dialects' in our study, then, were excerpts from dialect performances from young teenagers who had grown up in these communities, and whose dialects (especially in the presence of their peers) were less likely to be accommodated to the normative pressures of, say, careers, or to the social influences and demands of moving residence to other communities, etc. Having just two speakers from each community went some way to addressing the important methodological consideration of keeping the listening task manageable. In terms of the analysis of these speaker pairs, it would have been possible, as in Edwards and Jacobsen's study, simply to average the scores across each pair of speakers to arrive at a single score for each community (which, in their case, then allowed the possibility of conducting the conventional analysis of variance on the data). But such an approach would have concealed the very properties that were of particular interest to us: that is, the way in which local and individual features in spoken performance impinge upon community-level processes. Similarly, confronting the rhetorical and cultural qualities of performance events per se led us to ask further questions about social evaluation, for example about the 'demand characteristics' of performed narratives among young people; so it was necessary to explore alternative techniques of analysis that would allow these properties to reveal themselves. This is why we focused on different speakers of each dialect (even if, in this study, only two speakers), leading to analysis using cluster analysis and multidimensional scaling. By these means, it has proved possible to show how people's judgements can be influenced in different directions when dialect and communicative performance operate together and reveal systematic interaction, between phonological and other dialect- markers on the one hand, and features of content, context and performance on the other.

Our narratives study, then, has evidenced a need to go beyond designs using discrete dialects expressing apparently fixed meanings, as in the MGT, and it projects an argument for integrating dialect and attitudes into a sociolinguistic theory of language use, rather than leaving dialect study in its traditional place as an independent discipline. Moreover, the findings open up many possible ways forward to explore these interplays further. To include more speakers, both sexes, different age-groups, for example, from (if necessary, a smaller number of) communities could reveal more complexities in these interactions, with different aspects of performances gaining salience for different speakers. Similarly, reactions to more types of dialect performance than storytelling alone need to be investigated, including exploring the role of performance features and frames in everyday interactional talk.

Combining research techniques has also been of benefit in setting a context in which to study the interplays mentioned above. The conceptual data in the various strands of the questionnaire study have provided a vantage point by documenting attitudes towards more abstract notions of dialect and community than did the dynamic and more context-rich performances of our second study. The differences that emerged between the evaluations of pairs of speakers from the same dialect communities, as respondents this time heard them 'using' and 'doing things with' their dialects, were more striking when considered against the evaluative maps and community profiles from the questionnaire study (for example, the way in which the students' affiliative judgements split the north-east pair, the north-west pair, the south-west pair and the Cardiff pair into separate clusters – see the discussion of figure 7.4 in chapter 7).

Keywords

The use of scales in conjunction with open-ended data (this time, what we called 'keywords') in the narratives study has afforded the same sorts of advantages as those mentioned in relation to the scales and labels/characterizations in the earlier study. And it has been shown that the collection of keywords data only, when used as a preliminary for the design of attitudinal scales or other closed items, does not fully exploit the value of such data. It was seen how the keywords, like the free-discussion data from the focus groups, were an illuminating discursive shorthand, delving deeper into attitudes, emotional reactions, vivid stereotyping, and attitudinal processes than the scales did alone. They have revealed linguistic repertoires that reflect local differences in salient values and priorities across young teenagers in Wales and, in so doing, they have allowed more insight into the cultural worlds of these teenagers than have studies assuming a universal set of dimensions applied to a whole host of separate communities. Keyword and focus-group data, with their evaluative labels often allocating speakers to particular peer groups, have allowed greater access to in- and out-grouping processes that, as was shown in our review of the human communication literature on adolescence, are of such special importance during that life-period. In fact, these approaches display the theoretical link between attitudes and group membership. Although the conventional line of interpretation is that group membership dictates or influences attitudes, these data show how the expression of attitudes is part of the process of constituting groups, and is part of social belonging.

Similar data, analysed here in relation only to adolescents, could also usefully be collected in much other language attitudes work. As with the labels and characterization data in the questionnaire study, keywords give a more detailed picture than scales tend to achieve on their own. They may show not just whether a speaker with a particular accent is perceived to be, say, intelligent to a greater or lesser degree, but also what value listeners place upon this property: whether they are impressed by, dismissive, or resentful of it, for example, whether they attribute much importance to it, what they associate it with, whether they appear to be thinking in terms of a number of different kinds of intelligence, etc. The approach does have drawbacks, too, of course. In particular, we noted that keyword frequencies are less comparable across groups than are frequencies from forced-choice techniques. Free-discussion data similarly offset the advantages of vibrancy and categorization-in-action data against the disadvantages of being particularistic and context-bound.

Dialect recognition

In responding to Preston's call to include a dialect-identification item in language attitudes studies where respondents are played recordings of accents or dialects, we have been able to report some further interesting findings. Preston himself seemed to be seeing the identification of a speaker's dialect in terms of a process of cognitive mapping, where listeners either recognize, at some level of accuracy, or fail to recognize the dialect communities that the speakers are from, or are intended to represent. (Edwards and Jacobsen, 1987, who also found some relatively low rates of 'accurate' accent-identification in their data, saw recognition in similar terms.) However, evidence in our study supported the tantalizing interpretation that dialect recognition is part of a much more elaborate process of *social cognition*, reflecting ideologies and preferences in listeners' communities and strategies in representing them. Responding to the question of where they think a speaker comes from is likely to tap into the same intergroup processes that were influencing responses to the other evaluative tasks in both of our sets of studies. And, although such processes may also be at work amongst adult respondents with more experience of and access to a range of dialect speakers, our review of the communication literature on adolescence and our keywords and discussion-group results show that these intergroup processes, which underpin the building and refining of group priorities, are particularly active for the teenagers. The recognition item has revealed itself in part to be a further manifestation of evaluative reactions to language use, and not merely a reliability check on language attitudes data.

Summing up

The work we have set out here had, as a core part of its design, many methodological strands. It has been spread over a relatively large geographical area (depending on one's world-view), involving a large number of respondents. One might be entitled to ask, particularly if all research methods are in some way flawed and partial, whether the use of such a battery of methods to collect data is detrimental rather than advantageous, and whether it simply produces an overcomplicated and hopelessly confused picture. In this final chapter, we believe it is possible to say that this approach has *removed* some of the confusion that precipitated Price et al.'s (1983) call, and that, while these studies, like most others, have stimulated many further issues to be explored, it has been possible to achieve a sharper focus than existed earlier, and to find explanations for some of the lack of consistency in the findings of earlier studies. Despite this, sociolinguistic work in Wales needs to progress further, to include more social and cultural groups, and to continue to explore new approaches for linking linguistic, social and subjective factors.

The field of 'language attitudes' emerges from these studies in Wales as one that is still, conceptually and methodologically, in its early phase. Although language attitudes research tends to be construed within sociolinguistics as a discrete, banded and even dogmatic methodology, linked to specific analytic objectives of showing the status and social attractiveness of prototypical speakers, we believe that our review and critique show otherwise. Language attitudes research can develop with a richly differentiated set of techniques and perspectives able to fill out our understanding of the complex subjective worlds in which sociolinguistic varieties exist.

References

Aboud, F. E. (1976). 'Social and developmental aspects of language', *Papers in Linguistics*, 9, 15–37.
Aitchison, J. and Carter, H. (1994). *A Geography of Welsh*, Cardiff, University of Wales Press.
Ajzen, I. and Fishbein, M. (1980). *Understanding Attitudes and Predicting Social Behaviour*, Englewood Cliffs, NJ, Prentice-Hall.
Aldenderfer, M. and Blashfield, R. (1984). *Cluster Analysis*, Newbury Park, CA, Sage.
Alderfer, C. (1968). 'Comparison of questionnaire responses with and without preceding interviews', *Journal of Applied Psychology*, 52, 335–40.
Aldridge, M. and Wood, J. (1998). *Interviewing Children: a Guide for Child Care and Forensic Practitioners*, Chichester, UK, Wiley.
Allport, G. (1935). 'Attitudes', in C. Murchison (ed.), *A Handbook of Social Psychology, Vol. 2*, Worcester, MA, Clark University Press.
Appadurai, A. (1996). *Modernity at Large: Cultural Dimensions of Globalization*, Minneapolis, MI, University of Minnesota Press.
Baker, C. (1988). *Key Issues in Bilingualism and Bilingual Education*, Clevedon, Multilingual Matters.
Baker, C. (1992). *Attitudes and Language*, Clevedon, Multilingual Matters.
Ball, P. (1983). 'Stereotypes of Anglo-Saxon and non-Anglo-Saxon accents: some exploratory Australian studies with the matched-guise technique', *Language Sciences*, 5, 163–84.
Ball, P., Byrne, J., Giles, H., Berechree, P., Griffiths, J., McDonald, H. and McKendrick, I. (1982). 'The retroactive speech stereotype effect: some Australian data and constraints', *Language and Communication*, 2, 277–84.
Ball, P., Giles, H., Byrne, J. and Berechree, P. (1984). 'Situational constraints on the evaluative significance of speech accommodation: some Australian data', *International Journal of the Sociology of Language*, 46, 115–29.

Balsom, D. (1985). 'The three-Wales model', in J. Osmond (ed.), *The National Question Again: Welsh Political Identity in the 1980s*, Llandysul, Gomer.

Bauman, R. (1977). *Verbal Art as Performance*, Prospect Heights, IL, Waveland Press.

Bauman, R. (1992). 'Performance', in R. Bauman (ed.), *Folklore, Cultural Performances, and Popular Entertainments*, New York and Oxford, Oxford University Press.

Bauman, R. (1996). 'Transformations of the word in the production of Mexican festival drama', in M. Silverstein and G. Urban (eds), *Natural Histories of Discourse*, Chicago and London, University of Chicago Press.

Bauman, R. and Briggs, C. (1990). 'Poetics and performance as critical perspectives on language and social life', *Annual Review of Anthropology*, 19, 59–88.

Baxter, L. (1992). 'Root metaphors in accounts of developing romantic relationships', *Journal of Social and Personal Relationships*, 9, 253–75.

Baxter, L. and Wilmot, W. (1984). 'Secret tests: social strategies for acquiring information about the state of the relationship', *Human Communication Research*, 11, 171–201.

Bayard, D., Weatherall, A., Gallois, C. and Pittam, J. (2001). 'Pax Americana? Accent attitudinal evaluations in New Zealand, Australia and America', *Journal of Sociolinguistics*, 5, 22–49.

Bellenger, D., Bernhardt, K. and Goldstucker, J. (1976). 'Qualitative research techniques: focus group interviews', in J. Higginbotham and K. Cox (eds), *Focus Group Interviews: A Reader*, Chicago, American Marketing Association.

Bellin, W., Matsuyama, A. and Schott, G. (1999). 'Teaching a "dead" language, teaching through a "dead" language: conflict and consensus during language revitalisation', in Eusko Jauralitza and Gobierno Basco, *Proceedings of the Seventh International Minority Languages Conference*, Bilbao, Spain.

Bettinghaus, E. and Cody, M. (1994). *Persuasive Communication*, Fort Worth, TX, Harcourt Brace.

Bezooijen, R. van (1994). 'Aesthetic evaluation of Dutch language varieties', *Language and Communication*, 14, 253–63.

Bixenstine, V., DeCorte, M. and Bixenstine, B. (1976). 'Conformity to peer-sponsored misconduct at four grade levels', *Developmental Psychology*, 12, 226–36.

Blommaert, J. and Verschueren, J. (1998). *Debating Diversity: Analysing the Discourse of Tolerance*, London, Routledge.

Boster, F. (1990). 'Group argument, social pressure, and the making of group decisions', in J. A. Anderson (ed.), *Communication Yearbook*, 13, Newbury Park, CA, Sage.

Bourhis, R. (1977). 'Language and social evaluation in Wales', unpublished Ph.D. thesis, University of Bristol.

REFERENCES

Bourhis, R. (1983). 'Language attitudes and self-reports of French-English language usage in Quebec', *Journal of Multilingual and Multicultural Development*, 4, 163–80.

Bourhis, R. and Giles, H. (1976). 'The language of co-operation in Wales: a field study', *Language Sciences*, 42, 13–16.

Bourhis, R., Giles, H. and Lambert, W. (1975). 'Social consequences of accommodating one's style of speech: a cross-national investigation', *International Journal of the Sociology of Language*, 6, 55–72.

Bourhis, R., Giles, H. and Tajfel, H. (1973). 'Language as a determinant of Welsh identity', *European Journal of Social Psychology*, 3, 447–60.

Bradac, J. (1990). 'Language attitudes and impression formation', in H. Giles and P. Robinson (eds), *Handbook of Language and Social Psychology*, Chichester, UK, Wiley.

Bradford Brown, B., Mory, M. and Kinney, D. (1994). 'Casting adolescent crowds in a relational perspective: caricature, channel, context', in R. Montemayor, G. Adams and T. Gullotta (eds), *Personal Relationships during Adolescence*, Thousand Oaks, CA, Sage.

Breckler, S. (1984). 'Empirical validation of affect, behaviour, and cognition as distinct components of attitude', *Journal of Personality and Social Psychology*, 47, 1191–205.

Brehm, S. and Brehm, J. (1981). *Psychological Reactance: A Theory of Freedom and Control*, New York, Academic Press.

Brown, B., Strong, W. and Rencher, A. (1975). 'Acoustic determinants of the perceptions of personality from speech', *International Journal of the Sociology of Language*, 6, 11–32.

Burroughs, G. (1971). *Design and Analysis in Educational Research*, Birmingham, University of Birmingham Press.

Cacioppo, J., Petty, R., Losch, M. and Crites, S. (1994). 'Psychophysiological approaches to attitudes: detecting affective dispositions when people won't say, can't say, or don't even know', in S. Shavitt and T. Brock (eds), *Persuasion: Psychological Insights and Perspectives*, Boston, MA, Allyn and Bacon.

Calder, R. J. (1977). 'Focus groups and the nature of qualitative marketing research', *Journal of Marketing Research*, 14, 353–64.

Callan, V., Gallois, C. and Forbes, P. (1983). 'Evaluative reactions to accented English', *Journal of Cross-cultural Psychology*, 14, 407–26.

Cannon, A. (1994). 'Clinton's love of polls shows he can't stop campaigning, critics say', *Miami Herald*, 18 April 1994, 4a.

Cargile, A. (2002). 'Speaker evaluation measures of language attitudes: evidence of information-processing effects', *Language Awareness*, 11, 178–91.

Cargile, A., Giles, H., Ryan, E. B., and Bradac, J. (1994). 'Language attitudes as a social process: a conceptual model and new directions', *Language and Communication*, 14, 211–236.

Carranza, M. (1976). 'Language attitudes and other cultural attitudes of Mexican American adults: some sociolinguistic implications', unpublished Ph.D. thesis, Notre Dame, IN.

Carranza, M. and Ryan, E.B. (1975).'Evaluative reactions of bilingual Anglo- and Mexican-American adolescents towards speakers of English and Spanish', *International Journal of the Sociology of Language*, 6, 83–104.

Catan, L., Dennison, C. and Coleman, J. (1996). *Getting Through: Effective Communication in the Teenage Years*, London, The BT Forum.

Chambers, J. and Trudgill, P. (1980). *Dialectology*, Cambridge, Cambridge University Press.

Chandler, P., Robinson, P. and Noyes, P. (1988). 'The level of linguistic knowledge and awareness amongst students training to be primary teachers', *Language and Education*, 2, 161–73.

Cheshire, J. and Moser, L.-M. (1994). 'English as a cultural symbol', *Journal of Multilingual and Multicultural Development*, 15, 451–69.

Choy, S. and Dodd, D. (1976). 'Standard English speaking and non-standard Hawaiian English speaking children: comprehension of both dialects and teachers' evaluations', *Journal of Educational Psychology*, 68, 184–93.

CILAR (Committee on Irish Language Attitudes Research) (1975). *Report of the Committee on Irish Language Attitudes Research*, Dublin, Government Stationery Office.

Cohen, L. and Manion, L. (1994). *Research Methods in Education*, London, Routledge.

Connolly, J. (1990). 'Port Talbot English', in N. Coupland (ed.), *English in Wales: Diversity, Conflict and Change*, Clevedon: Multilingual Matters.

Cook, S. and Sellitz, C. (1964). 'A multiple-indicator approach to attitude measurement', *Psychological Bulletin*, 62, 36–55.

Cots, J. and Nussbaum, L. (1999). 'Schooling, language and teachers: language awareness and the discourse of the educational reform in Catalonia', *Language Awareness*, 8, 174–89.

Coupland, N. (1988). *Dialect in Use: Sociolinguistic Variation in Cardiff English*, Cardiff, University of Wales Press.

Coupland, N. (ed.) (1990). *English in Wales: Diversity, Conflict and Change*, Clevedon, Multilingual Matters.

Coupland, N. (2000). 'Sociolinguistic prevarication over Standard English', *Journal of Sociolinguistics*, 4, 614–21.

Coupland, N. (forthcoming). 'The discursive framing of phonological acts of identity: Welshness through English', in C. Evans-Davies, J. Brutt-Griffler and L. Pickering (eds), *English and Ethnicity*, London, Palgrave.

Coupland, N., Bishop, H. and Garrett, P. (forthcoming). 'Home truths: globalization and the iconizing of Welsh in a Welsh-American newspaper', *Journal of Multilingual and Multicultural Development*.

REFERENCES

Coupland, N., Williams, A. and Garrett, P. (1994). 'The social meanings of Welsh English: teachers' stereotyped judgements', *Journal of Multilingual and Multicultural Development*, 15, 471–91.

Coupland, N., Williams, A. and Garrett, P. (1999). 'Welshness and Englishness as attitudinal dimensions of English language varieties in Wales', in D. Preston (ed.), *Handbook of Perceptual Dialectology, Vol. 1*, Amsterdam, Benjamins.

Cremona, C. and Bates, E. (1977). 'The development of attitudes toward dialect in Italian children', *Journal of Psycholinguistic Research*, 6, 223–32.

Dailey-O'Cain, J. (1999). 'The perception of post-unification German regional speech', in D. Preston (ed.), *Handbook of Perceptual Dialectology, Vol. 1*, Amsterdam, Benjamins.

Davies, W. (2000). 'Language awareness amongst teachers in a Central German dialect', *Language Awareness*, 9, 119–34

Dawes, R. and Smith, T. (1985). 'Attitude and opinion measurement', in G. Lindzey and E. Aronson (eds), *Handbook of Social Psychology*, New York, Random House.

Day, R. (1980). 'The development of linguistic attitudes and preferences', *TESOL Quarterly*, 14, 27–37.

Day, R. (1982). 'Children's attitudes toward language', in E. B. Ryan and H. Giles (eds), *Attitudes towards Language Variation*, London, Edward Arnold.

Doise, W., Sinclair, A. and Bourhis, R. (1976). 'Evaluation of accent convergence and divergence in co-operative and competitive intergroup situations', *British Journal of Social and Clinical Psychology*, 15, 247–52.

Drury, J., Catan, L., Dennison, C. and Brody, R. (1998). 'Exploring teenagers' accounts of bad communication: a new basis for intervention', *Journal of Adolescence*, 21, 177–96.

Dunnette, M. and Heneman, H. (1956). 'Influence of scale administrator on employee attitude responses', *Journal of Applied Psychology*, 40, 73–7.

Eckert, P. (1989). *Jocks and Burnouts: Social Categories and Identity in the High School*, New York, Teachers College Press.

Edwards, J. (1982). 'Language attitudes and their implication among English speakers', in E. B. Ryan and H. Giles (eds), *Attitudes towards Language Variation*, London, Edward Arnold.

Edwards, J. and Giles, H. (1984). 'Application of the social psychology of language: sociolinguistics and education', in P. Trudgill (ed.), *Applied Sociolinguistics*, London, Academic Press.

Edwards, J. and Jacobsen, M. (1987). 'Standard and regional speech: distinctions and similarities', *Language in Society*, 16, 369–80.

Edwards, V. (1991). 'The Welsh speech community', in S. Alladina and V. Edwards (eds), *Multilingualism in the British Isles: The Older Mother Tongues and Europe*, London, Longman.

El Dash, L. and Tucker, R. (1975). 'Subjective reactions to various speech styles in Egypt', *International Journal of the Sociology of Language*, 6, 33–54.

Erickson, F. (1975). 'Gatekeeping and the melting pot: interaction in counselling encounters', *Harvard Educational Review*, 45, 44–70.

Everitt, B. (1993). *Cluster Analysis*, London, Edward Arnold.

Fairclough, N. (1995). *Critical Discourse Analysis*, London, Longman.

Festinger, L. (1957). *A Theory of Cognitive Dissonance*, Stanford, CA, Stanford University Press.

Gal, S. and Irvine, J. (1995). 'The boundaries of languages and disciplines: how ideologies construct differences', *Social Research*, 62, 967–1001.

Gallois, C. and Callan, V. (1981). 'Personality impressions elicited by accented English speech', *Journal of Cross-Cultural Psychology*, 12, 347–59.

Gardner, R. (1982). 'Language attitudes and language learning', in E. B. Ryan and H. Giles (eds), *Attitudes towards Language Variation*, London, Edward Arnold.

Gardner, R. and Lambert, W. (1972). *Attitudes and Motivation in Second Language Learning*, Rowley, MA, Newbury House.

Garrett, P. (1992). 'Accommodation and hyperaccommodation in foreign language learners: contrasting responses to French and Spanish English speakers by native and non-native recipients', *Language and Communication*, 12, 295–315.

Garrett, P. and Austin, C. (1993). 'The English genitive apostrophe: judgements of errors and implications for teaching', *Language Awareness*, 2, 61–75.

Garrett, P., Coupland, N. and Williams, A. (1995). 'City harsh and the Welsh version of RP: some ways in which teachers view dialects of Welsh English', *Language Awareness*, 4, 99–107.

Garrett, P., Coupland, N. and Williams, A. (1999). 'Evaluating dialect in discourse: teachers' and teenagers' responses to young English speakers in Wales', *Language in Society*, 28, 321–54.

Garrett, P., Coupland, N. and Williams, A. (forthcoming). 'Adolescents' lexical repertoires of peer evaluation: boring prats and English snobs', in A. Jaworski, N. Coupland, and D. Galasinski (eds), *Metalanguage: Social and Ideological Perspectives*, The Hague, Mouton.

Garrett, P., Griffiths, Y., James, C. and Scholfield, P. (1992). 'Differences and similarities between and within bilingual settings: some British data', *Language, Culture and Curriculum*, 5, 99–116.

Garrett, P., Griffiths, Y., James, C. and Scholfield, P. (1994). 'Use of mother-tongue in second language classrooms: an experimental investigation of effects on the attitudes and writing performance of bilingual UK schoolchildren', *Journal of Multilingual and Multicultural Development*, 15, 371–83.

Gass, R. and Seiter, J. (1999). *Persuasion, Social Influence, and Compliance Gaining*, Boston, MA, Allyn and Bacon.

Gavin, L. and Furman, W. (1989). 'Age differences in adolescents' perceptions of their peer groups', *Developmental Psychology*, 25, 827–34.

Genesee, F. and Bourhis, R. (1982). 'The social psychological significance of code-switching in cross-cultural communication', *Journal of Language and Social Psychology*, 1, 1–28.

Genesee, F. and Bourhis, R. (1988). 'Evaluative reactions to language choice strategies: the role of sociocultural factors', *Language and Communication*, 8, 229–50.

Giles, H. (1970). 'Evaluative reactions to accents', *Educational Review*, 22, 211–27.

Giles, H. (1971a). 'Patterns of evaluation of RP, South Welsh English and Somerset accented speech', *British Journal of Social and Clinical Psychology*, 10, 280–1.

Giles, H. (1971b). 'Teachers' attitudes towards accent usage and change', *Educational Review*, 23, 11–25.

Giles, H. (1990). 'Social meanings of Welsh English', in N. Coupland (ed.), *English in Wales: Diversity, Conflict and Change*, Clevedon, Multilingual Matters.

Giles, H., Baker, S. and Fielding, G. (1975). 'Communication length as a behavioural index of accent prejudice', *International Journal of the Sociology of Language*, 6, 73–81.

Giles, H., Bourhis, R. and Davies, A. (1979). 'Prestige speech styles: the imposed norm and inherent value hypotheses', in W. McCormack and S. Wurm (eds), *Language in Anthropology IV: Language in Many Ways*, The Hague, Mouton.

Giles, H., Bourhis, R. and Taylor, D. (1977). 'Towards a theory of language in ethnic group relations', in H. Giles (ed.), *Language, Ethnicity and Intergroup Relations*, London, Academic Press.

Giles, H., Bourhis, R., Trudgill, P. and Lewis, A. (1974). 'The imposed norm hypothesis: a validation', *Quarterly Journal of Speech*, 60, 405–10.

Giles, H. and Coupland, N. (1991). *Language: Contexts and Consequences*, Buckingham, Open University Press.

Giles, H., Coupland, N., Henwood, K., Harriman, J. and Coupland, J. (1990). 'The social meaning of RP: an intergenerational perspective', in S. Ramsaran (ed.), *Studies in the Pronunciation of English: A Commemorative Volume in Honour of A. C. Gimson*, London, Routledge.

Giles, H. and Farrar, K. (1979). 'Some behavioural consequences of speech and dress styles', *British Journal of Social and Clinical Psychology*, 18, 209–10.

Giles, H., Harrison, C., Creber, C., Smith, P. and Freeman, N. (1983). 'Developmental and contextual aspects of children's language attitudes', *Language and Communication*, 3, 1–6.

Giles, H. and Powesland, P. (1975). *Speech Style and Social Evaluation*, London, Academic Press.
Giles, H. and Sassoon, C. (1983). 'The effect of speaker's accent, social class background and message style on British listeners' social judgements', *Language and Communication*, 3, 305–13.
Gorter, D. and Ytsma, J. (1988). 'Social factors and language attitudes in Friesland', in R. van Hout and U. Knops (eds), *Language Attitudes in the Dutch Language Area*, Dordrecht, Foris.
Gould, P. (1977). 'Changing mental maps: childhood to adulthood', *Ekistics*, 255, 100–21.
Gould, P. and White, R. (1986). *Mental Maps*, Boston, MA, Allen and Unwin.
Granger, R., Mathews, M., Quay, L. and Verner, R. (1977). 'Teacher judgements of the communication effectiveness of children using different speech patterns', *Journal of Educational Psychology*, 69, 793–6.
Haarmann, H. (1984). 'The role of ethnocultural stereotypes and foreign languages in Japanese commercials', *International Journal of the Sociology of Language*, 50, 101–21.
Haarmann, H. (1986). 'Verbal strategies in Japanese fashion magazines: a study in impersonal bilingualism and ethnosymbolism', *International Journal of the Sociology of Language*, 58, 107–121.
Halliday, M. A. K. (1978). *Language as Social Semiotic*, London, Edward Arnold.
Hanson, D. (1980). 'Relationship between methods and findings in attitude-behaviour research', *Psychology*, 17, 11–13.
Hargreaves, D. (1967). *Social Relations in a Secondary School*, London, Routledge and Kegan Paul.
Hartley, L. (1999). 'A view from the West: perception of US dialects by Oregon residents', in D. Preston (ed.), *Handbook of Perceptual Dialectology, Vol. 1*, Amsterdam, Benjamins.
Heaven, P. (1994). *Contemporary Adolescence: A Social Psychological Approach*, Basingstoke, Macmillan.
Heise, D. (1970). 'The semantic differential in attitude research', in G. F. Summers (ed.), *Attitude Measurement*, New York, Rand McNally.
Henerson, M., Morris, L. and Fitz-Gibbon, C. (1987). *How to Measure Attitudes*, Newbury Park, CA, Sage.
Hewstone, M. (1989). *Causal Attribution*, Oxford, Blackwell.
Hewstone, M. and Giles, H. (1997). 'Social groups and social stereotypes', in N. Coupland and A. Jaworski (eds), *Sociolinguistics: A Reader and Coursebook*, Basingstoke, Macmillan.
Hidalgo, M. (1984). 'Attitudes and behaviour toward English in Juarez, Mexico', *Anthropological Linguistics*, 26, 376–92.
Hodge, R., and Kress, G. (1988). *Social Semiotics*, Cambridge, Polity Press.

REFERENCES

Hoenigswald, H. (1966). 'A proposal for the study of folklinguistics', in W. Bright (ed.), *Sociolinguistics*, The Hague, Mouton.

Hogg, M. (1992). *The Social Psychology of Group Cohesiveness*, London, Harvester Wheatsheaf.

Holmes, J. and Ainsworth, H. (1997). 'Unpacking the research process: investigating syllable timing in New Zealand English', *Language Awareness*, 6, 32–47.

Hughes, A. and Trudgill, P. (1979). *English Accents and Dialects*, London, Edward Arnold.

Huygens, I. and Vaughan, G. (1983). 'Language attitudes, ethnicity, and social class in New Zealand', *Journal of Multilingual and Multicultural Development*, 4, 207–23.

Hymes, D. (1971). 'Competence and performance in linguistic theory', in R. Huxley and E. Ingram (eds), *Language Acquisition: Models and Methods*, London, Academic Press.

Hymes, D. (1972). 'On communicative competence', in J. Pride and J. Holmes (eds), *Sociolinguistics*, Harmondsworth, Penguin.

Hymes, D. (1974). 'Ways of speaking', in R. Baumann and J. Sherzer (eds), *Explorations in the Ethnography of Speaking*, Cambridge, Cambridge University Press.

Inoue, F. (1999). 'Subjective dialect division in Great Britain', in D. Preston (ed.), *Handbook of Perceptual Dialectology, Vol. 1*, Amsterdam, Benjamins.

Irvine, J. (2001). 'Style as distinctiveness: the culture and ideology of linguistic differentiation', in P. Eckert and J. Rickford (eds), *Style and Sociolinguistic Variation*, Cambridge, Cambridge University Press.

Irvine, J. and Gal, S. (2000). 'Language ideology and linguistic differentiation', in P. Kroskrity (ed.), *Regimes of Language: Ideologies, Polities and Identities*, Santa Fe, NM, School for American Research Press.

Jaworski, A. and Coupland, N. (eds) (1999). *The Discourse Reader*, London, Routledge.

Jaworski, A., Coupland, N. and Galasinski, D. (eds) (forthcoming). *Metalanguage: Social and Ideological Perspectives*, The Hague, Mouton.

Jones, W. R. (1949). 'Attitudes towards Welsh as a second language: a preliminary investigation', *British Journal of Educational Psychology*, 19, 44–52.

Jones, W. R. (1950). 'Attitudes towards Welsh as a second language: a further investigation', *British Journal of Educational Psychology*, 20, 117–32.

de Klerk, V. (1997). 'The role of expletives in the construction of masculinity', in S. Johnson and U. Meinhof (eds), *Language and Masculinity*, Oxford, Blackwell.

Knops, U. (1988). 'Attitudes towards regional variation in Dutch pronunciation', in R. van Hout and U. Knops (eds), *Language Attitudes in the Dutch Language Area*, Dordrecht, Foris.

Knops, U. and van Hout, R. (1988). 'Language attitudes in the Dutch language area: an introduction', in R. van Hout and U. Knops (eds), *Language Attitudes in the Dutch Language Area*, Dordrecht, Foris.

Kothandapani, V. (1971). 'Validation of feeling, belief, and intention to act as three components of attitude and their contribution to prediction of contraceptive behaviour', *Journal of Personality and Social Psychology*, 19, 321–33.

Kramarae, C. (1982). 'Gender: how she speaks', in E. B. Ryan and H. Giles (eds), *Attitudes towards Language Variation*, London, Edward Arnold.

Kramer, C. (1974). 'Stereotypes of women's speech: the world from cartoons', *Journal of Popular Culture*, 8, 624–38.

Kristiansen, T. (1997). 'Language attitudes in a Danish cinema', in N. Coupland and A. Jaworski (eds), *Sociolinguistics: A Reader and Coursebook*, Basingstoke, Macmillan.

Kristiansen, T. (2001). 'Two standards: one for the media and one for the school', *Language Awareness*, 10, 9–24.

Kristiansen, T. (forthcoming). 'Attitudes and values in representations of language: their role in language variation and change', in A. Jaworski, N. Coupland and D. Galasinski (eds), *Metalanguage: Social and Ideological Perspectives*, The Hague, Mouton.

Krueger, R. (1981). 'Focus-group interviewing: a helpful technique for agricultural educators', *The Visitor*, 73, 7, 1–4.

Kruskal, J. and Wish, M. (1978). *Multidimensional Scaling*, Beverly Hills, CA Sage.

Kuiper, L. (1999). 'Variation and the norm: Parisian perceptions of regional French', in D. Preston (ed.), *Handbook of Perceptual Dialectology, Vol. 1*, Amsterdam, Benjamins.

Labov, W. (1965). 'Stages in the acquisition of standard English', in *Social Dialects and Language Learning*, Champaign, IL, National Council of Teachers of English.

Labov, W. (1966). *The Social Significance of Speech in New York City*, Washington, DC, Centre for Applied Linguistics.

Labov, W. (1972). *Sociolinguistic Patterns*, Oxford, Blackwell.

Labov, W. (1984). 'Five methods of the project on linguistic change and variation', in J. Baugh and J. Sherzer (eds), *Language in Use*, Englewood Cliffs, NJ, Prentice Hall.

Ladegaard, H. J. (2001). 'Popular perceptions of standard language: attitudes to "regional standards" in Denmark', *Language Awareness*, 10, 25–40.

Lambert, W. (1967). 'A social psychology of bilingualism', *Journal of Social Issues*, 23, 91–109.

Lambert, W., Anisfeld, M. and Yeni-Komshian, G. (1965). 'Evaluational reactions of Jewish and Arab adolescents to dialect and language variations', *Journal of Personality and Social Psychology*, 2, 84–90.

REFERENCES

Lambert, W., Giles, H. and Picard, O. (1975). 'Language attitudes in a French-American community', *International Journal of the Sociology of Language*, 4, 127–52.

Lambert, W., Hodgson, R., Gardner, R. and Fillenbaum, S. (1960). 'Evaluational reactions to spoken languages', *Journal of Abnormal and Social Psychology*, 60, 44–51.

Lee, D. (1992). *Competing Discourses: Perspective and Ideology in Language*, London, Longman.

Lee, R. (1971). 'Dialect perception: a critical view and re-evaluation', *Quarterly Journal of Speech*, 57, 410–17.

Levin, H. and Garrett, P. (1990). 'Sentence structure and formality', *Language in Society*, 19, 511–20.

Levin, H., Giles, H. and Garrett, P. (1994). 'The effects of lexical formality and accent on trait attributions', *Language and Communication*, 14, 265–74.

Lewis, E. G. (1975). 'Attitude to language among bilingual children and adults in Wales', *International Journal of the Sociology of Language*, 4, 103–21.

Lieberson, S. (1981). *Language Diversity and Language Contact: Essays by Stanley Lieberson*, Stanford, CA, Stanford University Press.

Likert, R. (1932). *A Technique for the Measurement of Attitudes*, New York, Columbia University Press.

Long, D. (1999a). 'Geographical perceptions of Japanese dialect regions', in D. Preston (ed.), *Handbook of Perceptual Dialectology, Vol. 1*, Amsterdam, Benjamins.

Long, D. (1999b). 'Mapping non-linguists' evaluations of Japanese language variation', in D. Preston (ed.), *Handbook of Perceptual Dialectology, Vol. 1*, Amsterdam, Benjamins.

Long, D. and Preston, D. (eds) (2002). *Handbook of Perceptual Dialectology, Vol. 2*, Amsterdam, Benjamins.

Macaulay, R. (1991). *Locating Dialect in Discourse: The Language of Honest Men and Bonnie Lasses in Ayr*, Oxford, Oxford University Press.

Mackie, D. and Hamilton, D. (eds) (1993). *Affect, Cognition, and Stereotyping: Interactive Processes in Group Perception*, San Diego, CA, Academic Press.

MacKinnon, K. (1981). 'Scottish Opinion on Gaelic', Hatfield Polytechnic Social Science Research Publication SS14.

Marcia, J. (1980). 'Identity in adolescence', in J. Adelson (ed.), *Handbook of Adolescent Psychology*, New York, Wiley.

Marston, P., Hecht, M. and Robers, T. (1987). 'True love ways: the subjective experience and communication of romantic love', *Journal of Social and Personal Relationships*, 4, 387–407.

Masterson, J., Mullins, E. and Mulvihill, A. (1983). 'Components of evaluative reactions to varieties of Irish accents', *Language and Speech*, 26, 215–31.

Mees, I. (1983). 'The speech of Cardiff schoolchildren: a real time study', unpublished Ph.D. thesis, University of Leiden.

Mercer, G. (1975). 'The development of children's ability to discriminate between languages and varieties of the same language', unpublished MA thesis, McGill University, Montreal.

Metcalf, A. (1985). 'Newspaper stylebooks: strictures teach tolerance', in S. Greenbaum (ed.), *The English Language Today*, Oxford, Pergamon.

Milroy, J. and Milroy, L. (1985). *Authority in Language: Investigating Language Prescription and Standardisation*, London, Routledge.

Milroy, L. and McClenaghan, P. (1977). 'Stereotyped reactions to four educated accents in Ulster', *Belfast Working Papers in Language and Linguistics*, 2, 4.

Mitchell, R. and Hooper, J. (1991). 'Teachers' views of language knowledge', in C. James and P. Garrett (eds), *Language Awareness in the Classroom*, London, Longman.

Morgan, D. (1997). *Focus Groups as Qualitative Research*, Thousand Oaks, CA, Sage.

Mosley, R. (1969). 'Development and application of a Spanish-English bilingualism attitude scale', unpublished Ph.D. thesis, Texas A. and M. University.

Myers, D. and Arenson, S. (1972). 'Enhancement of dominant risk tendencies in group discussion', *Psychological Reports*, 30, 615–23.

Myers, D. and Lamm, H. (1976). 'The group polarisation phenomenon', *Psychological Bulletin*, 83, 602–27.

Nesdale, D. and Rooney, R. (1996). 'Evaluations and stereotyping of accented speakers by pre-adolescent children', *Journal of Language and Social Psychology*, 15, 133–54.

Newman, P. and Newman, B. (1988). 'Early adolescence and its conflict: group identity vs. alienation', *Adolescence*, 11, 261–74.

Nickols, S. and Shaw, M. (1964). 'Saliency and two measures of attitude', *Psychological Reports*, 14, 273–4.

Niedzielski, N. and Preston, D. (2000). *Folk Linguistics*, New York, Mouton.

Norušis, M. (1990). *SPSS Advanced Statistics Student Guide*, Chicago, SPSS Inc.

Oppenheim, A. (1992). *Questionnaire Design, Interviewing, and Attitude Measurement*, London, Pinter.

Oppenheim, B. (1982). 'An exercise in attitude measurement', in G. Breakwell, H. Foot, and R. Gilmour (eds), *Social Psychology: a Practical Manual*, Basingstoke, Macmillan.

O'Riagain, P. (1993). 'Stability and change in public attitudes towards Irish since the 1960s', *Teangeolas*, 32, 45–9.

Osgood, C., Suci, G. and Tannenbaum, P. (1957). *The Measurement of Meaning*, Urbana, IL, University of Illinois Press.

Oskamp, S. (1977). *Attitudes and Opinions*, Englewood Cliffs, NJ, Prentice-Hall.

Osmond, J. (ed.) (1985). *The National Question Again: Welsh Political Identity in the 1980s*, Llandysul, Gomer.

Ostrom, T. (1969). 'The relationship between the affective, behavioural, and cognitive components of attitude', *Journal of Experimental Social Psychology*, 5, 12–30.

Ostrom, T., Bond, C., Krosnik, J. and Sedikides, C. (1994). 'Attitude scales: how we measure the unmeasurable', in S. Shavitt and T. Brock (eds), *Persuasion: Psychological Insights and Perspectives*, Boston, MA, Allyn and Bacon.

Paltridge, J. and Giles, H. (1984). 'Attitudes towards speakers of regional accents of French', *Linguistische Berichte*, 90, 71–85.

Parry, D. (1990). 'The conservative English dialects of north Carmarthenshire', in N. Coupland (ed.), *English in Wales: Diversity, Conflict and Change*, Clevedon, Multilingual Matters.

Parry, D. (ed.) (1999). *A Grammar and Glossary of the Conservative Anglo-Welsh Dialects of Rural Wales*, University of Sheffield, National Centre for English Cultural Tradition.

Pavitt, C. (1994). 'Another view of group polarising: the 'reasons for' one-sided oral argumentation', *Communication Research*, 21, 625–42.

Peate, M.R., Coupland, N. and Garrett, P. (1998). 'Teaching Welsh and English in Wales', in W. Tulasiewicz and A. Adams (eds), *Teaching the Mother Tongue in a Multilingual Europe*, London, Cassell.

Penhallurick, R. J. (1991). *The Anglo-Welsh Dialects of North Wales* (University of Bamberg Studies in English Linguistics, Vol. 27), Frankfurt am Main, Peter Lang.

Perloff, R. (1993). *The Dynamics of Persuasion*, Hillsdale, NJ, Lawrence Erlbaum Associates.

Petty, R., Cacioppo, J. and Heesacker, M. (1981). 'The use of rhetorical questions in persuasion: a cognitive response analysis', *Journal of Personality and Social Psychology*, 40, 432–40.

Potter, J. and Wetherell, M. (1987). *Discourse and Social Psychology: Beyond Attitudes and Behaviour*, London, Sage.

Preston, D. (1989). *Perceptual Dialectology: Nonlinguists' Views of Areal Linguistics*, Dordrecht, Foris.

Preston, D. (1993). 'The uses of folk linguistics', *International Journal of Applied Linguistics*, 3, 181–259.

Preston, D. (1996). 'Whaddayaknow? The modes of folklinguistic awareness', *Language Awareness*, 5, 40–74.

Preston, D. (ed.) (1999). *Handbook of Perceptual Dialectology, Vol. 1*, Amsterdam, Benjamins.

Price, S., Fluck, M. and Giles, H. (1983). 'The effects of language of testing on bilingual pre-adolescents' attitudes towards Welsh and varieties of English', *Journal of Multilingual and Multicultural Development*, 4, 149–61.

Price-Jones, E. (1982). 'A study of some of the factors which determine the degree of bilingualism of a Welsh child between 10 and 13 years of age', unpublished Ph.D. thesis, University of Wales.

Rampton, B. (1995). *Crossing: Language and Ethnicity among Adolescents*, London, Longman.

Rickford, J. and Traugott, E. (1985). 'Symbol of powerlessness and degeneracy, or symbol of solidarity and truth? Paradoxical attitudes toward pidgins and creoles', in S. Greenbaum (ed.), *The English Language Today*, Oxford, Pergamon.

Rokeach, M. (1973). *The Nature of Human Values*, New York, Free Press.

Rosenberg, M. and Hovland, C. (1960). 'Cognitive, affective, and behavioural components of attitude', in M. Rosenberg, C. Hovland, W. McGuire, R. Abelson and J. Brehm (eds), *Attitude Organisation and Change: An Analysis of Consistency among Attitude Components*, New Haven, CT, Yale University Press.

Rosenthal, M. (1974). 'The magic boxes: pre-school children's attitudes toward Black and Standard English', *The Florida Reporter*, 12, 55–62.

Ryan, E. B. and Carranza, M. (1980). 'Language and other cultural attitudes of bilingual Mexican-American adolescents', *Ethnicity*, 7, 191–202.

Ryan, E. B., Giles, H. and Hewstone, M. (1988). 'The measurement of language attitudes', in U. Ammon, N. Dittmar and K. Mattheier (eds), *Sociolinguistics: An International Handbook of the Science of Language and Society*, Berlin, Walter de Gruyter.

Ryan, E. B., Giles, H. and Sebastian, R. (1982). 'An integrative perspective for the study of attitudes toward language variation', in Ryan, E. B. and Giles, H. (eds), *Attitudes towards Language Variation: Social and Applied Contexts*, London, Edward Arnold.

Sarnoff, I. (1970). 'Social attitudes and the resolution of motivational conflict', in M. Jahoda and N. Warren (eds), *Attitudes*, Harmondsworth, Penguin.

Saville-Troike, M. (1982). *The Ethnography of Communication: An Introduction*, Oxford, Blackwell.

Schmied, J. (1991). *English in Africa*, London, Longman.

Schneiderman, E. (1976). 'An examination of the ethnic and linguistic attitudes of bilingual children', *ITL Review of Applied Linguistics*, 33, 59–72.

Sears, D. (1983). 'The persistence of early political predispositions: the role of attitude object and life stage', in L. Wheeler and P. Shaver (eds), *Review of Personality and Social Psychology, Vol. 4*, Beverly Hills, CA, Sage.

Sears, D. and Kosterman, R. (1994). 'Mass media and political persuasion', in S. Shavitt and T. Brock (eds), *Persuasion: Psychological Insights and Perspectives*, Boston, MA, Allyn and Bacon.

Seggie, I. (1983). 'Attribution of guilt as a function of ethnic accent and type of crime', *Journal of Multilingual and Multicultural Development*, 4, 197–206.

Seligman, C., Tucker, R. and Lambert, W. (1972). 'The effects of speech style and other attributes on teachers' attitudes toward pupils', *Language in Society*, 1, 131–42.

Sharp, D., Thomas, B., Price, E., Francis, G. and Davies, I. (1973). *Attitudes to Welsh and English in the Schools of Wales*, Basingstoke/Cardiff, Macmillan/University of Wales Press.

Sherif, M. (1967). 'Introduction', in C. Sherif and M. Sherif (eds), *Attitude, Ego Involvement and Change*, New York, Wiley.

Sherif, M. and Sherif, C. (1967). 'Attitudes as the individual's own categories: the social judgement approach to attitude and attitude change', in C. Sherif and M. Sherif (eds), *Attitude, Ego-involvement, and Change*, New York, Wiley.

Smith, E. and Mackie, D. (2000). *Social Psychology*, New York, Worth.

Stewart, M. and Ryan, E. B. (1982). 'Attitudes toward younger and older adult speakers: effects of varying speech rates', *Journal of Language and Social Psychology*, 1, 91–109.

Tajfel, H. (1974). 'Social identity and intergroup behaviour', *Social Science Information*, 13, 65–93.

Tajfel, H. (1981). 'Social stereotypes and social groups', in J. Turner and H. Giles (eds), *Intergroup Behaviour*, Oxford, Blackwell.

Tench, P. (1990). 'The pronunciation of English in Abercrave', in N. Coupland (ed.), *English in Wales: Diversity, Conflict and Change*, Clevedon, Multilingual Matters.

Thakerar, J., Giles, H. and Cheshire, J. (1982). 'Psychological and linguistics parameters of speech accommodation theory', in C. Fraser and K. Scherer (eds), *Advances in the Social Psychology of Language*, Cambridge, Cambridge University Press.

Thomas, A. R. (1973). *The Linguistic Geography of Wales*, Cardiff, University of Wales Press.

Triandis, H. (1959). 'Differential perception of certain jobs and people by managers, clerks, and workers in industry', *Journal of Applied Psychology*, 43, 221–5.

Triandis, H. (1971). *Attitude and Attitude Change*, New York, Wiley.

Trudgill, P. (ed.) (1978). *Sociolinguistic Patterns in British English*, London, Edward Arnold.

Trudgill, P. (1990). *The Dialects of England*, Oxford, Blackwell.

Urban, G. (1993). 'The represented functions of speech in Shokleng myths',

in J. Lucy (ed.), *Reflexive Language: Reported Speech and Metapragmatics*, Cambridge, Cambridge University Press.
Urban, G. (1996). 'Entextualization, replication and power', in M. Silverstein and G. Urban (eds), *Natural Histories of Discourse*, Chicago, University of Chicago Press.
Van de Velde, H., van Hout, R. and Gerritsen, M. (1997). 'Watching Dutch change: a realtime study of variation and change in standard Dutch pronunciation', *Journal of Sociolinguistics*, 3, 361–91.
van Lier, L. (1988). *The Classroom and the Language Learner*, London, Longman.
Vaughn, S., Schumm, J. S. and Sinagub, J. (1996). *Focus Group Interviews in Education and Psychology*, Thousand Oaks, CA, Sage.
Waterman, A. (1982). 'Identity development from adolescence to adulthood: an extension of theory and a review of research', *Developmental Psychology*, 18, 341–58.
Webster, C. (1996). 'Hispanic and Anglo interviewer and respondent ethnicity and gender: the impact on survey response data', *Journal of Marketing Research*, 33, 62–72.
Weksel, W. and Hennes, J. (1965). 'Attitude intensity and the semantic differential', *Journal of Personality and Social Psychology*, 2, 91–4.
Wicker, A. (1969). 'Attitudes versus actions: the relationship of verbal and overt responses to attitude objects', *Journal of Social Issues*, 25, 41–78.
Widdowson, H. (1979). *Explorations in Applied Linguistics*, Oxford, Oxford University Press.
Williams, A., Garrett, P. and Coupland, N. (1996). 'Perceptual dialectology, folklinguistics, and regional stereotypes: teachers' perceptions of variation in Welsh English', *Multilingua*, 15, 171–99.
Williams, A., Garrett, P. and Coupland, N. (1999). 'Dialect recognition', in D. Preston (ed.), *Handbook of Perceptual Dialectology, Vol. 1*, Amsterdam, Benjamins.
Williams, A. and Garrett, P. (2002). 'Communication evaluations across the lifespan: from adolescent storm and stress to elder aches and pains', *Journal of Language and Social Psychology*, 21, 101–26.
Williams, C. (1979). 'An ecological and behavioural analysis of ethnolinguistic change in Wales', in H. Giles and B. Saint-Jacques (eds), *Language and Ethnic Relations*, Oxford, Pergamon.
Williams, C. (1985) 'On culture space: perceptual culture regions in Wales', *Études Celtiques*, 22, 273–95.
Williams, C. (1990). 'The anglicisation of Wales', in N. Coupland (ed.), *English in Wales: Diversity, Conflict and Change*, Clevedon, Multilingual Matters.
Williams, C. (1995). 'Questions concerning the development of bilingual Wales', in B. Morris Jones and P. Singh Ghuman (eds), *Bilingualism, Education and Identity*, Cardiff, University of Wales Press.

Williams, C. (ed.) (2000). *Language Revitalization: Policy and Planning in Wales*, Cardiff, University of Wales Press.

Williams, G. (1987). 'Bilingualism, class dialect, and social reproduction', *International Journal of the Sociology of Language*, 66, 85–98.

Windsor Lewis, J. (1990). 'The roots of Cardiff English', in N. Coupland (ed.), *English in Wales: Diversity, Conflict and Change*, Clevedon, Multilingual Matters.

Winford, D. (1975). 'Teacher attitudes toward language varieties in a creole community', *International Journal of the Sociology of Language*, 8, 45–75.

Wolfson, N. (1976). 'Speech events and natural speech: some implications for sociolinguistic methodology', *Language in Society*, 5, 189–209.

Woolard, K. (1998). 'Introduction: language ideology as a field of inquiry', in B. Schieffelin, K. Woolard and P. Kroskrity (eds), *Language Ideologies: Practice and Theory*, New York, Oxford University Press.

Wray, A., Evans, B., Coupland, N. and Bishop, H. (2003). 'Singing in Welsh, becoming Welsh: "turfing" a "grass roots" identity', *Language Awareness*, 12, 33–58.

Yin, R. (1989). *Case Study Research: Design and Methods*, Newbury Park CA, Sage.

Zahn, C. and Hopper, R. (1985). 'Measuring language attitudes: the speech evaluation instrument', *Journal of Language and Social Psychology*, 4, 113–23.

Zanna, M. and Rempel, J. (1988). 'Attitudes: a new look at an old concept', in D. Bar-Tal and A. Kruglanski (eds), *The Social Psychology of Knowledge*, New York, Cambridge University Press.

Index

acquiescence bias 8, 27, 29, 31, 219
adolescent crowds 86–8
affiliative/affective judgements 106, 119–27, 150–5, 161–4, 207–8
Africa 31
Anglicization 20, 176, 192
anonymity *see* data gathering
antonyms 65–6
attitudes
  across generations 214
  and behaviour 7–9, 12, 27
  and beliefs 10
  definitions, components and nature of 2–7, 37–8
  and habits 9–10
  and ideology 11, 83
  main research approaches 14–18
  and opinions 10
  reasons for studying 11–14
  stability and durability of 5, 9
  and values 10
attitude rating scales
  intensity and directionality 41–2, 65–6, 195–6
  Likert scales 39–43
  numbers of points on 41–2
  semantic differential scales 39, 41, 43, 52, 56, 61, 212, 221–2
  scale-labels 56, 63–6, 80, 181, 184, 195, 221

Thurstone scales 39–40, 43
Australia 54, 214

behavioural measures 56–7, 69–70
Birmingham 55
'boasters and bullshitters' 172, 194
'boring', 174, 183–5

Canada 15, 17, 59, 84, 90, 216
Cardiff
  conceptual presentation of 93–5
  judgements about 129–34, 138–44, 150–78, 173–4, 182–95
  label set 121–2
  narratives 99–100, 103–4
  previous studies 69–70
  recognition 199–207
  socio-cultural characteristics 96–7
  speech 72–4
Census
  (1991) 215
  (2001) 20
children's language awareness 85–6
combining research techniques 221–2, 225–8
conceptual presentation 79–80, 146–7
'cool Cymru' 21, 219
'crossing' 87

data gathering
  anonymity 34
  distance 28, 34
  individuals and groups 32–3
  interaction and response rates 34–5
  numbers of respondents 33–4
  open and closed items 36–8
  researcher characteristics 29–30
  structured and unstructured designs 35–6
  types of closed items 38–9, *see also* attitude rating scales
  uniformity 34
data summary 109–10
debriefing 17
deindividuation 8
Denmark 55, 144
dialect, nature of 61–3
dialect performance 62, 223–5
  see also narratives
dialect recognition 58–9, 81, 88–90, 106, 226–7
  and dimensions of language awareness 204–6, 208–9
  rates of 198–203
  see also ingrouping and outgrouping processes
direct methods 15, 16, 24–50
draw a map 45–6
drugs 193, 196
dynamism 63, 130–3, 137–9, 173

educational contexts
  other attitudinal research in 6, 13, 14, 15, 18, 19, 25, 83–4, 86–8
  previous research in Wales 25, 42–4
Egypt 54
EPA (evaluation, potency and activity) 65
ethnography 15, 36
evaluative dimensions 53, 57, 63, 65, 106, 129
  see also prestige; social attractiveness; dynamism
evaluative profiles of Welsh English communities
  focus groups 168–75
  keywords 180–95
  label-sets 120–7
  narratives scales 150–68
  questionnaire scales 130–4, 137–43
  'social advantage' item 135–43
expletives *see* pejoratives

familiarity effects 133–4, 138
focus groups 22, 26, 29, 32–3, 35, 36, 168–75
folklinguistics *see* perceptual dialectology
French 15, 26, 54, 56, 59, 85, 89–90

Gaelic 25, 28, 36
Germany 84
globalization 214
'good at school' judgements 84, 150–5, 164–6
gradeability 65–6
Greece 90
group polarization phenomenon 29, 31

Hawaii 84
hypothetical questions 27

identity dynamics in teenagers 19, 86, 88, 213, 218–19
identity moratorium 180, 197
imposed norm hypothesis 90
indirect methods 15–18
  see also matched guise technique
ingrouping and outgrouping processes 3–4, 30, 48, 142, 183, 193, 196, 206–10, 226–7
inherent value hypothesis 89

'interesting story' judgements 150–5, 157–61
Interviewer's Paradox 29
Ireland 25, 46–7, 54

judgements on Welshness *see* Welshness

keywords 106, 109, 179–97, 225–6

language attitudes *see* attitudes
language ideology *see* attitudes

map labelling
  characteristics of labels 118–20
  dialect zones 112–13
  labelling of Wales regions 120–7
  label sets 113–16
  territorial span of zones 116–18
matched guise technique 17–22, 29, 51–70, 74–81, 146, 219–20
  collection of evaluations in 55–7
  commonly claimed successes of 57
  presentation of varieties in 51–5, 223–5
  problems with 57–63, 79–81
mid-Wales
  conceptual presentation of 93–5
  judgements about 129–34, 138–44, 150–78, 182–95
  label set 123–4
  narratives 102, 105
  recognition 199–207
  socio-cultural characteristics 97
  speech 73
modes of language awareness 204–5
multiple questions 28

narratives 22
  as performance 148–9, 168–75, 176, 223–5
  collection and preparation of 98–100
  collection of reactions to 105–10
  teachers' and teenagers' evaluations of 150–5, 157–77
  teenagers' normative demands of 168–75
  transcriptions of 100–5
National Assembly for Wales 20, 78
  referendum for 50, 141–2
negativity 150, 180, 182, 197
New Zealand 54, 214
non-attitudes 5, 38
north-east Wales
  conceptual presentation of 93–5
  judgements about 129–34, 138–44, 150–68, 175–8, 182–95
  label set 122, 124–5
  narratives 99, 100–1, 103
  recognition 199–207
  socio-cultural characteristics 97
  speech 72–4
north Wales attitudes compared with south 116, 133–5, 213, 215
north-west Wales
  conceptual presentation of 93–5
  judgements about 129–34, 138–44, 150–78, 182–95, 219
  label set 122
  narratives 99, 102–3
  recognition 199–207
  socio-cultural characteristics 97
  speech 72–4

pejoratives 180–3
perceptual culture regions 48–9, 75
perceptual dialectology 16, 22, 24, 44–50
  and descriptive dialectology 142–3

earlier work on Wales 46–50
future work 222–3
perceptual English dialect zones in Wales
  data collection 92–6
  evaluations of 118–27, 214–16, 220–1
  identification of 112–16
  territorial span of 116–18
performance *see* narratives
political aspirations and map boundaries 139–42, 215
prestige 63, 67–70, 93–4, 106, 119–21, 127, 129–38, 144–6, 216–18, 220, 222
  see also 'good at school' judgements
prior discussion, effects of 30–1

Received Pronunciation
  compared with Welsh Englishes 71–3
  conceptual presentation of 93–5
  judgements about 129–34, 150–5, 157–78, 182–95, 213
  narratives 99, 101, 104
  previous attitudinal research 14, 18, 19, 58, 67–70
  recognition 199–207
  and standardness in Wales 143–4, 216–17
research questions and issues 21–2, 79
'rich/posh' 193

'sad' 66, 179
Scotland 25, 28, 36, 46
see-saw effect 44
sexuality 192
'sheepshagger' 190–2, 196, 213
social acceptability and social advantage items 135–8, 219
social attractiveness 63, 67–9, 106

  see also affiliative affective judgements
social desirability bias 8, 28, 29, 38, 57, 146
social judgement theory 6
societal treatment 14–16, 24, 25
socio-cultural characteristics of Welsh regions 96–7
south-east Wales
  conceptual presentation of 93–5
  judgements about 129–44, 150–68, 175–8, 182–95
  label set 120–1
  narratives 99, 102, 103
  recognition 199–207
  socio-cultural characteristics 97
  speech 72–4
south-west Wales
  conceptual presentation of 93–5
  judgements about 129–44, 150–78, 182–95, 216
  label set 124
  narratives 99, 101, 104
  recognition 199–207
  socio-cultural characteristics 97
  speech 72–4
Spanish 25, 30, 54
sport 192
Standard Welsh English 143, 216
statistical analysis 25, 52–3
  MANOVA 129
  multidimensional scaling and cluster analysis 155–7, 177
status *see* prestige
strongly slanted questions 27
superiority *see* prestige
Switzerland 15

teacher-student comparisons 217–18
teachers' attitudes
  narratives study 151–5, 157–68, 175–8, 217–18

INDEX

previous research 83–4
questionnaire study 144–6
teachers' awareness 217
teenagers' attitudes
  keywords 179–97
  scales in narratives study 150–1, 153–5, 157–78, 217–18
teenagers' awareness of language 85–7
theory of reasoned action 8
'three Wales' model 75–6, 126, 140, 214–15
Trinidad 84
'troublemaker' 174, 194–5
two Wales model 75, 126

USA 13, 25, 28, 30, 46, 59, 84, 85, 214, 216

validity and reliability 29, 39–40, 51, 54–5, 58–63, 65, 220
verbal guise technique 53–4

Wales
  previous language attitudes research 18–22, 42–4, 46–50, 67–70
  issues to be addressed in present research 74–81, 211–14

Welsh Assembly Government 215–16
Welsh English dialect communities
  mapping task profiles 93–127
  narrative scale profiles 150–78
  questionnaire scale profiles 129–47
  regional dialect features 14, 70–4
Welsh language 6, 14, 18–21, 40, 42–4, 48–50, 215–16
Welsh Language Act 21
Welsh speakers compared with non-Welsh speakers 132–3, 213
Welshness 74–6, 106, 113, 115, 116, 119–20, 126, 130–4, 138–44, 150–5, 166–8, 185–9, 203–6, 212–17, 219
  and affect 139, 220
  and Englishness 125–6, 185–9, 196
  and globalization 214
  varieties of 20–1, 49, 175, 189, 212–16, 219
word of mouth and written response techniques 25, 31–9

Y Fro Gymraeg 75–6, 97, 139–40, 214–15